JUST ASPIRE

Advance Praise for *Just Aspire*

Ajai is a highly acknowledged leader, who has been the foremost evangelist for making India an Electronics Product Nation. This book is a must for all budding entrepreneurs, managers, and anyone who is aspiring to reach greater heights. Ajai has delivered a captivating account of his life's journey, interspersed with important lessons for achieving success.

Vinod Dham, father of the Pentium chip

Pathbreaking, passionate, persevering and purposeful—Ajai has woven a delightful tapestry of personal experience and professional achievement. *Just Aspire* is a portrayal of him being at the forefront of creating and building an institution, by spotting opportunities, developing and nurturing relationships, and taking risks with great conviction and commitment. Ajai is amongst the many visionaries who continue to take forward the dream of building India through both technological and entrepreneurial excellence, by service and philanthropy. An inspiring read for everyone with national pride who believes in sound family values and lifelong learning.

M.M. Murugappan, former chairman, Murugappa Group

I have nothing but the deepest admiration for Ajai's passion and commitment to the cause of electronics hardware in India. He has never given up. His recipe is impressively uncluttered and I cannot but completely agree with it. The stars are lining up for us in this space but to win, we need to focus on skills, capital, conducive policies and all stakeholders coming together to create the renaissance for manufacturing which the country critically needs. This book is an absolute must read.

Saurabh Srivastava, cofounder, NASSCOM and Indian Angel Network

It's truly remarkable to read about Ajai's achievements and contributions to the Indian IT industry. His ideas transformed not only the company where he worked for over three decades but also the Indian IT and hardware industries. His life story is inspirational. His passion and drive to achieve and learn are evident in the book. It's a warm and fun book, which will inspire many young minds to strive for excellence.

Neelam Dhawan, former managing director, HP

Infused with experience, learnings and memories, *Just Aspire* captures Ajai's wealth of wisdom, his sense of curiosity and his towering leadership that make him one of the most brilliant professionals and coaches of our country. He is a huge believer in the India story and his biggest asset is his conviction and capability to convert dreams into reality. Ajai seamlessly blends the personal with the professional and has been my guru who taught me to be bold, to be a learner and to be relevant ... I owe it to Ajai. Read this book and learn from one of the best.

C.P. Gurnani, CEO and managing director, Tech Mahindra

Ajai's journey from Jabalpur to be the cofounder of HCL as also chairman of several reputed institutions has been astoundingly remarkable. The best thing about *Just Aspire* is that it is provocative and written in a bold way—truly a book of transformation and guidance.

Harshavardhan Neotia, chairman, Ambuja Neotia Group

JUST ASPIRE

Notes on Technology, Entrepreneurship and the Future

AJAI CHOWDHRY

Cofounder of HCL

HARPER BUSINESS

An Imprint of HarperCollins *Publishers*

First published hardback in India in 2023 by Harper Business
An imprint of HarperCollins *Publishers*
4th Floor, Tower A, Building No. 10, DLF Cyber City,
DLF Phase II, Gurugram, Haryana – 122002
www.harpercollins.co.in

This edition published by Harper Business 2024

2 4 6 8 10 9 7 5 3

P-ISBN: 978-93-6213-912-2
E-ISBN: 978-93-5629-662-6

Typeset in 11/15.5 Sabon LT Std at
Manipal Technology Ltd, Manipal

Printed and bound at
Saurabh Printers Pvt. Ltd.

FSC
www.fsc.org
MIX
Paper | Supporting responsible forestry
FSC® C195953

This book is printed on FSC® certified paper
which ensures responsible forest management

HarperCollins *Publishers*, Macken House, 39/40 Mayor Street Upper, Dublin 1, D01 C9W8, Ireland

To the aspirational Indians, the millions who have the courage and self-belief to follow their dreams

CONTENTS

Be our strength in hours of weakness
In our wanderings be our guide
Through endeavour, failure, danger
Father, be thou at our side

– Prayer, Christ Church Boys' Senior Secondary School, Jabalpur

AUTHOR'S NOTE

I HAVE HAD THE PRIVILEGE of spending thirty-six years of my life helping to create businesses within HCL (originally Hindustan Computers Ltd). Today, HCL is a thirteen-billion-dollar corporation with an approximate market capitalization of fifty-billion dollars, and I am proud to have been a cofounder.

When I left Jabalpur, the small town in Madhya Pradesh where I grew up, to pursue a career, I could not have dreamt that I would find myself at the vanguard of pathbreaking revolutions that would transform India.

My story is interleaved with my experiences and learnings at HCL. It is also about my life, pre- and post-HCL. In Jabalpur, I acquired the academic foundation and aspirational spirit that eventually led me to cofound HCL, where I helped shape India's 'PC revolution' and later, the revolution in mobile telephony.

None of it would have been possible without the support of HCLers and the intrepid visionaries who founded HCL: the enigmatic and brilliant Shiv Nadar, who mentored and guided me throughout my career; the affable tech-wizard Arjun Malhotra; sales virtuosos Yogesh Vaidya and Subhash Arora; and the insightful, irrepressible D.S. 'Pammi' Puri.

In the process of nudging India towards a knowledge economy, we cofounded the Manufacturers' Association of Information Technology (MAIT). Then, to help create the right ecosystem to bring mobile phones to the masses, we cofounded the Indian Cellular Association (ICA), which played a significant role in enabling conducive rules for the growth of the industry, as well as reasonable product prices.

As early as 1995, along with Nokia, we led the movement towards broad phone adoption by making them affordable, accessible and repairable all over the country, with breakthrough distribution strategies. Our success can be gauged from the fact that at one time, seventy out of a hundred phones were Nokia/HCL. Today, the transformative effect of the telecom revolution across all sectors of the economy, not to mention its social and cultural impact, is self-evident.

Parallel to this, I strove towards creating the Electronics System Design and Manufacturing (ESDM) industry in India. To that end, I have worked relentlessly since 1999 with doyens like N. Seshagiri and R. Chidambaram. As a member of several government committees, I've helped bring out a series of reports that found reflection in the breakthrough National Policy on Electronics, 2019.

The ESDM aspect of my work has picked up momentum in the last year with the creation of the EPIC Foundation, a non-profit organization that I have founded along with leading luminaries of the electronics hardware sector. It serves as a think tank for electronics and enables the growth of ESDM in India. I am excited about the future of the industry and I dream about making India an Electronics Product Nation.

Looking back, I feel that my success as a business leader is owed in large measure to the interdisciplinary mindset that I was encouraged to cultivate in my youth. My interests were wide and varied—spanning the spectrum from sports, music and art to solid state physics, software and space technology—and this gave me a panoramic worldview and an ability to think laterally.

Today, business leadership is increasingly about sifting for solutions from masses of data. It mandates an ability to connect the dots—one that has always come naturally to me (thanks to the plethora of whodunits I read!)—to the point where I can reflexively solve complex problems linked to management and technology.

Wide-ranging knowledge enables you to step back and look at the big picture objectively, to see how the various components complement each other and how they can be adjusted to improve the whole. The capacity to integrate learnings across seemingly unrelated domains and from a variety of people in different fields contributes to effective strategies.

It is important to have passions outside the job, to keep the brain agile and the spirit humble with the knowledge that other people can outperform you in their respective fields. This motivates you to better yourself. To stop learning is to stop living so I am constantly teaching, fostering innovation and nurturing talent, and in the process, reinventing myself, my skills and my business.

I have worn many hats: entrepreneur, sportsman, salesperson, engineer, educationist, jazz aficionado and consultant on population stabilization. As an investor, I go from SAAS (software services) to pharma, from QSRs (quick service restaurants) to deep tech, and from furniture to space tech with equal ease.

My journey from a small-town boy to a CEO of a global company has enabled me to view the world from different angles and adapt to diverse environments. I've been as comfortable dining on the floor of a village hut as cochairing the World Economic Forum in Africa.

My advice: never let your aspirations die or your passions dim, for they are the soul of entrepreneurship.

INTRODUCTION

IF I COULD CHOOSE A career all over again, what would it be? My school friend, the thespian Sharat Saxena, put that question to me at an event celebrating the release of this book, *Just Aspire*. Without hesitation, I replied that I'd be a singer. An odd thing for an entrepreneur and a technology maven to say, but I've always had a passion for music. As luck would have it, I'm stuck with being an amateur crooner.

But all my many passions—music, technology, futurology, sales and reading—came together in the writing of this book, the unexpurgated story of my life: the journey from small town India to being the founder of Hindustan Computers Limited (HCL), the 'second innings' as an institution-builder, investor, mentor, philanthrope and advisor to the government, the hard-won wisdoms and heartfelt beliefs.

Just Aspire came out in early 2023, and I was surprised and gratified at the enthusiastic response. 'Inspiring', 'path-breaking', 'mesmerising', 'one-of-a-kind', 'visionary', 'must-read' were some of the more flattering descriptors. What mattered most was that many found the book relatable. They 'got' me. They understood the underlying philosophy that aspiration is greater than resources, and saw the book as 'a road map for people who want to reach their full potential'.

As I traversed the country for successive book launches, I was deeply moved to find cohorts of HCLers (past and present members of the HCL family) and colleagues from my college days in attendance. It gave me the opportunity to reconnect with them, and for that I am grateful. When the 2024 HCL Alumni reunion was held in New Delhi, I had a wonderful time with my co-founders Arjun Malhotra, Yogesh Vaidya and the inimitable Shiv Nadar.

Of the thirty-plus book-related events, my absolute favourite was the one organized in my home town, Jabalpur, by my alma maters: Christ Church Boys' Higher Secondary School and Jabalpur Engineering College (JEC). It was a heartwarming homecoming. The list of 150 invitees ballooned to 360. Mothers showed up with children in tow, and converged onstage to introduce them to me. The publisher had been kind enough to provide 100 copies of my book; they sold out in record time and the audience clamoured for more. Deeply touched at the unlooked-for reception, I told them that growing up in Jabalpur, I'd never dreamed of scripting technology revolutions in India. All I did was focus on making a meaningful contribution to India's progress, and that thinking got me where I am today.

Another event that warmed the cockles of my heart—and tested my vocal chords—was organized by my music group, Lutff, to mark the 100th anniversary of Dev Anand and to celebrate my book (in which the great actor features prominently). In front of an audience of 350—more than twice the number invited—I was called upon to render two of my favourite songs from Dev Anand films: the sublime '*Phoolon ke rang se*' from *Prem Pujari* and the light-hearted '*Ae meri topi*' from *Funtoosh*.

I found myself in demand as a speaker at various institutions and forums, as well as TV shows and YouTube channels. I'm no prophet of technology or Captain Marvel of industry, but ended up being treated like one! My social media following ballooned, from a few hundred followers to hundreds of thousands. My ET Masterclass training programme on innovative product development, sales tactics, start-up funding and so forth saw more than half a million downloads. The level of feedback was remarkable—my interview with YouTuber Raj Shamani, my post on 'retire retirement' and my Josh Talk went viral, attracting millions of views.

Time and again, I addressed a sea of expectant faces—students, professors, IT professionals, salespeople, entrepreneurs, journalists, bloggers and science enthusiasts. I told them the feel-good success story that they wanted to hear: how a garage (or barsati) start-up with an initial capital of Rs 1.8 lakh went on to become the $13 billion company that HCL is today. Then I told them how they could craft their own stories.

The challenges confronting them are big but the opportunities are bigger. The Next Big Thing is not around the corner; it is already upon us. Those who get in on the ground will ride a wave the like of which humanity has never seen. The transformative potential of artificial intelligence and quantum-based systems is unparalleled, and perhaps unimaginable. It will radically reshape our world, our lives and our thought processes.

Parallel to my speaking commitments, I was privileged to contribute my mite to the vision of a developed India. In addition to my role as advisor to the National Semiconductor Mission, I was appointed chairman of the National Quantum Mission's governing board and drafted as a member of the Ministry of Electronics and Information Technology (MeitY) Task Force on making India a product nation. Some months later, I joined NITI Aayog as a distinguished fellow. For the first time, I found myself in possession of a government office. (It is rather unsettling to be on the other side of the desk, after a lifetime in the corporate world, so I prefer to work from home.)

A great churn was happening at this time. The thinking folk on Raisina Hill were increasingly aware that a huge opportunity was knocking at our door, in terms of India's integration into global value chains (GVC). Weak GVC linkages have been a consistent handicap, despite India's manufacturing capability. To drive growth, exports and job-creation, India must emerge as a global manufacturing hub. This thinking dovetailed beautifully with the last chapter of my book, which calls for India to become a product nation.

I have long held that we must pivot from services to products, and become self-reliant in electronics. In contrast to India's robust share in IT/ITeS, that of electronics stands at a humble 3 per cent, pointing to enormous untapped potential. While we pride ourselves on $11 billion worth of mobile phone exports annually, the fact is that our value addition is marginal, barely 6–8 per cent. NASSCOM pegs India's IT exports at $250 billion, but hidden in this figure is the export of R&D worth $39 billion. We must apply our manifest capacity for innovation to designing and value-addition, not just manufacturing. A combination of our software skills and hardware/R&D capability will translate into unmatchable global products.

Identification of sectors with high potential, be it semiconductors, biotechnology, telecom, defence or electronics, is a priority. Providing infrastructure support, conducive policy frameworks and a rejigged regulatory environment are challenges that must be addressed, and I believe they will be.

If we miss the boat, we might be stuck in a middle-income economy for the forseeable future.

I am gratified at the recent policy thrust on electronics and welcome the resolve to leverage India's strengths in engineering and design services to become a leader in electronics and hardware. The electronics sector requires fast movement of components and products, so I appreciate the new logistics policy aimed at dramatically improving connectivity.

It was to this end that I took the initiative to work towards bringing Taiwanese investment to India. Taiwan is the world's top chipmaker, so while addressing the India-Taipei Association's Supply Chain Summit, I made a pitch for India to be part of the Taiwanese GVC. I pointed out that with the government giving an upfront 70 per cent incentive on capex for chip manufacture, 'there is no better deal in the world'. In my view, bringing Taiwanese SMEs to India will be mutually beneficial. India represents a huge market opportunity, after all.

In conjunction with electronics product design and manufacturing, I hope to see three significant initiatives. First, the state must intervene to scale demand. The government is the biggest buyer, and demand aggregation will ensure the viability of start-ups. Second, Indian companies must realign their thinking towards creating global brands. We have global businesses, but lack brand sensibility. Third, we need a right to repair (RTR) framework, for which I have lobbied strenuously. I'm glad the Ministry of Consumer Affairs has taken a step forward with the launch of an RTR portal, where hundreds of companies have uploaded product information, including repair manuals.

As I keep reminding audiences across the country, the opportunity size in electronics is enormous, at an estimated 4 trillion dollars. Margins are already being squeezed in services, and opportunities in software and analytics are decreasing. I am not predicting an AI-mediated software apocalypse in the near future, but there is no doubt in my mind that hardware and electronics will be much bigger.

If we are to be a product nation, we must inculcate skillsets beyond those offered at engineering schools today. This calls for an updated curriculum in product design, manufacturing and management. I have urged engineering institutions to come up with customized programmes for each vertical—from drone manufacture, medtech, spacetech, EV (electronic vehicles) technology, VLSI (Very Large Scale Integration) design and semiconductor fab, to building small nuclear reactors.

At Chitkara University near Chandigarh, which was kind enough to honour me with the title of Doctor of Literature (honoris causa)—my fifth doctorate—I urged students to take advantage of their proximity to India's first semiconductor foundry, the Semiconductor

Laboratory (SCL) located at Mohali, and gain first-hand experience of the design, fabrication, assembly, packaging and testing of chips.

I also had a sit-down session with the faculty. 'Do you have a marketing department?' I asked. They were a bit foxed. I explained that merely introducing new courses, say a master's degree in quantum or even a minor at the B. Tech. level, was not enough. Marketing these courses requires outreach, particularly to parents of hopeful engineering aspirants, who might not find value in unfamiliar programmes. A strong marketing campaign will go a long way in correcting perceptions that such courses are not career-oriented.

The opportunities in R&D will certainly expand. The announcement, in the interim budget for 2024, of a Rs 1 lakh crore corpus for long-term financing of research and innovation in sunrise sectors is a potential game-changer. A publically funded, privately managed fund will encourage the private sector to scale up R&D in diverse fields. This is a model that has yielded spectacular results.

Consider the Defense Advanced Research Projects Agency (DARPA), the US agency tasked with investing in breakthrough technologies. It was the force behind the creation of the Internet, global positioning system (GPS), voice recognition systems and dozens of other transformative technologies. The model owes to Vannevar Bush's post-World War II manifesto, written at the behest of President Franklin D. Roosevelt and calling for a sci-tech policy that would put the US at the forefront of technology and innovation. The DARPA's primary objective was national security, but the ecosystem of public, private and academic partnerships in R&D that it fostered literally changed the world. It sought out the best and brightest, in the US and abroad, and nurtured their creativity.

A similar example is the creation of India Stack, acknowledged as the world's best digital public infrastructure (DPI). It was publicly developed and privately provisioned. Thousands of Indian Software Products Industry Round Table (iSPIRT) volunteers worked on application programming interface (APIs) for India Stack, and the result was a globally successful, breakthrough product that is increasingly being adopted by countries across the world. It has shown that our engineers can make world-beating products. The more I talk to young people, the more confident I am of India's ability to innovate.

Many friends and associates have asked me why I don't just take it easy, focus on my singing and on my philanthropic foundation, Swayam. I devote time to both. My foundation has recently started a Rs 9 crore 'Aspire' scholarship for deserving students, in addition to ongoing projects. And I never let up on my singing practice!

But I am driven to put India at the forefront of technological innovation. I think L. Venkata Subramaniam put it best in his book *Quantum Nation*, where he says that my chairmanship of the National Quantum Mission and the current focus on this critical and emerging technology sector represents a 'second chance for HCL's founder and for India'.

HCL was founded as a computer hardware manufacturer, and we proved that Indian technology could compete with the best in the world. But India missed the opportunity to become a leader in hardware, thanks primarily to the increasing focus on software, lack of a conducive policy environment and the failure of domestic industry to recognize its potential. HCL itself made a strategic pivot to software and is now one of the leading providers of IT services globally.

Rather than mourn the missteps of the past, we must look to the future. Sharat Saxena recently threw a quote from his film *Baabul* at me: 'Sach to sirf tumhara aaj hai aur tumhara aane wala kal.' Your present and future are the only reality. Look forward, not back. So, if I truly believe India has the capacity to become a technology hub, I must embrace my role in NQM as a 'second chance', and steer the country towards a vibrant quantum ecosystem!

As I have often said, we are behind the times in quantum, but we can certainly catch up. The progress in quantum computing has been spectacular, with new leaps forward announced every other week. The US, thus far in pole position, has put considerable resources behind quantum information sciences (QIS) and quantum-resistant cryptography. As the head of the US Cyber Command observed, a sufficiently powerful Cryptanalytically Relevant Quantum Computer (CRQC) could render a nation's civil and military systems vulnerable to a crippling mega-hack.

From a national security perspective, it must be pointed out that China has committed $15 billion to quantum computing. It has made great strides in quantum communication, through the Beijing–Shanghai Quantum Secure Communication Backbone. At 2,000-odd kilometres, this is the world's longest stable quantum key distribution (QKD) network, an ultra-secure form of communication. India has so far achieved 250 kilometre (by the IIT-Madras incubated start-up QNu). In video game terminology, we must 'power up' or 'get fragged'.

In some areas, the gap is narrow and in others, it is wider. The NQM intends to set up four thematic hubs in select institutions, dedicated to quantum computing, sensors, communication and materials. There are perhaps 30 or 40 start-ups in quantum, but we need at least 500 more. A government-sponsored scheme to nurture and promote start-ups in the quantum space would help, and I am working towards that goal.

The thousands of youngsters I have addressed in the last year are avid to understand the shape of things to come. I tell them that they are fortunate to live in a time of burgeoning opportunities and myriad possibilities. 'I wish I were younger,' I said during one such interaction. Doesn't everybody? In my case, it has to do with my passion for technology and its capacity for shaping a brave new world. The privilege of contributing to the development of new technological frontiers in India has made me feel young. There is a long road ahead, and the digital afterlife is still far away.

1

JABALPUR: THE WONDER YEARS

MOST BOYS GET A DOG for a pet. I had a tiger cub. My father, the then commissioner of Bundelkhand and Baghelkhand, gifted it to me when I was recovering from measles. Alas, the cub fell prey to the vagaries of India's malaria control programme. While romping around the grounds of our sprawling bungalow in Rewa, it ingested a lethal dose of pesticide. For years, I couldn't think of my lost pet without a pang.

There were other pets: rabbits, a deer and the stray puppies gambolling around the servants' quarters of our home. Rewa, once a princely state known as the 'land of the white tiger', offered many amusements for a young boy, but very little by way of education. After my father, Jai Krishna Chowdhry, retired from the Indian Administrative Service in 1961, we moved to Jabalpur, which combined the gentle, laidback ambience of a small town with one of the finest educations India had to offer.

Surrounded by highlands and nestled in the valley of the Narmada, the town had passed from Maratha to British rule in the early nineteenth century. It had multiple claims to fame: the fabulous Dhuandhar waterfall and Marble Rocks gorge, central India's first ordnance factory (GCF or Gun Carriage Factory), and a rich history dating back to pre-Mauryan times.

Jabalpur, or Jubbulpore as the British called it, expanded in the twentieth century. The clement climate attracted a large migrant population. To this day, the names of many of its localities reflect the town's long colonial past, such as Lordganj named for Governor-General William Bentinck, and Miloniganj, Jonesganj and Napier Town, each named for a former British commissioner of Jabalpur.

The cultural impact of the British was visible in the emphasis on an 'English' education and an inclusive, open-minded social milieu. With its strong sense of community, relaxed pace of life, access to amenities and high standard of education, Jabalpur was an idyllic setting for my journey through boyhood and adolescence.

We stayed at Sarguja House while my father negotiated the purchase of his retirement home in Napier Town, appropriately named 'Ashiana' (nest). Fortuitously, he was offered a two-year extension and the post of Jabalpur municipal commissioner, which he accepted with alacrity.

The decision to settle in Jabalpur followed naturally from my father's long stint in Madhya Pradesh and the fact that as a Partition refugee, he had no 'home' to which he could return. His family was originally from Tank, in the North West Frontier Province (carved out of British Punjab in 1901, now Khyber Pakhtunkhwa in Pakistan). The rolling tract between the Hindu Kush mountains and the plains of Punjab has long served as a confluence of cultures, having been ruled by the Persians, Greeks, Mauryans, Sikhs, British, and finally, the sovereign state of Pakistan.

At the time my father was born, Indian nationalism was charting a new destiny for the subcontinent. As a young man, his first karmabhoomi (land where he worked) was Abbottabad, where he set up a thriving practice as a criminal lawyer. The family lived in a beautiful house opposite the Abbottabad Club, framed by tall poplars, with white rose bushes wreathing the large verandah. The library was well stocked with books in Persian, Urdu and

Sanskrit, apart from the vast array of legal volumes my father needed for his work.

A fervent nationalist, he joined the freedom struggle and became the president of the Hazara District Congress Committee. Partition was a shattering blow. Overnight, Jai Krishna Chowdhry the freedom fighter became a nameless refugee.

ABBOTTABAD TO ABU

At the urging of well-wishers, the family boarded the last train from Pakistan, fleeing with the clothes on their backs, clinging to the hope that Partition would be short-lived and they would return in due course. The train left from Haripur at dawn. The coaches were jam-packed, with hundreds perched precariously on the roofs. It was a journey fraught with terror. Frenzied mobs on either side of the rail track were baying for their blood. Thousands had already perished in the infamous 'blood trains' ferrying refugees to India and, but for the contingent of brave Gorkha soldiers on board, this bunch of passengers would also have been slaughtered.

My grandmother did not survive that horrific journey; she passed away just as the train arrived at Ferozepur cantonment. Here, the Sutlej river, mirroring the turmoil of the times, overflowed, causing a terrible flood. As the waters receded, cholera stalked the refugee camps. My parents made their way to Delhi, where they found a home of sorts in premises vacated by a coal and scrap merchant who had departed for Pakistan. It was a grimy, noxious hellhole, located six kilometres from the Viceroy's House (now Rashtrapati Bhavan).

Fortunately, my father found employment as assistant commandant of the Kingsway Camp for refugees, helping other displaced people find their feet. His performance was noted with appreciation, and he was appointed assistant regional commissioner of the Rajputana states, tasked with persuading the princes to sign the instrument of accession and integrate with the Republic of India before 26 January 1950. He was posted at Mount Abu, where I was born in August 1950, in a lavish bungalow called 'The Wilderness', overlooking the Nakki Lake. The youngest of seven children, and the second boy, I was the pink-cheeked, chubby little apple of the family's eye.

Senior officials of the British Raj had enjoyed a luxurious lifestyle, which the Chowdhry family inherited. With the bungalow came a large staff, including a cook, masalchis (spice blenders), numerous bearers, a dhobi (washerman) and several others with miscellaneous jobs. Soon after, while I was still an infant, my father was posted to Jaipur. His ardent nationalism had survived the rigours of Partition, and he wanted to play a role in establishing the sovereign Republic of India on firm footing. To that end, he applied to the Indian Administrative Service (IAS), the successor to the Indian Civil Service (ICS), whose British members had been repatriated. His education and administrative experience made him an ideal candidate, and after nine months of training at the Metcalfe House Academy in Jaipur, he joined the first batch of the IAS, at the age of forty-five.

Allotted the Vindhya Pradesh cadre, he was sent to Jabalpur for nine months of field training, before being posted as district magistrate of Shahdol, a heavily forested tribal area. Electricity had yet to reach this remote district, so the DM's bungalow had no power, and hence, no electrical gadgets, not even fans. Tarred roads were non-existent and sanitation was decidedly old-school—thunderboxes rather than water closets.

It was hard on my older siblings, but I, as a three-year-old, was more concerned with escaping their attempts to teach me the alphabet, so that I could ride my tricycle. Frustrated, my sister Sneh would lock me up in the bathroom. If the objective was to frighten me into learning my ABCs, it failed. Even as a toddler, I had a sanguine temperament. They would invariably find me sitting calmly on the bathroom floor, waiting to be let out. That innate composure, which I owe to the stable emotional environment created by my family, has proved invaluable throughout my life.

I have pleasant, if rather vague, memories of our next home in Nowgong. My father was divisional commissioner of Bundelkhand, so we lived in a fabulous British Residency, which had six bedrooms with attached bathrooms; a durbar hall; a vast, chandeliered dining room; a swimming pool; a summerhouse and tennis courts. After Shahdol, it was a veritable paradise.

The previous incumbent seemed to have departed precipitously, as he left behind a fully equipped home, right down to a dinner service and library. It was an estate in itself, with orchards, fields, outhouses and acres of lawn. One of my sisters was married there and the guests, I imagine, must have been suitably impressed by the venue.

JAWAHARLAL NEHRU AND THE PHATPHATI

A few months after we had settled into Nowgong, Prime Minister Jawaharlal Nehru and his daughter, Indira, came to dinner. Nehru's interest in the development of Khajuraho as a tourist destination is well-documented. He declared his desire to see the temple complex, which was part of my father's jurisdiction. Ahead of the visit, my father undertook a preparatory tour of the area.

Captain T.S. Burt had rediscovered the Chandela temple complex, dating from the ninth to the eleventh centuries CE, in 1838. He brought it to the attention of eminent archaeologists, such as Sir Alexander Cunningham. But when my father saw the site over a century later, he found it utterly neglected, overgrown with vegetation, and encrusted in bat guano. So foul were the interiors of the temples that one couldn't stand there without holding one's breath.

He initiated a mammoth effort to clean it up before the PM arrived. Even so, Nehru was shocked when he saw the temple complex in decay and disrepair. As a result, Khajuraho became one of the first sites in India to be developed for tourism.

After the tour, the PM and his daughter came to the Residency for dinner. The top brass of the state was in attendance—the lieutenant governor, the chief minister and the home minister. Also in attendance was the PM's head of security, one Mr Handoo. After a guard of honour by the police contingent, the family lined up to greet the Nehrus.

Clutching the red rose I had been given, I looked wide-eyed at the prime ministerial cavalcade of motorcycles and cars, so much more interesting to a juvenile than the distinguished visitors. I was introduced to Nehru, who wore a benign smile. He accepted the rose and spoke to me kindly, quite tickled by my obvious fascination with the phatphatis (motorcycles).

He promised me a phatphati of my own someday.

'*Aap ke haath ko kya ho gaya hai*?' (What happened to your hand?) I asked, distracted by a bandage on his finger.

'It got caught in the car door,' he said ruefully.

The Nehrus stayed for dinner, before leaving for Jhansi to travel to Delhi by saloon. The PM was gracious, but my sisters found his daughter rather remote. She walked past them, failing to notice the malas (garlands) they had painstakingly strung for her!

My father's next posting was in Rewa, where I was enrolled in a Hindi-medium school. I had no interest in books, but developed a love for music. As far back as I remember, music was always in the backdrop of our lives. Morning ragas wafted gently through the house at dawn, up-tempo songs from Hindi films enlivened the day, and meditative Urdu couplets lent a tranquil touch to the twilight. As we moved from place to place, music was the constant, permeating our homes and our hearts. If it wasn't my sister diligently practicing her swaras (musical notes), it was Papaji humming along to K.L. Saigal on the radio, or my brother whistling a tune from Kishore Kumar's latest romantic comedy.

The Chowdhry family's musical inclinations stemmed from Papaji's passion for poetry. Educated in Urdu and English, he demonstrated a talent for Urdu shayari early on. By the time Partition brought him to India, he was a noted litterateur, having published numerous books, including collections of poetry. Like all poets of the genre, he adopted a takhallus (pen name). His was 'Habib' (Arabic for friend), and he was indeed a friend to the musical arts.

Regular mehfils (gatherings) were held at our home, where my father and his fellow poets would recite or sing their latest compositions to the accompaniment of a harmonium. As is the custom, a candle or lamp would pass from poet to poet. Towards the end, it would be placed before Papaji, and he would render a nazm or ghazal, to great acclaim. We also attended the mushairas (poetic gatherings) that were frequently held in Rewa.

My first onstage appearance was in Rewa, as a tabla mouth percussionist. Let me explain. By this time, my older siblings had moved out to pursue higher studies, leaving my sister Indu and me at home. The two of us became close. So, when she trained in Hindustani classical singing at the instance of our mother, she prompted me to pick up an instrument. I opted for the tabla, but my performance was indifferent, so I tried mouth percussion instead. I accompanied my sister's vocals with great aplomb, and to my delight, I could keep up with her.

'YOU ARE A HANDSOME BOY'

In Jabalpur, I was enrolled at the Christ Church Boys' Senior Secondary School, an English-medium institution founded in 1870 and regarded as the finest in the region. I was nine years old. My early education had been in Hindi, at a school in Rewa set up by Maharani Pravin Kumari of the erstwhile princely state. Realizing that I needed to upgrade my English skills very quickly, my father engaged a tutor to give me a three-month crash course. As a result, I have two native tongues—I often think in Hindi and speak in English, and vice versa.

Christ Church school was a revelation. It was a Christian institution, with all the characteristic emphasis on strict discipline. The principal, whose residence adjoined the school, was an English canon, Reverend J.E. Robinson. He was an upright, rather heavy-handed gentleman, as students who found themselves at the business end of his cane could testify. Our vice-principal was the worthy Donald Beatson, known for his fluent Hindi.

The school day began with an assembly in the main hall, where a brief address by the principal was followed by the school prayer and hymns. On Christmas day, we went to church. We knew all the rituals—how to make the sign of the cross, dip our fingers in holy water before entering the chapel, and kneel at the pews.

The emphasis was on all-round character-building. Enrolment in the National Cadet Corps (NCC), which aimed to turn out disciplined and patriotic citizens, was mandatory. Sports received a lot of weightage; in fact, our school was regarded as one of the best in the country in that respect. For one thing, it had a long-standing culture of hockey. In the 1920s, a team of Christ Church old boys won India's premier hockey tournament, the Agha Khan trophy, three times.

Competition in sports with other schools was intense. Racquet games were my forte. I had picked up table tennis in Rewa; when I first started playing, I had to stand on a stool to reach the table! I continued to play in Jabalpur, where I would go to the club after school to practice. It soon became an obsession and I would play for two to three hours a day, reaching home so late that I didn't have time to study. My mother would yell at me, to no avail.

The practice paid off, and I won a number of competitions. At one time, I was ranked number two in the state of Madhya Pradesh. I tried my hand at tennis as well, mainly because my father played regularly, and at badminton. Many years later, I would pick up squash while living in Singapore.

Christ Church school also had the advantage of a superb faculty. Among our favourite teachers was the mathematics don, and later mayor of Jabalpur, R.P. Guru, fondly referred to as 'Guruji'. Another was the inimitable Mr Shinde, the English teacher, who would close the doors and windows of the classroom and regale us with the plot of the latest movie he had watched. He was a superb orator; I remember him bringing every scene of *The Horror of Dracula* to life.

One of the teachers gave me a reason to smile. She was beautiful, the object of many a secret adolescent crush. One day, as I was lounging with my friends, she summoned me.

'What is your name?' she asked.

'Ajai Chowdhry, ma'am.'

'You are a handsome boy, Ajai. But I have never seen you smile. Why is that?'

I found myself smiling bashfully. From then on, I made it a point to smile more, especially when she was in the vicinity.

Being an affable chap, I quickly forged lasting friendships. Sharat Saxena (who went on to become a popular Bollywood actor) was a great buddy and the strongman of our group. I actually saw him break a brick in two with his bare hands.

The highlight of the year was Annual Day, when the school's unique 'torch drill' was performed. We got to participate in and witness competitive sports, but more importantly, to interact with girls. The Christ Church girls' school was right opposite ours on Sleeman Road (named after Sir William Sleeman, the British officer who wiped out the 'thuggee'). It was sequestered behind a high wall, and intermingling was possible only on that one day.

I am proud to have sported the Christ Church boys' khaki uniform and green-and-yellow school tie. The school has produced a number of politicians, war heroes, sportsmen and academics. There was Frank Anthony, member of Parliament, educationist and adviser to Indira Gandhi; the sons of Crown Prince Abdullah of Afghanistan, as well as members of India's Olympic hockey squad and an honour roll of World War II heroes.

A HOME OF OUR OWN

Our home in Napier Town—a quiet neighbourhood—was a pretty cottage, roofed with terracotta tiles. It had been dilapidated when we first acquired it, but my mother and sisters had it renovated and restructured. It was set in landscaped gardens designed by Papaji, with a profusion of flowers and several trees. All in all, it was a charming home—a far cry from the splendid bungalows where I had spent my early years, but the first that our family could call its own.

Adding a serene touch to the gardens was a tenth century Buddha statue resting on a raised platform, under a beautiful gulmohar tree. It was the first object that caught a visitor's eye. Antiques were one of Papaji's hobbies; he was an avid collector of old books, photo-frames and ancient idols.

After his term as municipal commissioner, he resumed his legal practice, which had come to an abrupt halt with Partition. He practiced in the Madhya Pradesh High Court at Jabalpur, and was much sought-after. Mahakoshal, where Jabalpur is located, is a mining region, so he numbered several collieries among his clients.

Having a house with a large garden meant that I could keep a dog. Enter Tiger (named in memory of my long-lost tiger cub). He was tall, dark and handsome—a regular heartthrob—and when he entered a room, he owned it. A tad short-tempered, he was perfectly amiable if you were courteous, but fiercely intolerant of disrespect. I saw no flaw in him, for I loved him and he loved me back.

Tiger, like most Alsatians, was a one-man dog. Once he had decided that I was his human, he gave unstintingly of himself. I was his to protect and play with, and he was my faithful companion in good times and bad. He would greet me exuberantly when I returned from school, bounding up to the gate and barking as if to say, 'Hello! You're back! I missed you'.

Alsatians, or German Shepherds, are highly intelligent and courageous. But they tend to be a bit aloof, and one cannot take liberties with them. My little niece Sonali once teased him by pulling his tail, as children do. Irritated, he went for her face and nipped her before I could pull him off.

Tiger's guarding instincts were so strong that even when he was very ill, I couldn't stop him from rearing and barking his head off when he spotted a stranger at the gate. The strain was too much. He collapsed, and within seconds, I had lost him.

My English teacher at school, Mr Shinde, having learnt about the sad event, introduced me to a poignant poem about a dog. Oliver Goldsmith's *An Elegy on the Death of a Mad Dog* (produced below) is a satire. The principal takeaway is that man, however 'good' by his own standards, is so toxic that he can poison even a rabid dog. In other words, dogs are purer creatures.

An Elegy on the Death of a Mad Dog

Good people all, of every sort,
Give ear unto my song;
And if you find it wondrous short,
It cannot hold you long.

In Islington there was a man
Of whom the world might say,
That still a godly race he ran—
Whene'er he went to pray.

A kind and gentle heart he had,
To comfort friends and foes;
The naked every day he clad—
When he put on his clothes.

And in that town a dog was found,
As many dogs there be,
Both mongrel, puppy, whelp, and hound,
And curs of low degree.

This dog and man at first were friends;
But when a pique began,
The dog, to gain some private ends,
Went mad, and bit the man.

Around from all the neighbouring streets
The wond'ring neighbours ran,
And swore the dog had lost its wits
To bite so good a man.

The wound it seemed both sore and sad
To every Christian eye;
And while they swore the dog was mad,
They swore the man would die.

But soon a wonder came to light
That showed the rogues they lied,—
The man recovered of the bite,
The dog it was that died!

– Oliver Goldsmith

POWS, DINOSAURS AND BOOKS

Jabalpur was a lively town; at least for a gregarious, energetic boy with varied interests. In a world without internet and TV, there was so much to do: hanging out with friends or playing with pets, reading storybooks, practicing sports, tinkering with this or that and, very occasionally, studying. There was simply no time to be bored. My friends and I were always on the go, riding our bicycles around town or to the famous tourist spots like the Marble Rocks, Balancing Rock and the Madan Mahal, with its ancient fort, named for the sixteenth century Gond queen Durgawati.

I also enjoyed going to the Jabalpur Cantonment, which is located on high ground (as was the British custom) to the south of the Omti Nala and the main town. The army brass was accommodated on 'The Ridge', which overlooks the city and offers panoramic views. One of my sisters, Manorama, had married a doctor in the Indian Army, who was, fortuitously, posted at Jabalpur Cantonment. I often went to visit 'Nomaji', called so because as a child I found her name a tongue-twister and shortened it to Noma.

It was at Jabalpur Cantonment that Pakistan's top military commanders were held after their surrender in the 1971 India-Pakistan war. The most high-profile among them was Lt Gen. Amir Abdullah Khan Niazi, commander of the Pakistani forces on the eastern front, who had signed the instrument of surrender.

Another notable—and notorious—prisoner of war was Maj. Gen. Rao Farman Ali, best known for his involvement in the execution of pro-liberation intellectuals in Bangladesh. The other senior officers held at the POW camp from January 1972 to April 1974 included Major Generals M. Jamshed, Q.A. Majid Khan, N. Hussain Shah and M.H. Ansari; Rear Admiral Mohammad Shariff; Air Commodore Inamul Haque Khan, and seventeen brigadiers of the Pakistan Army. Naturally, the 'VIP' POWs were a talking point in Jabalpur, although no one outside the military establishment actually got to see them.

In the vicinity of the cantonment lies Sir William Sleeman's discovery, in 1828, of the first dinosaur fossils in India. The *Titanosaurus indicus* is believed to have been twelve metres tall and twenty-five metres long. This area, known as the Lameta formation (after Lamheta Ghat in Jabalpur), is said to be the richest source of Cretaceous-period dinosaur fossils in India. A century and a half later, eminent paleontologist Ashok Sahni found dinosaur eggs close to the same spot.

Having read Michael Crichton's 1990 novel *Jurassic Park*, in which genetically engineered dinosaurs are recreated from the DNA found in fossils (as I write, scientists are working on the genetic resurrection of the Woolly Mammoth), I was intrigued to learn about Jabalpur's wealth of dinosaur remains. In 2022, the Geological Survey of India (GSI) announced plans to set up the country's very own 'Jurassic Park'—known as a 'geo park'—at Lamheta, on the banks of the Narmada.

In the 1960s, living as we did in a snug, small-town bubble, books, magazines and newspapers were our window to the world. It was my older brother Vijay who introduced me to the limitless world of the written word. In the 1950s, access to Hindi fiction was limited, so I barely read outside of school. It was only after we moved to Jabalpur that I discovered the joys of reading. There were libraries, where one could borrow a book for ten paise a day, devour it and come back for more. Then there was the pleasure of discussing books with friends and exchanging notes on what each of us was reading.

Vijay was in Delhi, majoring in English literature. When he came home on vacations, we would sit together on the porch of our house and talk about books. I looked forward to those conversations all year, and more so, to the stack of books and magazines that he brought for me to read.

In school, we read Shakespeare and were fortunate to have a teacher who brought the characters to life. Reading satisfaction comes from getting to know the characters intimately, speculating on their motives, and sharing their emotions. To this day, I can reel off passages of *Macbeth* from memory.

Early on, I developed a fascination for mystery novels. I explored Kirrin Island with the Famous Five in Enid Blyton's *Five on a Treasure Island*. I was a fly on the wall as Hercule Poirot crouched over a corpse in Agatha Christie's *Murder in the Mews*. I stood at Sherlock Holmes' shoulder as he confronted the fire-breathing *Hound of the Baskervilles*.

Like many of my peers, I read Westerns as well—a genre that appealed to the pioneering spirit of my generation. Curled up in my room, I would step into the American Old West, with its audacious cowboys, gunfighters, explorers, settlers and native Americans. Zane Grey and Max Brand were my favourite authors.

I read classics with the same verve as popular fiction: *Lolita*, *Madame Bovary*, *Moby Dick*, *To Kill a Mockingbird* and so on. I steadily worked my way through Jane Austen, Charles Dickens and Ernest Hemingway. For a while, I was hooked on Norman Mailer. The reading habit expanded my vocabulary, along with my mind.

Given the opportunity, I would have read all day. At home, I would find places to hide where I could read undisturbed. Whenever I was feeling low, I would reach for a book. I called it 'reading your blues away'.

Another of my favourite extra-curricular activities was photography. My friend Rajnikant's brother was an ace photographer, so we would tag along on his shoots, accompanied by his models. One time, I was asked to model and wound up with my pictures in *The Illustrated Weekly of India*, back then India's most popular magazine.

An outing I looked forward to was to the Kanha Tiger Reserve, just a few hours from Jabalpur. On one of our trips there, we had a close encounter with a tiger. We sat atop an elephant, which trundled up to a ditch. A tiger was curled up there, deep in slumber. Our elephant clearly didn't believe in letting sleeping tigers lie, and nudged the big cat with its trunk. It woke up and growled at us.

My older brother and brother-in-law occasionally went on hunts, and I would sometimes tag along. The thrill of sitting on a machan in a dense forest, with the bait tied up below, waiting for the predator to show up, really gets the adrenalin pumping. I tried my hand at shooting birds, with guns borrowed from my brother, but proved an indifferent marksman. I never took to hunting, but I loved reading Jim Corbett's books. *Man-Eaters of Kumaon* was my favourite.

Jabalpur offered an uncomplicated but full life, replete with simple pleasures. No child could have asked for more; I had a loving home, wonderful friends and good teachers. We had few worries and lots of time for ourselves and other people. We found excitement in the little things; a phone call from out of town, the release of a new movie or a picnic with friends and family.

Indu and I looked forward to the visits of our older siblings in the summer. As the youngest, I was the gofer, constantly fetching glasses of water for my thirsty siblings. In the evenings, I was dispatched to pick up mangodas, savouries made of green gram flour. I had to wind my way through the narrow lanes of the old town to the home of the venerable lady who produced the best mangodas Jabalpur had to offer. I didn't grudge the effort, because I loved them too.

Another delectable gastronomic experience was Parsi jalebis. My sister's friend belonged to a Parsi family and their version of the coiled and syrupy sweet was the best I'd ever had—plate-sized whorls of thin, crisp, golden strands.

School segued smoothly into college. After graduating from Christ Church, I had decided to become an engineer and applied to the Jabalpur Engineering College (JEC) for admission. It was at this stage that I casually made what would prove to be a life-changing decision, by opting for a programme in telecommunications bundled with an entirely new course: electronics.

It seemed like a good idea, given my fascination with rapid developments in the field. The miniaturized transistor, invented just a couple of years before I was born, had captured my imagination. The world's very first mass-market portable transistor radio had been introduced just about a decade earlier, and the silicon chip followed a few years later. The era of consumer electronics was just beginning.

I was among the first batch of students at JEC to take up the newly introduced programme in electronics in 1966. At the time, I had no idea whether it would translate into a job. As it turns out, it was to define the entire course of my life.

2

COMING OF AGE

'*BAAP IAS, AUR BETA TELI!*' (The father is an IAS, and the son will sell oil!) Papaji was furious when my brother Vijay landed a prestigious job with Caltex, back then one of the largest oil companies in the world. For my father, a civil servant who had served in the top echelons of the government, a private sector employee was no better than a shopkeeper.

Like most parents in the 1960s, Papaji wanted his sons to follow in his footsteps. That meant joining the Indian Administrative Service or the Indian Foreign Service, which offered a social standing, influence and lifestyle that only the very wealthy could afford. In his book, my brother would be coming down in the world by working for an employer other than the President of India. It took quite a while for Papaji's anger to subside.

I chose to disappoint him as well, as I was determined to become an engineer, owing to my fascination with telecommunications, and increasingly, with electronics. The field was young, although the science behind it was old. My early infatuation with electronics owed itself to the Boolean binary, the '0' and the '1'. As any schoolkid knows, binary numbers are the basis of digital systems. The philosophical dimension of Boolean logic appealed to my youthful mind. A thing was either '1' or '0', true or false, open or shut, positive or negative, on or off, yin or yang. In a fuzzy and uncertain world, here was a total lack of ambiguity (at least in the macro-universe; the weirdness of quantum mechanics is another story altogether).

Jabalpur Engineering College, established in 1947, was a highly regarded institution, and gaining admission there was creditable in itself. The first to offer a course in telecommunications, it was also ahead of the curve in introducing electronics. An added attraction for me, apart from the course itself, was that I could stay in Jabalpur with my parents, who were getting on in years. As the last of my siblings in the nest, I couldn't bear the thought of leaving them alone.

Looking back, it was the best decision I could have made. My college years were a halcyon experience, thanks to a wonderful group of friends. Psychologists say the role of the peer group is critical in adolescence. As youngsters become more independent of their parents, they increasingly forge social and emotional bonds outside the family. A supportive community of friends will help you resolve your confusions and figure out who you are to make the difficult transition into adulthood.

In college, I was part of a gang of four, which included my friends Chintan, Ashok and Suresh. The 'G 4' was known for pranks and high jinks. I had never been a troublesome child; I was organized and maintained a fixed routine, which included ironing my own clothes and doing odd jobs around the house. Nor did I shy away from doing chores for my parents. But when high-spirited adolescents get together, trouble is bound to follow.

Chintan and I met on 17 June 1966. He remembers the date, because that's when the HSC (Higher Secondary School certificate) results were announced. I'd read in the newspaper that he had aced the exam, so when I spotted him cycling up the road, I flagged him down and offered my congratulations. Then I invited him home.

I was regarded as a rather 'snooty' chap (according to Chintan), so he was surprised by my affability and the warm welcome by the Chowdhry family. It was the beginning of a lifelong friendship.

Suresh was our comrade-in-arms. He was a great tinkerer—he could fix anything electronic—and a diehard fan of film music. He knew every Bollywood song you could think of. The three of us—Chintan, Suresh and I—did everything together, from cycling to college (ogling girls along the way) and group study to bunking classes and getting into tight spots. Every evening, we met at a coffee house and spent hours discussing girls, movies, music and campus gossip over idlis, vadas and dosas. In the midday break, we shared our lunches at Shuklaji's canteen, washing them down with his 'special chai'.

The fourth member of our group was Chintan's neighbour, Ashok. He was so brilliant that, unlike the rest of us, he never needed to study. Gifted with a near-eidetic memory, he only had to scan a page once to remember it. He would show up on the eve of an exam and nonchalantly suggest, 'Let's go see a movie.'

We had to cycle thirteen kilometres to college, often with a precariously balanced drawing board. The highlight of the trip was encountering college girls headed to their respective campuses. Only during the examinations was I allowed to borrow my father's car. All my friends would pile in and we would set off, passing the famous ordnance factory on the way.

MOVIE MAGIC

Movies were our passion and we were constantly scrounging for money to buy tickets. Chronically short of cash, we always bought the cheapest seats, so close to the screen that the mole on actor Jeevan's cheek was football-sized. We would scan *Screen*, the weekly film magazine published by the *Indian Express* group, for information on new releases. It became a tradition to watch a movie after every exam.

The 1960s matinee idol Dev Anand was our favourite actor. We never missed any of his films, and were always desperate to catch them first day, first show. I unashamedly tried to copy the hero's flamboyant sartorial style, and could quote all his dialogues by heart. Clad in Dev Anand's trademark checkered shirt, beret and scarf, I would declaim dramatically, '*Na sukh hai, na dukh hai, na deen hai, na duniya, na insaan, na bhagwan, sirf main hoon, main hoon, main hoon*' (There is no joy, no sorrow, no world, no man, no god, only I, only I, only I). My friends would whistle and applaud for this dialogue from the 1965 superhit *Guide* was a favourite.

On Thursdays, we had drawing classes at college. Typically, the teachers gave us our assignments and then disappeared, leaving us to our own devices. It was a golden opportunity to bunk and catch a matinee show. Just before the interval, we would slide out of the hall to steal cold drinks. Suresh recalls Chintan and Ashok displaying their bravado by opening bottle caps with their teeth.

English movies were generally screened at around 6 p.m., so we would tell our respective parents that we were going out for a combined study session, and then head to the Empire or Delight theatre. To catch late night shows of old Hollywood movies, we would sneak out of our homes after everyone else had gone to bed. We would leave the lights on in our rooms to signal that we were studying, just in case someone woke up.

A frequent nocturnal activity in the summers was stealing mangoes from our neighbours' trees. One time, Chintan shimmied up the tree while I shone a narrow beam of light at the dangling fruits. Suddenly, the garden was flooded with light and yells of '*chor, chor, pakdo, pakdo*!' (catch the thief) came from the lady of the house. We scampered and scaled the compound wall, landing bruised and bleeding on the other side, but with the mangoes intact. We kept them on the roof of Chintan's house. Being stolen fruit, they were doubly delicious.

We were also shameless peeping toms. One night, we congregated outside the window of the newlywed tenants who had moved into a neighbour's house. We jostled with each other trying to get a better look at what was going on inside. The commotion alerted the neighbour, and we had to run for our lives.

Money was tight, but that didn't stop us from having fun. None of our pleasures were expensive. For the grand sum of one and a half rupees, we could get coffee and dosas at the Indian Coffee House, our daily adda (meeting place). We often pooled what little money we had and shared the food and beverages. Occasionally, we would be able to afford a cutlet.

It was Ashok who introduced me to the joys of pen friends. In the 1960s, before PCs and the internet and email and social media, making transcontinental connections was incredibly exciting. It was our window to other cultures, with all their exotic customs, fashions and cuisines. Of course, for my pen friends in France, the US, Germany, Japan and the Philippines, India was equally exotic.

Snail mail, i.e., handwritten letters, was the only viable form of long-distance communication, so good penmanship was prized. To make a pen friend, one had to either put an ad in a magazine or newspaper, or respond to one. My first friend was Annie Veckens, who was based in France. I then found Jeri-Lynn White in the US, Marietta in the Philippines and Eiko Hirata in Japan.

We would exchange pictures, and I was blown away by Eiko's supermodel good looks. If most of my pen friends were girls, it was simply because they were more inclined to write letters (it was one way to improve their English). I did, however, have a male pen friend in Rheinhausen, Germany.

Pen friends came with benefits, namely, shaving blades. The quality of blades available in India those days was very poor, so we would ask our pen friends to send us Schick blades, the top brand at the time. We also exchanged gifts and cards on birthdays and Christmas.

I tried to satisfy their insatiable curiosity about India, writing about and enclosing pictures of the places I'd been to, the widely differing cuisines of the North and South, and the jungle wildlife we took for granted but they had only seen in zoos. I may have busted a myth or two about 'the land of snake-charmers and yogis'. After all, my friends and I were studying electronics, sported bell-bottoms and dog-ear collars, and listened to Western music.

THE SOUND OF SHORTWAVE MUSIC

Growing up in the neolithic age of electronics, when the nearest thing to a mobile phone weighed 30 kilograms, and a tablet was something your mother shoved down your throat when you were ill, we had a magic box. It was called the radio and it was a rich part of our lives.

It had shiny glass tubes on the inside and knobs on the outside. There were two knobs, one for volume control and another to select the frequency band, an exercise that involved endless twiddling.

After minutes of gentle coaxing, the box would emit a throat-clearing crackle and speak up: 'This is Melville de Mellow speaking to you from the ramparts of the Red Fort in New Delhi ... It's pouring heavily ... umbrellas, umbrellas, umbrellas ...' (from his 1966 Independence Day broadcast on All India Radio). It was de Mellow who had covered Mahatma Gandhi's funeral after his assassination, on 30 January 1948.

The AIR had been around for at least a quarter of a century before I entered my teens, but in far-flung Jabalpur, the broadcasts still crackled. Radio Ceylon, on the other hand, offered high-quality transmission. English pop songs wafted to us from across the Gulf of Mannar in the *Binaca Hit Parade*, a countdown show hosted by Greg Roskowski.

Radio Ceylon then launched the cult show *Binaca Geetmala*, a weekly countdown of the most popular Bollywood songs presented by Ameen Sayani. In 1963, I recall, the top song was the Sahir Ludhianvi-penned '*Jo wada kiya woh nibhana padega*', in the unforgettable delightful voices of Mohammed Rafi and Lata Mangeshkar. We swooned and bought Binaca toothpaste, which came with a little freebie: a trinket attached to a rubber-band.

Our thirst for good English music remained unslaked, so we hunted for international radio stations with shortwave transmission. Unlike mediumwave, the shortwave band can be reflected or refracted from the ionosphere, a layer of electrically charged atoms in the upper atmosphere. Thus, shortwave transmissions have tremendous range, extending thousands of miles across geographical and political boundaries.

Discovering new radio stations became a hobby with us. Much later, I got to know that there was a term for it: DXing. 'DX' refers to distance. Unbeknownst to us, we were members of a global club called SWLers or DXers. They still exist.

Suresh, whose father owned Jabalpur's largest radio repair store, kept my beat-up old radio set in good order. It was a vacuum tube model and the tubes had a tendency to heat up and develop glitches, but Suresh could generally fix them. I would trundle up to the storefront on my bike and signal to Suresh, who was always in the workshop on the first floor. We would set off and spend many happy hours twiddling dials in search of new radio stations, and scribbling down frequencies. We listened to Voice of America, BBC, Radio Philippines, Radio Mauritania, and a score of other stations.

For shortwave, we needed a good antenna. So, we would shin up a tree or scramble onto the roof of a house to position it, in such a way that it was protected from strong winds. Sometimes, we would stumble on mysterious signals of the 'Lima, Charlie, Bravo, Zulu' variety, because the shortwave band was also used for police and military broadcasts (the phonetic alphabet—Alpha, Bravo, Charlie, Delta, Echo and so on—allows for clear communication).

All through college, my room was flooded with music. Apart from the radio, I also had a record player, and saved up pocket money to buy vinyl. My friends and I even studied to music, solving math problems while the AIR Urdu service or Radio Ceylon warbled in the background.

As teenagers in the 1960s, we were naturally exposed to jazz, rock, blues and country. The Beatles blew our minds, from *Please Please Me* to the seminal *The White Album*. But the staple of our get-togethers was always Hindi film music. Kishore Kumar rocked our world, Lata Mangeshkar moved us to tears, and Mohammed Rafi's incredible versatility left us awed and intoxicated.

Several of my friends were good singers, and no festive occasion was complete without a couple of hours of full-throated collective crooning. The undisputed star of these evenings was Chintan, a natural-born singer and the life and soul of every party. His rendition of Kishore Kumar's hilarious '*Yaar tum shaadi mat karna*' from *Parivaar* was a favourite, and he was made to perform it at all our parties. Thanks to these convivial get-togethers, I learnt to sing. I wasn't very good, nowhere near Chintan's class, but I could carry a tune.

HAM radio, which allowed two-way communication, was another popular hobby in those days, but our purpose was to find good music or sports commentaries, so we stuck to SWLing. It was shortwave that enabled us to listen in to the most seminal broadcast of our time: the Moon landing.

MAN ON THE MOON

Ashok and I shared a mutual passion for space travel. All through school and college, zero-gravity dreams took me skyward. I dreamt of hovering above the earth, looking down on people and the technicolour patchwork below, being the only person in the whole wide world who could fly without wings.

Ashok, who was pursuing mechanical engineering, taught me a lot about space research and we had endless discussions on the technological breakthroughs that came hard and fast in the 1960s. The Soviet Union's launch of the beach ball-sized Sputnik in 1957, which orbited Earth in ninety-eight minutes flat, was followed by the first human spaceflight on 12 April 1961. Cosmonaut Yuri Gagarin became the first man in space, 'orbiting Earth for 108 minutes'.

Three weeks later, Alan Shepard became the first American in space. And three weeks after that, US President John F. Kennedy famously committed his nation 'to achieving the goal, before this decade is out, of landing a man on the moon'. The space race heated up, even as Cold War tensions dialled down after the Bay of Pigs.

I followed the Gemini and Apollo missions with a passion, from the first orbital manoeuvre (change of orbit) by a crew in 1965, to the first crewed orbit of the Moon in 1968. I wrote letters to NASA, asking for material, which they were kind enough to supply. It became a regular correspondence and all four walls of my room were soon plastered with NASA posters: astronauts like John Glenn, Gus Grissom and John Young; maps of the near and far side of the Moon with every sea and crater clearly marked; and the Saturn and Delta series of rockets.

Kennedy's dream was realized six years after his death, testifying that political will can achieve the seemingly impossible. The day 16 July 1969 found Ashok and me huddled around our radios in our respective homes. Three Moon-bound US astronauts had blasted off in the Saturn V rocket from Merritt Island, Florida, with the Apollo Lunar Module 'Eagle' on board. Over the next four nail-biting days, we followed the Apollo 11 mission, from Neil Armstrong's 'Good morning, Houston' on Day Two to 'The Eagle has landed' on Day Five.

Early morning on 21 July, we waited breathlessly for the denouement. Armstrong said, 'I'm going to step off the LM now'. Then, with his left boot on the lunar surface, he spoke those immortal words, 'That's one small step for man; one giant leap for mankind'.

Like millions of those glued to Voice of America, I was almost moved to tears. Ashok and I met the next morning, still overwhelmed by that poignant moment. It was beyond words, so we just hugged.

I have always been passionate about my interests, be it music, sports, space exploration, electronics, future technologies or sales. It is a defining trait that I have brought to bear on all my ventures. My great fortune has been that my friends and family have encouraged me to nurture my passions, rather than the other way around.

GOODBYE JABALPUR, HELLO BOMBAY

All too soon, it was time for all of us to take our own 'giant leap'. Our idyllic boyhood was coming to an end. We were on the cusp of adulthood, and all the responsibilities that this implied. We would soon graduate, become job seekers and leave the safe environs of the college campus and our hometown for the big, bad world of metropolitan India. Delhi, Bombay and Madras beckoned, and we looked forward with trepidation and excitement in equal measure.

But first, we gave ourselves a royal send-off. Our final year of college had been fraught with tension, as exams were frequently postponed and the results delayed by several months. So, at the Annual Day function, my buddies and I decided to stage a valedictory musical performance celebrating the ups and downs of college life. We reworked the lyrics of '*Jeena yahan marna yahan*' from Raj Kapoor's *Mera Naam Joker* to say 'Postpone *yahan*, postpone *wahan*'. As we took the stage and launched into the song, the auditorium erupted with laughter and applause. The staff and student body loved the parody, and called for repeated encores!

The prospect of finding a job weighed heavily on me and my fellow graduates. In those days, the concept of campus placements didn't exist, and most jobs for telecom graduates were in the government or the public sector. JEC was the main supplier of engineers to the Department of Telecommunications (DoT). But I had something different in mind.

My brother was in sales and marketing at Caltex and had introduced me to the subject. I was immediately intrigued. He had learnt the basic concepts during his training in Calcutta. Fortunately for him, the training supervisor, Krishna Kumar, was a superb teacher. He introduced his charges to Peter Drucker, Robert Blake and other wise men of management and marketing, illustrating each point with a practical example. All of these learnings were passed on to me.

Once, my friends and I decided to go on a cycling trip from Jabalpur to Bhopal, a distance of 330 kilometres. But how was I to convince my parents? Given that I was the youngest of seven siblings, they were very protective. It was my first conscious attempt at salesmanship, and I pulled it off with aplomb.

Vijay gifted me Peter Drucker's *Managing for Results,* among other books. Once I had absorbed them, we spent hours talking about the techniques and niceties of marketing. It occurred to me that I could make a career of it. So, I scanned newspaper ads for jobs in sales and marketing, and sent off a number of applications.

For several months there was no response. My friends were in the same boat, all of us eagerly awaiting gainful employment. We'd meet up in a park at night to exchange notes. Lying on the grass under the star-speckled night sky with my buddies, I would wonder how my life would pan out.

All at once, there was a barrage of letters summoning me to Delhi for interviews. I set off, feeling chipper. I was quite familiar with the capital, having spent many holidays with my sister Pammi, who had settled there. Three interviews later, I had three job offers. The first was from J.N. Marshall, a small Pune-based company, while the other two were from DCM, India's fifth largest corporate house (I had the option to join DCM as an executive trainee, or DCM Data Products as a sales executive).

I chewed it over and decided DCM DP's offer was the most attractive, because it allowed me to combine both my passions, electronics and sales. I'd heard that DCM DP was moving into electronics, so the '0' and '1' would continue to be a part of my life. That was just as well; if I hadn't joined DCM DP, the HCL story may never have happened, because that's where I met Shiv Nadar and Arjun Malhotra, who floated the idea of striking out on our own.

Parting from my friends was as big a wrench as leaving home. Two of us—Sharat Saxena and I—were heading to Bombay. Given Chintan's musical gifts, he could have had a shot at becoming a playback singer, but it was Sharat—my oldest friend—who aspired to make it in Bollywood. We had spent two years together in Christ Church and another four at JEC. Apart from being physically strong, he was very bright, so his parents had insisted that he complete his education.

After he obtained his degree, he told his father, 'I did what you wanted. Now I'm going to do what I want', and off he went to Bombay. Sharat was convinced that he was great-looking, every inch a hero, and would make it big in films. He did, but is best known for his roles as the villain. In those days, muscle-bound, tough-looking actors were typecast as cops or bad guys.

I was truly lucky to have had Chintan, Suresh, Ashok and Sharat in my life. Thanks to them, my coming of age was a pleasant adventure, and prepared me to navigate the world with confidence, open-mindedness and honesty. Most important of all, it taught me the value of building relationships, a practice that has served me well ever since.

We may have traded in our bicycles for cars and Shuklaji's masala tea for first flush Darjeeling Oolong, but wheels are wheels and chai is chai. And friends are friends. So, no matter where we are and who we've become, the bond remains. We may not meet often, but we start off from wherever we left off when we do.

UNBOXING SOLUTIONS

Sales training was conducted in Delhi, after which two other executives and I were posted to Bombay. Brought up in the comfort of a sarkari home, I was faced with the challenge of living on a modest income of Rs 600 per month, the equivalent of Rs 24,000 today, in India's most expensive city. One of my colleagues had a home in Bombay, so that left the two of us. We decided to share accommodation, to keep rental costs down.

Our office was on mezzanine floor of the DCM cloth store at Churchgate, where we met a business manager with the textiles division. He offered us the use of his first-floor apartment in the middle-income suburb of Ghatkopar. We thought we were in luck, until we saw our new digs. They were, in a word, disastrous. The place was encrusted in dust and festooned with spider webs. Most of the glass in the windows was broken, so the premises were a roosting ground for pigeons. We were knee-deep in bird guano.

The only positive was an Udupi restaurant on the ground floor, where palatable, inexpensive and hygienic meals were available. That didn't make up for the fertilizer on the floors, so we moved out, to a two-bedroom in the rather more upmarket area of Juhu. My colleague was married, so he naturally took the larger room.

I began my career by selling electronic calculators, which were bulky, box-like gadgets priced at Rs 10,000, the equivalent of Rs 4 lakhs today (yes, the free app on your phone performs the same functions). Bear in mind that businesses and government departments did complex and extensive calculations manually, or with mechanical Facit machines. The cost in terms of man-hours was tremendous. But that didn't mean clients were lining up, panting for our product. We had to go to them, not the other way around.

To understand the challenges, picture a world without internet, email, mobile phones and a sparse and erratic telecom network, where an intercity phone call involved an operator and several hours of delay. Physical connectivity was just as poor—roads were rough; bus and train services infrequent; hotels and eateries few and far between.

Brainstorming with my boss, Yogesh Vaidya, I identified a business where rapid and accurate calculations were crucial. These were the sugar mills. The chemist at the mill determines the amount of sucrose in sugarcane juice, the yield of sugar, the processing losses, and the efficiency of extraction. The mill manager needs quick access to the information on all these counts, to recover maximum sugar at minimum cost. During crushing season, the chemist is the most important person at the mill.

I figured out how to do all the requisite number crunching on the calculator, thereby saving the chemist considerable time and effort, and eliminating inaccuracies. My product was no longer a box; it was a solution. And that's what I sold to my customers. It was my first and most important lesson in sales. Present the product as the solution, the fix, the panacea for all problems. Focus on the benefits, not on the attributes. While selling computers a few years later, we didn't rhapsodize about the cutting-edge nature of our technology, but what it could deliver to our clients.

That said, my first years in sales were the classic 'baptism by fire'. I must have visited every sugar mill of Maharashtra, and all of them were located in remote areas. We travelled and slept rough, ate at dhabas (roadside eateries), and hung around for hours waiting to see the mill managers.

Typically, there would be just one bus from Bombay to the town nearest the mill. It usually left early in the morning, so I would get there by the afternoon. My first port of call was the chemist. Convincing him was easy. I would demonstrate our product, using his figures, and this invariably did the trick. Now came the hard part.

The sugar mills were cooperatives, so the chairperson made the final call on purchases. Taking appointments was unheard of, as the telecom network was still a work in progress. I would loiter in tea shops, or take advantage of the mill's hospitality, while waiting for 'sahib' to show up. I learnt to carry a book to while away the time.

The boss usually rolled in by the evening. After he had settled in and attended to the urgent business of the day, I would be summoned. Post the introductions, the chemist would be called in and, forty-five minutes later, the chairperson would graciously give me the nod. The next step was to get the order, which would be typed up by a reluctant clerk and then whisked back and forth for approvals.

By the time I had the order in hand, it would be dusk and the bus to Bombay would've left. Heading to the local mandi, I would ask around for a Bombay-bound truck. The truck drivers were large-hearted, convivial chaps, and I rarely met with a refusal. Ensconced in the cabin of the vehicle, I would rattle home, with stopovers for naps, food and most important of all, the fortifying 'hundred-mile' chai.

The other customer niche we addressed were irrigation engineers, who determined the water requirement for crops based on a whole host of variables. Complex calculations were involved. Yogesh met the head of the state's water resources division, who was so fascinated by our product that he dashed off a strong letter of recommendation, mentioning its price and manifest advantages. Armed with the letter, we secured our first order. This had a domino effect, and we cut a swathe through all the irrigation offices in the state.

Agricultural universities were added to our growing list of clients. In a matter of three years, I traversed the length and breadth of Maharashtra, learning about rural and small-town India from the ground up. At the end of it, we had far and away the best sales numbers in the country.

The job didn't stop with a purchase order. We also had to deliver. One time, I had to personally carry four calculators to the Mahatma Phule Krishi Vidyapeeth at Rahuri, some 50 kilometres south of the temple town of Shirdi. They were high-value items and it wasn't as if logistics companies were available to make the delivery.

My train reached Rahuri at 1.30 a.m. A couple of other passengers disembarked along with me and went their way. I had nowhere to go; there was no question of finding transportation, or a hotel, at that time of the night. The station master had illuminated the platform when the train arrived, but switched the lights off immediately after and disappeared into his office.

In the darkness, I, the doughty salesperson, settled on an unforgiving platform bench. My precious calculators were stacked below it. I barely slept, for fear they might be stolen. A couple of stray dogs kept me company. At sunrise, I hefted my boxes to the road, wondering how to cover the four kilometres to the university. A bullock-cart trundled by.

'*Ram-ram, Kaka*,' I said, greeting the driver. 'I have to go to the university. Is there a bus?'

He shook his head laconically and offered me a lift. To cut a long story short, DCM DP's state-of-the-art electronic calculators were delivered by bullock cart.

Meanwhile, change was afoot at DCM DP. The company was growing fast, but cash flow was a constraint. While Vinay Bharat Ram, the eldest son of the group's founder, was committed to developing the electronics division, no one outside it shared his vision. Although we had a crack R&D team and were well on the way to create an indigenous microprocessor-based computer, money was not forthcoming.

Fed up with the naysayers, Shiv and Arjun floated their idea of an independent company to manufacture and market computers. They approached a dozen people, but ultimately, only four of us agreed to cofound the new venture. The rest, I imagine, must have kicked themselves a few years down the line.

3

THE TECHNO DREAMERS

A LOT OF PEOPLE I know are in the habit of reading their weekly horoscopes. I am not, because the forecast is always generic, along the lines of 'a significant change in your life' or 'a romance in the offing'. In 1976, however, both predictions would have been absolutely true for me. That year, I drastically altered the course of my career, and met the love of my life.

The 'significant change' was my decision to quit DCM DP and leap headfirst into the uncharted waters of entrepreneurship, along with Shiv Nadar, Arjun Malhotra, Yogesh Vaidya, Subhash Arora and D.S. Puri. In the 1970s, start-ups were a virtually unknown phenomenon, so my family and friends naturally thought I was being irresponsible at best, and crazy at worst. To add to their fears, they had only the vaguest notion of what a computer was.

Brimful of aspiration, the six of us—HCL's founders—quit stable, salaried jobs with one of India's biggest brands to chase our own rainbow. The sheer romance of that narrative—six dreamers with pockets to let, creating a global giant—would capture the imagination of journalists and aspiring entrepreneurs in the decades to come. For them, it was a classic rags-to-riches start-up story. The tears and toil that went into actualizing the dream are rarely talked about.

The times were turbulent, as Emergency had been imposed, but we were driven by our belief in the transformative potential of the microprocessor. The goal was to develop an indigenous microcomputer, so we called ourselves 'Microcomp'. We hadn't yet heard of 'Microsoft', a start-up founded in Albuquerque, New Mexico, US by college dropouts Bill Gates and Paul Allen a year earlier.

Like all entrepreneurs, we faced the question of resources. At the time, venture capitalists (VCs) and angel investors didn't exist, and banks did not give loans to entrepreneurs with no collateral or track record. Between us, we raised the grand sum of Rs 1.87 lakhs by borrowing, pooling our savings, and in one case, selling a car. Other than that, we had a very minor loan from Syndicate Bank. We were a garage start-up, pure and simple, operating out of a barsati (a small room on the roof of a house) in Golf Links, one of New Delhi's most posh residential areas.

Fortuitously, Televista gave us the marketing rights to its calculators, with a sweet sixty days' credit deal. This allowed for a negative cash conversion cycle (long before Michael Dell famously used it to fuel his company's growth). We sold like demons and raised enough capital to stay afloat. But we still didn't have the mandatory manufacturing licence. So, we approached the Uttar Pradesh Electronics Corporation Limited (UPTRON). They had the licence, we had the tech expertise. Hindustan Computers Limited was born as a joint sector company.

We were careful in our choice of name and logo. Only PSUs and the biggest companies incorporated 'Hindustan' in their name. We got away with it thanks to our collaboration with a state-owned entity. The name conjured power, patriotism and progress, size and solidity. It made us look larger than life and endowed us with a weight and credibility way beyond our track record.

Bureaucrats and executives were suitably impressed by the 'HIKA' logo in Hindi and the legend 'A joint sector company' emblazoned on our cards, which eased access everywhere. Cold calls and walk-ins by our sales force were rarely rebuffed; in fact, they were given preference.

Names have power, and a logo is a visual connect with customers. Consider Xerox—the 'Xs' make it memorable. In later years, I would tell the aspiring entrepreneurs among my students and mentees to pick a name for their company that would convey brand positioning, enhance credibility and leave a mental imprint.

GUTS AND GLORY

As the new kids on the block, we had to power ahead or perish. Even as our four-bit Micro 2200 desktop for engineers/scientists was still on the drawing board, we began selling. Armed with our brochure, a thing of beauty with a mock-up of the product, our sales force fanned across the country, with the founders leading from the front. I was asked to base myself in Madras and head sales in South India.

The message here is gumption; having the chutzpah to sell a product without a product. As one of our later print ads proclaimed, 'At HCL, there's only one thing more important than brains. Guts'.

We trained our sales team in transactional analysis techniques, which call for an assessment of, and adaptation to, the potential buyer. For instance, when you meet a professor, become a student. Interpersonal communication is the key to sales.

Arjun Malhotra, who'd been my boss at DCM DP, swore he would get the first order—and he did, from his alma mater, IIT Kharagpur. I secured another for six machines from IIT Madras. We were on our way.

The Emergency was followed by the Janata Party government, and industries minister George Fernandes lost no time in asking multinationals to dilute their equity. IBM refused, preferring, like Coca-Cola, to exit the Indian market. This offered a great opportunity to us, and indeed, to all indigenous computer manufacturers, to fill the vacuum left by the multinational giant. Even without IBM, our competition was stiff. It included our old employer DCM DP, Tata's

NELCO, Sarabhai's ORG and the United Kingdom's ICL, which had set up an Indian arm, ICIM.

Our 8C, an eight-bit model, had the added advantage of data entry and battery backup. That was our USP, so to speak. In a market accustomed to mainframes, we consciously focused on first-time users. A powerful advertising campaign, intended to demystify computer technology and bust the myth that it was far too complicated for non-techies, piqued interest tremendously. The headlines read 'HCL introduces a computer which even your typist can operate ... come and see it'; 'Even if your yearly sale is Rs 50 lakhs, HCL computers can bring you profits'; and 'Now you can buy a computer for as little as Rs 3,500 a month ... HCL shows you how'.

Of the many things HCL did right, two stand out as object lessons to entrepreneurs. First, be restless; keep looking for opportunities and gaps in the market and innovate, innovate, innovate. Second, find the right people. Early on, we took a conscious decision to hire the best, regardless of cost. We looked for recruits who were cowboys at heart. 'It's not a job, it's an adventure' was the message. Years later, the media was fascinated by the number of HCL employees who went on to become successful entrepreneurs.

I set up our office in Madras, in a rented space that we redesigned and painted in bright colours to infuse a sense of optimism and cheer. I hired a team of young people and trained them, imparting the techniques I had learnt at DCM DP. Our first job was to create a list of prospects. The challenge was formidable: the computer was entirely new, more a concept than a product, and we were operating in a highly conservative environment.

To overcome the inherent resistance to change, we positioned the computer as a smart investment. To that end, we introduced a return-on-investment (RoI) calculator, which worked out the savings a business could make by using computers. For the first six months, however, there were no sales. Every other region in the country was far ahead of us.

My boss Arjun called from Delhi, complaining, 'You haven't sold a thing! What's wrong with you guys?' He decided to send our Bombay business head, a former IBM employee, to Madras to lecture us on sales. The gentleman arrived and subjected us to long sermons on how well his team in Bombay was doing, at the end of which we got the distinct feeling of having been belittled.

My team was naturally crestfallen, so after he left, I called them. 'Look, he hasn't told us anything we don't already know. I know that you are all good salesmen. Now, we need to turn things around. We absolutely have to make it happen,' I said. That was the turning point. With great determination, they went out and sold aggressively. In six months, we had outsold everyone else. It's amazing what people can do with the right motivation and leadership.

My next target was Coimbatore, a thriving textile hub with warm and friendly people and a classy ambience, but every bit as conservative as Madras. DCM DP was our major competitor and enjoyed the advantage of a parent company that was in the textile business. The group was the fifth largest in the country at the time, and by comparison, we were nobodies. Our prospects would invariably mention their comfort factor with DCM when we met them.

Clearly, the challenge was to build relationships. We focused our efforts towards developing a rapport with prospective clients. We differentiated ourselves from the competition and explained why we were better. If the objection was that we were small fry, we would point out that we were a joint sector company, set up in collaboration with the Uttar Pradesh government. We would cite our existing customer base and references.

Our breakthrough came when we went head-to-head with DCM DP in a large deal with Premier Mills, one of the leading textile firms in the city. I distinctly remember sitting in their reception area, while the team from DCM DP went in to make its pitch. We went in second, but we closed the deal. It was a great reference to have, and we finally cracked the Coimbatore market. That one order got us five more, then ten, and after that, we never looked back.

Premier Mills was family-owned, headed by three brothers, who had taken the call to go with us. One of them became a friend and we are still in touch. Building relationships is good for business, because it ensures your venture's sustainability.

'IF MUSIC BE THE FOOD OF LOVE, PLAY ON'

When I moved out of home and to metropolitan India for work, I took my abiding love of music with me. But the escalating pressure of work and frequent changes of locale—Delhi, Bombay, Madras—didn't allow as much scope for the pursuit of music as I would've liked.

While still a trainee with DCM in Delhi, I found the time to attend a number of late-night baithaks (musical sittings) at Modern School. The programme typically commenced after 9 p.m., and the audience would sit on the floor, which was deathly cold in the winters. Mesmerized by the likes of Ustad Vilayat Khan, I was oblivious to the chill; the cockles of my heart warmed by the electrifying strains of his sitar.

All through, I continued to serve as an amateur entertainer at parties. I would always be called upon to sing, and found myself improving gradually. The fact that I didn't have a shred of stage fright helped. My impromptu performances must have been memorable, because old friends often remember me belting out film songs with gusto. Trouble was, I could never remember the lyrics. I'd scribble them down on chits of paper, which I fished out of my pockets when asked to sing. But on the day I met my wife, I sang effortlessly.

'Love is friendship set to music' is a quote often attributed to the artist Jackson Pollock. It certainly brought my wife and me together. I was lounging at Shiv Nadar's home on a trip to Delhi, while working with DCM DP in Bombay. Shiv's wife, Guddu, came in with a young woman in tow, and introduced her as 'my cousin, Kunkun'. I looked into a pair of beautiful eyes, set under a mop of curly hair, and immediately liked what I saw.

We started to talk and I was bowled over by her impeccable English, picked up at the Lawrence School in Sanawar in the Kasauli Hills, the most prestigious of the private boarding schools at the time. She had a habit of giggling, which I found enchanting. I was soon sitting on the floor next to her, singing. It was an electric moment, because I realized all at once that I was singing just for her, and that she probably knew it.

Kunkun was staying with her famous grandmother, the eminent classical vocal artiste, Naina Devi, at her house in Delhi's Kaka Nagar. I was posted in Bombay. On the face of it, there was no scope for further meetings, so the question of a relationship didn't arise. Fortunately, Kunkun decided to visit Bombay to spend some time with her uncle, a big wheel in Voltas who lived in the city's posh Malabar Hills. That's when I really got to know her.

I took a bus to see her and quickly discovered that romancing a girl was an expensive exercise. On a salary of Rs 600 a month, I had become accustomed to public transport, but Kunkun was appalled when I suggested taking a bus into town, to take a seaside stroll on Marine Drive. So, we took a taxi. Over the next few days, I spent my entire salary on cabs. I was broke for the rest of the month, but it was worth it. We had become comfortable with each other and tentatively embarked on a romance.

After she returned to Delhi, we kept in touch through letters. In those days, a long-distance relationship was intensely frustrating, but at the same time, incredibly romantic. Phone calls were prohibitively expensive and slow. A 'lightning' trunk call would take three or four hours to come through. The internet was still fifteen years in the future, so we relied—perforce—on snail mail. This involved days of fevered anticipation and nail-biting suspense as I waited for the next letter—a far cry from the instant gratification afforded by a WhatsApp call today. I would pounce delightedly on the thick envelope with Kunkun's, by then familiar, left-handed scrawl and tear it open, hoping for long, long strings of sweet nothings—only to find that she had written all of five lines on a single page! I have kept those letters to this day.

The following year, in 1976—just before we founded HCL—I was posted to Delhi. Kunkun was staying with her maasi (mother's sister), Billy, a famous interior designer, in the capital's upmarket Sunder Nagar. Over the next few months, we met practically every evening. Billy Maasi welcomed me into her home, always insisting that I stay for dinner. She introduced me to her fascinating guests, many of whom were from erstwhile royal families. I would stay on after they left, chatting with Kunkun far into the night.

I was deeply in love and wanted to marry Kunkun (although I never proposed explicitly), and everyone knew that. She wasn't quite as sure. I suspect that Billy Maasi and the rest of the family prompted her to make up her mind in my favour. One day, out of the blue, she said, 'Alright, Ajai. Let's go ahead. Let's get married.'

Ecstatic, I took her out that evening to celebrate with Shiv, Arjun and Guddu. We decided that the momentous occasion demanded a splendid venue, so we headed to the ultra-expensive Chinoiserie restaurant at the Oberoi, New Delhi. The maître d' looked us up and down.

'Sorry, sir. I'm afraid you cannot enter,' he said.

'Don't you have a table available?'

'We do, sir. But there is a dress code. And none of you gentlemen is wearing a jacket.'

'But it's a special occasion. We are celebrating an engagement.'

The maître d' immediately relented, and along with his congratulations, offered to lend us jackets. We gratefully seized the offer, donned the jackets and entered the restaurant, where we spied the famous thespian Shashi Kapoor in his shirtsleeves!

We turned at once to the maître d' and pointed out, 'Shashiji is here, and he isn't wearing a jacket!'

Flustered, he seated us and then repaired at once to Shashi Kapoor's table. He whispered into the celebrated actor's ear.

A few minutes later, as we were scanning the menu, we heard a familiar voice. 'Hello,' said Shashi Kapoor, in the clear tone that had delivered one of the most iconic film dialogues of the time, '*Mere paas maa hai*'. He had donned a jacket, and had graciously come over to wish us. We were overwhelmed. He was a superstar, having co-starred with Amitabh Bachchan in the previous year's box-office hit, *Deewaar*.

Blissful as I was at the prospect of marrying Kunkun, there was a major fly in my ointment. Papaji's health was failing. Fortunately, Vijay had been posted to Jabalpur as ITC's branch manager in early 1976, and was able to keep a close eye on our parents. He and his wife Kukoo were installed in the lavish ITC bungalow, Sona House, just a few kilometres from my parents' home in Napier Town. Kunkun and I decided that our formal engagement should take place there in the month of August 1977, as Papaji was too unwell to travel.

Kunkun's family was put up at the Jacksons hotel, a beautiful nineteenth century heritage property owned by Kukoo's friends. The ceremony itself was held on the vast terrace of Sona House. We kept it short and sweet, but followed it up with a swinging party, in the presence of my parents. Sadly, it was the last time that I saw my father. He passed away within the month.

The wedding was planned for November and we couldn't postpone it, as all the arrangements had already been made. It was held at the house of Kunkun's didima (grandmother), Naina Devi, back then India's best known exponent of thumri. The baraat (groom's wedding procession) left from my sister Pammi's house. Among the guests was Bubbles, the 'maharaja' of Jaipur, who was well known to the family. He took me to his family temple to seek the deity's blessings, and insisted that I wear a Rajasthani saafa (turban). I found it tough to handle; it kept falling off.

Apart from the eminent musicians of the day, a number of 'royals' attended the wedding, as Nainaji, who was from the famous Calcutta family of social reformer Keshub Chandra Sen, had married into the

Kapurthala royal family. She was then known as Nilina and was already a great classical singer, but could not perform because her father-in-law wouldn't allow it. After he passed away, she changed her name to Naina Devi and emerged as the thumri queen of India.

Over the years, before and after we got married, we attended many a baithak at her home, where we were privileged to hear the top classical musicians of the day. She had created an organization called Raag Rang, which held monthly concerts. I made it a point to attend whenever I was in town.

Kunkun and I settled happily into married life in Madras, where I was posted. She had never before stepped into the kitchen in her life, so I had to teach her how to make tea. We hired a cook and my mother came down for a bit to coach her on how to make the dishes I liked. Kunkun had other skills, though. She was an excellent money manager, and while we were always short on cash, she somehow managed to stretch our budget to cover a fairly decent standard of living.

Luckily for us, her grandfather had given her a fixed deposit of Rs 11,000 as a wedding present, and we used that to buy a second-hand Fiat. It was a rather beat-up old vehicle, but it allowed us to be mobile. We made 'couple friends', as married people tend to do. In Madras, we met Kailash and Sajida Sharma, who lived in the same apartment building, Cambrae East. We became close over the years. Through Kailash, we met Steve and Asha Pinto, who continue to be good friends to this day. We also got to know the Murugappa family, which runs the highly diversified conglomerate of that name. Alagappan and Murugu became close friends.

We had many get-togethers, and were constantly on the lookout for ways and means to procure alcohol, because Tamil Nadu was a dry state in those days. Kailash was with Philips and became quite the hero in my eyes when he arranged a TV for us to watch cricket. I was desperate to see the matches, but neither of us could afford a TV at the time. So, he asked a dealer to give him one, and we happily binged on cricket for a few days. Sadly, Kailash is no longer with us, but Sajida remains a dear friend.

The birth of our first son, Kunal, in 1979 put the seal on our marital happiness. Kunkun did not go back to her maternal home to have the baby. Her mother and grandmother came to Madras for the birth. They kept us both in good spirits as we waited for the D-day. As soon as Kunkun went into labour, she developed a food craving and insisted on eating a dish she particularly liked before going to the hospital for her delivery, much to the amusement of her grandmother.

Kunkun was wheeled into the maternity ward, leaving me to pace outside as expectant fathers always do. We kept on waiting, but there was no news from within. For first-time mothers, labour can last for quite a long time, I was told in consolation. Finally, just as I was ready to tear my hair out, came the good news: we had had a healthy baby boy, born through caesarean section. It would take Kunkun a few days to recover from the surgery, but she was doing fine.

I was an unashamedly doting dad, rushing home from work in the evenings to be with my infant son. The demands of work were intense at the time, as we were building HCL from scratch. I was travelling constantly, usually by bus or train. Hyderabad, a frequent destination, involved a sixteen-hour bus journey. But no matter how exhausting the journey, the joy of coming home to the welcoming smiles of my wife and son never failed to lift my spirits.

EASTWARD HO!

Soon, another big change was in the offing. HCL was doing well, thanks to our strategy. Leveraging our understanding of purchase decisions within organizations, we zeroed in on those with individual decision-makers, and where the computer could contribute to higher productivity. We targeted lower-end markets, including small businesses, for our products, holding roadshows in Tier II cities.

In a highly competitive environment, we stayed ahead of the curve with our proprietary hardware and software systems and application packages.

End result: while our competitors sold a couple of hundred computers a year, we sold a thousand. By 1980, the year Indira Gandhi swept back to power, we had beaten DCM DP.

The next leap forward was overseas. I had been happily ensconced in Madras for two years, settling into the joys of married life and enjoying the heady success of breaking into the South Indian market. Enter Shiv Nadar. He was very keen that HCL should go international. The opportunity had come up in talks with Singapore's Economic Development Board (EDB). In keeping with their policy to promote electronics, they had invited us to set up a manufacturing unit in Singapore.

It was a bold move; a giant leap of faith for our four-year-old company. I would go so far as to dub it a 'man on the moon' moment, because no Indian tech company had ventured into Singapore until then. Subhash Arora and I, with our senior colleague Raj Mahajan, were asked to relocate there within the month.

At 29, I had never set foot beyond the subcontinent, so Singapore's multi-cultural, cosmopolitan milieu came as a bit of a culture shock. The island had once been under the cultural sway of the Indian subcontinent, but the tide had turned many times since its conquest by the Chola king Rajendra I in the eleventh century CE. Ethnic Chinese were in majority and Mandarin the most commonly spoken language.

Leaving my wife and infant son in Madras, I moved into the Oberoi group-owned Imperial Hotel in Singapore, which offered Indian food. My family joined me after I found an apartment at Dragon Court (we later moved to Mandalay Court). I knew that our salaries would be at rock bottom and we would be living hand to mouth for the foreseeable future, but I was confident that Kunkun would manage our finances with her customary aplomb.

We pondered over the name of the new company. Obviously, Hindustan Computers wouldn't do, so we settled on Far East

Computers. Subhash was to be the overall head while I, the marketing director.

From the outset, we knew that money would be a major constraint. In those days, the Reserve Bank of India (RBI) was very reluctant to part with foreign exchange. Shiv gave us a target: one million dollars' worth of business in six months. We had no choice in the matter; to generate enough cash flow to keep our Singapore operations going, we had to meet our target.

For Far East Computers, and HCL as a whole, the success of the Singapore operation demanded all the blood, sweat, tears, toil and ingenuity we could summon. It was make or break, and we were determined for it to be the former.

4

WINDOW TO THE WORLD

'AT LAST, A COMPANY THAT offers computerization, not just computers,' read the banner headline in *The Straits Times*. The full-page advertisement in Singapore's leading daily, with the strapline 'Introducing Far East Computers', included a little cut-out form for inquiries about our 'comprehensive computerization package', alongside a picture of Subhash Arora exuding gravitas. It had panache, it had flair, and it generated all the noise and attention we could have hoped for.

The ad created the impression that we were a much larger company than we actually were, a tactic we had employed in India by incorporating 'Hindustan' into our name. Determined to make a big splash in the Singapore market, we had decided that however tight our finances, there would be no stinting on advertising and public relations. We decided to engage Ogilvy & Mather for the former and Burson-Marsteller for the latter—the leaders in their respective fields at the time. It was well worth it.

Fortunately, we had the advantage of a zero-tax regime for five years, given that we were setting up Singapore's very first electronics factory to manufacture our 8C computers, to be sold under the brand name Abacus. The plant was located at the industrial estate in Red Hills (Bukit Merah in Malay) in central Singapore, where the government had built flatted factories. All we had to do was to move in with our equipment.

We found a small office in the Tunas building and bought second-hand cars to get around, because Singapore's mass rapid transit system was still in the planning stages. Shiv moved to Singapore for a while to help us get off the ground. We had to set up operations from scratch, including getting the company registered, and installing telephones. To our surprise, all of this was accomplished smoothly. Singapore rightly prided itself on ease of doing business.

We began selling from the get-go. Rain or shine—and it was mainly rain—we were out on the road, selling. Gaining a foothold in Singapore was by no means easy, as India had yet to make its presence felt internationally in the IT sector. The software boom was still a couple of decades in the future. So, customers, particularly government agencies, were surprised and even sceptical to hear of an Indian company at the cutting edge of technology—designing and manufacturing state-of-the-art hardware. The typical Indian, in their general perception, was the guy who ran the corner shop.

To meet our target, we needed to pull a rabbit out of a hat. And we did, by creating an opportunity where none existed. We had heard that the Singapore and Ngee Ann polytechnics were coming out with a tender for a large number of IBM PCs, as they wanted one for each of their engineering students. It was a big order. We were determined to get it, in the teeth of fierce competition. In terms of size, we were tiny compared to our rivals, so we relied on a strategy that differentiated us from the rest of the field.

My colleague Peter Purushottama and I had been following the development of workstations, specifically for engineering and scientific applications. It was actually an offshoot of our shared interest in future technologies. For instance, we were fascinated by the concept of relational databases long before people realized its business potential. So, when Larry Ellison and his coworkers released Oracle in 1979 and changed the face of business computing, we decided to pay them a visit. This eventually led to us creating a business around Oracle in ASEAN and India.

The idea of a workstation—a single-user product configured for engineers and scientists—was revolutionary. First off the blocks was Apollo, a company set up in 1980 by Bill Poduska, an MIT-trained electronics engineer, and Dave Nelson. Bill called his company Apollo because he'd worked with NASA's Electronics Research Centre during the Apollo space programme, which he regarded as a 'seminal point in the history of man'.

We met him in Chelmsford, Massachusetts, where Apollo was headquartered. Sun Microsystems had also come up with a workstation, but we were greatly impressed by Apollo's token ring networking technology. Bill invited us to his home and there, sitting in his basement along with his cofounder Dave, we had a thrilling conversation on technology. At the time, Apollo produced much of its own hardware and software.

So impressed were we that we signed up for a fifteen-day training programme with Apollo. It was the middle of winter, so every morning, I had to scrape snow off our car and then manoeuvre carefully over roads slick with ice, all the way from our hotel to Chelmsford. The precarious journeys were worth it, just to watch the creation of a world-class tech company from scratch. I learnt a lot about technology from Bill, and it stood me in good stead in the years that followed (Apollo was eventually acquired by Hewlett Packard in 1989).

The Singapore government order opened up the possibility of marketing the Apollo workstations, so we approached them with a question. 'Why specifically an IBM PC? Why not an engineering workstation?'

'Because they are appropriate for our students,' came Singapore's reply.

Our challenge was to prove that we had a better alternative. We knew that Apollo's 'token ring' technology-based workstations were ideal for engineers, but we had to sell the idea to the buyers. Subhash and I worked in tandem. He created a rapport with the buyers while I handled the technology aspect.

I realized that the big difference between the IBM PC and the Apollo workstation was the operating system. The former used MS-DOS, and the latter UNIX. I did some research and learnt that UNIX had originally been developed by AT&T for engineers. I pointed out this very pertinent fact to the buyers. 'Using MS-DOS rather than UNIX, which is designed for engineers, would be a mistake,' I said confidently. Pat came the reply: 'What is UNIX?'

I was stumped. So, I placed a call to AT&T. It was a behemoth of a company, and I had no clue what I was looking for, but after several calls, I discovered that they had an instructional video on UNIX. I placed an order for it, and it was delivered by courier five days later.

I made copies and handed them over to the relevant people, saying, 'You wanted to know about UNIX. This is it.'

They were quite intrigued and wanted to know more. I got back to Apollo and asked them for references. They suggested two universities that were already using their products to teach engineering: Oxford in the UK and Brown in the US. We even managed to get some white papers on Brown University's experience with the workstations. But we needed something more, a pièce de résistance that would clinch the deal.

'ROYALL' FLUSH

Our ace in the hole turned out to be an Englishman by the name of Ken Royall, who was running the workstation facility at Oxford. He was obviously the foremost expert on the subject. What if we were to hire him? It was a bold decision, but I was convinced that if he were on board, it would seal the deal, and in all likelihood, generate a lot more business in the future.

I flew to London and put up at a fancy hotel that I could ill afford, ostensibly to interview people for HCL. I called Royall and told him I was looking to hire people and would love to meet with him. He came over and we had a long chat. Then I put my cards on the table, and explained that we needed his help to sell the idea of UNIX-based workstations in Singapore.

I discovered that Royall was married to an Indian and used that to sell him on Singapore. 'Your wife would be happy there. Help is easily available and it's close to India. It's a great life,' I pointed out. Royall agreed. It was an important step forward, because I knew his word would carry a lot of weight in Singapore. I was right.

To put it in perspective, we were (barely) a million-dollar company that had won a three-million dollar contract, competing against a global hardware giant. Soon after, we introduced the product in India and set up a joint manufacturing facility with Apollo. Indigenously manufactured workstations were a big step forward for us, and for India's IT sector as a whole.

Apart from Apollo, Far East Computers looked at two other US-based companies. One of them was a pioneering ODM (original design manufacturing) vendor by the name of Convergent Technologies. Long before Taiwan became the ODM/OEM hub of the world, Convergent was supplying hardware to customers like Prime, Mohawk, AT&T and Burroughs, who sold the computers under their respective brands.

I had reached out to the CEO, Allen Michaels, who had earlier worked with the Digital Equipment Corporation and Intel, because I'd heard they were working on an easily programmable, multitasking business computer. We had taken the lead in engineering and science workstations, but we felt the need for a UNIX-based business computer. Convergent's Motorola 68000-based system ran on UNIX, and we figured it might fit the bill. Off we went to California to meet the Convergent team.

I took to Allen immediately. His work ethic was incredible; he put in fifteen-hour days, fuelled by fast food. Explaining his dynamic leadership style to me, he said, 'As CEO, I take very quick decisions. If I take ten rapid decisions, chances are two will be wrong, but I can rectify those later.' I took this lesson in timely decision-making to heart; I have never sat on decisions since.

The other company was Fortune Systems, where I met Rich Siegel, their global sales head and perhaps the best salesperson I have ever known. It was a US-based start-up, among the first to market multi-user computer systems tailored to business applications. In 1981, the company had made a big splash with the prototype of its low-cost, business-oriented, Motorola 68000 microprocessor-based computer that worked on UNIX. The design was wonderfully aesthetic. I am reminded of Steve Jobs's comment on the MacOS X, 'We made the buttons on the screen look so good you'll want to lick them.'

Fortune had reverse-engineered Wang Laboratories' world-beating word-processing software and produced a very user-friendly version called 32:16. We met with the CEO, Gary Friedman, and arrived at a deal. We took the product to Singapore. I was continually impressed by Siegel's sheer dynamism. I would call in the middle of the night with a query or request, and by the next morning, I would get a callback. It taught me the importance of being responsive. Fortune Systems eventually sold its hardware business to SCI in 1987. Many years later, SCI would become one of HCL's customers when we set up operations in the US.

THE CITY OF LIONS

Far East Computers proved to be a turning point for HCL. Singapore, Sanskrit for 'lion city', was our window to the world, and our success in the South and Southeast Asian markets catapulted us into the big—or at least bigger—league. In the backdrop of that success was Singapore PM Lee Kuan Yew's vision to bring his country into the global mainstream.

It was still a work in progress when I landed there for the first time. The legendary Lee, founder prime minister of the city state, had scripted an economic boom, but it was a long way from becoming the internationalized financial hub and architectural wonderland that it is today.

When the island became independent in 1965, Lee didn't have very much to work with. Originally a small settlement, it had become an important port under British rule, but fell to Japan during World War II. A period of political turmoil followed, from which Singapore emerged in desperately straitened circumstances, with a high unemployment rate, poor health and educational infrastructure and constant threats of annexation.

'LKY', as Lee was known, wasted no time. His first move was to join the Commonwealth and the United Nations, simultaneously focussing on a rapid build-up of Singapore's economy. The country positioned itself as a trans-shipment hub, and became an attractive destination for foreign investment. It set up industrial estates and oil refineries and invested heavily in education and skill development. LKY inculcated a work ethic based on the core concepts of efficiency, honesty, discipline, cleanliness, motivation and merit-based status.

The country lacked natural resources and land was limited, so promoting the electronics sector was seen as the best way forward. In a matter of ten years, it became the largest producer of disk drives. The Tandon Corporation, a US-based company set up by the Indian-born engineer Sirjang Lal 'Jugi' Tandon, was the first to establish HDD manufacturing in Singapore in 1983.

LKY was a problem-solver par excellence. If land was needed, you reclaimed it. If skills were required, you developed them. If drugs were a problem (given that Singapore was cheek by jowl with the golden triangle), you came down on offenders like a tonne of bricks. And if the birth rate was low because people were too career-oriented to opt for marriage, well, you encouraged romance! One year, LKY conceived of an experiment to boost the birth rate: a bunch of very bright youngsters were sent off together on a cruise in the hopes that proximity would lead to love affairs, marriages and eventually, very bright children. I call it the 'Lee Genes' programme!

A significant aspect of the Singapore miracle was the fact that in a city of varied ethnicities, there was absolute harmony. One reason for this may have been that the ethnic balance in the city state was maintained in a natural way, not as a matter of state policy. Singapore was not concerned with provenance; it wanted talent and skills. If you contributed, you were offered permanent residency (as I was).

Kunkun adjusted to Singapore easily, one major blessing being that we were permitted to take our ayah from India. For her, a big challenge was the fact that she still hadn't learnt to cook, but thanks to our ayah and the mother of one of our Chennai friends, who laboriously wrote down some thirty recipes by hand, she coped very well. Despite her careful management, we were always overdrawn, so we discovered the virtues of a credit card.

Kunal, when he was old enough to go to school, was enrolled at the local primary, where he picked up Mandarin. We eventually moved him to the prestigious Tanglin International School. Kunkun, when she had time on her hands, began working with children who had autism.

When Kunkun was expecting once more, Rose David entered our lives. My wife had gone off to India, leaving me to look for a nanny. Rose had been working for another family, and had just become available. She was the ideal candidate: she spoke English, was a great cook and an accomplished nanny. I called Kunkun with the good news, and Rose became a part of our family.

Kunkun and I found plenty of scope for entertainment in Singapore, even in the early 1980s. The Hawker Centre's food court was one of our favourite haunts. It offered excellent and inexpensive food, but one had to get used to the pervading smell of pork and lard, and learn how to use chopsticks.

A renowned tourist hub was Bugis Street, famed for its nightly gathering of transvestites. The atmosphere was perpetually festive; food and liquor flowed, music blared, the night market did brisk business and the glamourous Asian queens danced. The principal queen presided over the revelries. On my very first visit there, I got my picture taken with the queen!

Occasionally, we would drive to Johor via the causeway linking Singapore to the mainland, cross the border into Malaysia, and visit Malacca or Kuala Lampur. Genting Highlands, the charming hill station on Mount Ulu Kali, was a favourite weekend destination. We also went to Thailand and Indonesia. We were fascinated by Bali. Predominantly Hindu, it had a strong cultural affinity to India, and extended us a warm welcome. Reminders of the Ramayana were everywhere. We ran into a server at a bar who proudly proclaimed that his surname was Gandhi!

One of my important learnings while working in Singapore was the concept of 'face'. In the course of negotiations, you were never aggressive. Etiquette demanded that you spoke softly, appeared humble and did not directly contradict the client. If they got cornered and had no choice but to accede to your terms, you always provided a face-saver that made it appear as if they were getting their way. The lesson came in handy, especially during my frequent trips to China.

Far East Computers had successfully penetrated the Southeast Asian market, covering Malaysia, Indonesia, Thailand and Hong Kong, and had even opened an office in Australia. However, these were relatively small markets. So, we started looking towards China, a huge emerging market with enormous potential.

IN THE DRAGON'S MOUTH

Deng Xiaoping's 'four modernizations' programme had been launched in 1978, and China was looking to become a modern, industrialized country. After the US granted the PRC full diplomatic recognition in 1979, it opened up to foreign investment, and forged trade and diplomatic ties with the rest of the world. The Maoist notion of economic self-reliance was left where it belonged, in the past.

Multilateral agencies like the UN were investing big in China in those days. Universities, in particular, were receiving funding and technological inputs. Our entry into the Chinese market started in 1983, with a bid on a UNDP (UN Development Programme) tender for a computer system to conduct a population census.

We were one of forty competitors, but we won the deal. That same year, we secured a second contract, and within two years, another two. All told, it added up to six-and-a-half-million dollars' worth of business, the equivalent of seventeen million dollars today. It was a good beginning.

We set about creating a sales and service relationship with our clients, primarily the universities of Beijing and Shanghai. As Mandarin was the local language, we had to draft people from our Singapore office who were fluent in it, to serve as interpreters. Peter Chang, who accompanied me on my China travels, was invaluable in liaising with the universities.

In China, I acquired a Sinicized name, 'Chow Ta Lee', as my Indian surname was a tongue-twister for our Chinese partners. To better connect with existing and potential clients, I had business cards proudly bearing the name printed up, and handed them out while visiting the country.

China was opening up, but had yet to emerge from decades of conservatism and socio-political conformity. Nothing underlined the fact more than the Friendship hotel, the one hostelry in Beijing city that was not at all habitable. The rooms were small and depressingly utilitarian, but at least there was attached bathroom.

Board and lodging were the least of my problems. I was mystified and unsettled by the Chinese methods of negotiation. As one of the first Indian businesspersons to venture into mainland China, I found their tactics unfathomable. We were constantly kept off-balance, and never knew where we stood. In later decades, Chinese-style negotiations and business culture would become the subject of academic research and numerous books.

Typically, the meetings were held in a stark conference room, featureless except for a black board and a long table with ergonomically challenged chairs. In the winters, physical discomfort was magnified because there was no heating, even when the mercury fell to twenty degrees below zero. To make matters worse, there was no glass in the windows, and our multiple layers of clothing were ineffective against the chill wind blowing through the room.

The two of us would sit on one side of the table, facing the negotiators. There would be five to ten of them, as if to overpower us through sheer numbers. It was hard to settle down, because discussions were frequently interrupted. At 11 a.m., they would depart for lunch, followed by a long siesta. We would kick our heels for several hours, until deliberations resumed in the evening.

When we got down to the commercials, it typically played out like this:

I say, 'So, that's our number.'

Dead silence for a few minutes. Then, 'Price is too high.'

One of them gets up, walks over to the board and with great deliberation, scrawls a much lower number.

'I'm sorry but that's impossible,' I say.

Silence. Then, as one, they all get up and leave the room.

I look at Peter Chang in silent enquiry. Are they going to come back? Is the meeting over? Is the deal dead in the water? He shrugs.

We go back to our hotel and wait. I am fidgety, well aware that these are psychological tactics aimed at softening us up, but I can't help myself.

Chang and I try to work out a strategy. But how do you strategize when you can't figure out the variables?

At 7 p.m., the phone rings, summoning us for a meeting at 10 a.m. the following day. We show up, hoping things will go better this time.

I say, 'We have talked to our people and we have another number.'

I quote a price 15 per cent lower than the original. Chang translates.

In total silence, they get up and depart en masse.

On the third day, they lowball us once again.

'Last price,' we are told.

We shake our heads. They exit stage left.

The following day is our last in Beijing, and they know it. We absolutely have to make our flight because we don't have a hotel booking for the next day. Discussions drag on and on, and we keep glancing anxiously at our wristwatches. Finally, we cave in, and agree to a price 30 per cent lower than our original quote.

After several such encounters with Chinese negotiators, I figured out that only one member of their team really matters. The rest are there to exert pressure. Zeroing in on the decision-maker is tricky, because he is careful not to stand out. One time, when we were discussing the sale of high-tech equipment with university representatives, I saw them glancing surreptitiously at a quiet gentleman sitting at one corner of the table. We later discovered that he was a People's Liberation Army general in civvies, who was passing himself off as a member of the team. We surmised that the purchase, ostensibly meant for the university, may have military application.

There were other reminders that we were in a communist regime. On one occasion, the Chinese team decided to meet with us in my hotel room. We were discussing technology, and I was liberally throwing around the ten odd tech terms in Mandarin that I had picked up, to their obvious enjoyment.

All at once, one of them got up and left without a word. After a while, he reappeared. Immediately, another disappeared. He returned, and a third one left. The musical chairs continued until the meeting was over. I was shocked; every one of our guests had vanished by turns for a good fifteen minutes.

I turned to Chang, 'What was all that about?'

'Didn't you guess? They went to the bathroom, to use the shower!'

Appalled, I stuttered, 'Wh-aa-t! You mean they had a bath there? With my soaps and towels? All of them?'

'Communal baths are the norm here. None of their homes have baths. A hot shower in an individual bathroom is a luxury. I think that was the whole idea of having the meeting here,' said Chang.

Sharing a bathroom with ten acquaintances is where I draw the line on socialism. I immediately called the reception and had my room changed.

Another time, I found myself at the receiving end of the Chinese bureaucracy. Entering the country wasn't easy. You needed a sponsor to get a permit, which awaited you at the port of entry. My secretary in Singapore had booked me on a flight to Beijing via Shanghai (commercial air services from Singapore to mainland China had commenced in 1985), so my papers were at Beijing airport.

At Shanghai, all the passengers were told to disembark and go through security and immigration. I tried to explain to the airline personnel that I was en route to Beijing. My lack of Mandarin was a severe handicap; they stared at me uncomprehendingly and gestured towards the exit door.

One by one, the passengers exited the cabin, until I was the only one left. Three uniformed persons, obviously policemen, entered. They pointed imperatively to the door. I was marched off the aircraft, clutching my briefcase and book, and taken to immigration. Fortunately, one of the officials there spoke English. He expressed great interest in the novel I was holding (China had emerged from the Cultural Revolution and its public book burnings just a decade earlier).

We chatted about the book and he was perfectly bonhomous, but firmly refused to allow me back on the aircraft. It took half an hour of cajoling before he relented. I was put back on the flight, which by this time was chock-a-block with passengers and enveloped in a thick haze of smoke. The Chinese loved their cigarettes and smoking on flights was not yet taboo.

My most memorable experience was a visit to the Great Wall, courtesy of a university liaison official. It was so spectacular that we lost track of time and walked for miles. At noon, we suddenly realized that we very hungry. Our host took us for lunch and only after the meal did we ask what we had eaten. Mule meat, he said.

THE GREAT BANQUET

Indeed, the culinary challenges involved in breaking into the Chinese market cannot be overstated. Pan masala was my constant companion in China. Often, I'd find myself at a formal banquet with an indeterminate chunk of meat quivering at the end of my chopsticks (for which my Singapore years had trained me). Under a score of curious eyes, I'd deftly transfer it into my mouth and swallow it whole, praying that my gastrointestinal lining wouldn't revolt.

The great Chinese banquet, a necessary feature of doing business in the PRC in the 1980s, was a gracious tradition, imbued with dignified rituals. The primary host and guest would sit facing each other. Protocol demanded that the host serve a bite-sized portion of the first dish to the chief guest. Next, the host served himself a similar portion. Only then could the rest of the company begin their meal.

The trouble was that the feast typically featured eleven to twenty-one dishes. If you were the chief guest or the chief host—and I was invariably cast in either one of those roles—it was mandatory to take a bite of each course. For a stomach unaccustomed to large quantities of non-vegetarian fare, it was a gruelling test.

The mega-meals were accompanied by three kinds of alcoholic beverages. The shots were at least 120 proof and burned all the way down.

I would return to my hotel after dinner and swallow a spoonful of that wonderful digestive pan masala. At times, when banquets were held in quick succession, even the pan masala would not be enough.

Food was always a problem for our team, because of the wide array of unfamiliar meats. The cuisine varied from province to province, and except for the Szechuan (or Sichuan) which I relished, the fare was rather bland, a far cry from the Indian 'Chinese' to which we were accustomed. Breakfast consisted of Chinese porridge, so heavy with meat that I preferred to start my day with bread. Occasionally, Chang and I would repair to the airport Hilton, which had an Indian restaurant and also served a very decent Peking duck.

There were virtually no vegetarian options. I once took a team from the UK to China, and the CAD/CAM (computer-aided design and computer-aided manufacture) expert, a vegetarian, couldn't find a thing to eat, except bread. On the fourth day, our Chinese sponsors took pity on him and bore us off to a banquet at a vegetarian restaurant. The meal consisted of mock meats, made of soya. There were thirty-one dishes in all. It felt like death by soya.

I was a regular visitor to China for five years. In those days, the mainland was decades behind Hong Kong. The island's booming economy had translated into edgy lifestyles and famously outré nightclubs, where international superstars dropped in on the regular.

I got a taste of Hong Kong's nightlife when one of our partner companies invited us for a tour, and insisted on taking us to a 'hostess bar' for drinks and dinner. 'It's huge! You could drive up and down in a car,' I said when we entered the bar.

'People do,' my host replied with a smirk. He had his arms around two of the hostesses, who were popping little morsels of food into his mouth. I figured he was going to take them home, to continue the party on the company's dime. So, we left him to his carousing and returned to our hotel.

Many years later, I took my wife to Beijing. I pointed out the Friendship hotel, and recapped my many adventures in the city. She had a wonderful time; we ate a lot of Peking duck, visited the Great Wall, did a ton of shopping, and took home an array of beautiful artefacts.

In 2008, we went back for the Beijing Olympics. I was stunned by the transformation. The city had fast-forwarded a century in a matter of a decade, and become a vibrant vista of soaring skyscrapers. There were automobiles of all shapes, sizes, colours and brand logos. The paradigm shift in street fashions was downright dazzling.

Shanghai was shock and awe. The infrastructure was futuristic, the hotels and restaurants among the best I'd seen. We could have been anywhere in the world. A friend took us to Xin Tian Di street, an affluent, car-free shopping area, with ravishing little cafés, restaurants playing jazz and beguiling European-style bistros with tables on the pavement. It was an unforgettable evening of beer, delectable food and music.

5

INDIA UNBOUND

I'M AN ARDENT INDOPHILE. NINE pleasant years of working overseas and decades of travel across the globe have only strengthened my conviction that there's no place quite like home. My father, Jai Krishna Chowdhry—freedom fighter, refugee, bureaucrat, poet, patriot—instilled in all his children an indelible pride in being Indian. So, when Kunkun and I had to decide between living in the US or in India, it was a no-brainer.

It was 1989, and HCL was growing exponentially. Shiv Nadar was clear that either Subhash or I would have to quit Singapore and lend a hand. I volunteered, because Subhash's wife was unwell and unfit to move at the time. That's when Shiv offered me a choice. 'We definitely need someone in the US as well, so you could go there if you prefer,' he said.

I didn't have to think it over. I told Kunkun, 'The US is a great place to visit, but I wouldn't want to live there.' She agreed, and I informed Shiv that we would prefer to move back to India.

For the family, it represented a radical change. Kunal had been a toddler when we moved to Singapore and Akshay hadn't lived anywhere else. As for Kunkun and me, we had thoroughly enjoyed our stint in the island city. For all that we were looking forward to upon moving back, leaving Singapore and its vibrant social life would be hard.

Our very first friends in Singapore had been the Sehgals, Manju and Lal, whom a mutual friend introduced to us. They, in turn, drew us into their wide social circle. There was Rafiq Jumabhoy, who headed Scotts Holdings, the then largest Indian family-owned corporation in the city, and Sajjad Akhtar who was a partner with American accounting firm Arthur Andersen, and his wife Ruby. We met and became close to a distant relative of Kunkun, Jayanti Rehman, and her husband Maif. She was a dynamic businesswoman who lived in a huge penthouse not too far from our modest home. Maif was godfather to our sons.

We also got to know Ranjan Kapur, banker turned advertising maven who was then head of O&M in Singapore, and his wife, Lorraine (better known as Jimi). Coincidentally, we met the Soods, Bhushan and Urvashi, who were with the Oberoi group at the time and whose daughter was destined to marry our son, Akshay. Among our other friends were Ali and Kinny Kapur, and Vikram and Nina Srihari. Vikram had worked with us in Far East Computers. We became close and remain so.

Our close-knit little expat community had frequent get-togethers, featuring bowling, dinners and long sessions of board games, mainly Trivial Pursuit. We had picked up bowling and Kunkun, being a left-hander, proved to be an ace. We played almost every Sunday. I was fond of racquet games, so I learnt squash, and this further expanded our social circuit.

When word got around that we would be leaving, Ranjan and Jimi threw us a farewell party. He walked in with a box, ceremoniously handed it over and announced, 'This is your farewell gift. You are going to need it in Delhi.'

'What is it?' I asked.

'It's a puppy kit.'

'A puppy kit? We don't have a dog!'

'Puppy', it turned out, was an acronym for 'prosperous urban Punjabi who is young', New Delhi's take on 'yuppy' (young upwardly mobile professional). The capital's Punjabi nouveau riche was known for its flashy spending habits and ostentatious displays. The typical puppy blared loud music from his air-conditioned Maruti (or Toyota) car, sported expensive watches and sunglasses and wafted cloying aftershaves. Ranjan claimed he had given me all I needed to pass myself off as a true-blue puppy.

To this day, I look back on my time in Singapore with fondness. A melting pot where East met West in an atmosphere of undiluted bonhomie, the city opened up our minds and hearts. We were there for nearly a decade, and watched it grow and evolve into an international hub. Changi airport was inaugurated in 1981 and became one of the largest globally. Even while creating world-class modern infrastructure, Singapore preserved its eclectic architectural and cultural heritage. Small wonder then that it had become an international tourist destination, charming visitors with its multicultural milieu.

During our time there, it was a favourite destination for global musicians. Kunkun and I, with our shared love of music, made it a point to take in as many live shows as we could and were able to sample a wide range of genres. My taste spanned from classical to pop, and while in Singapore, I developed a deep fascination with jazz. We were also privileged to hear Mehdi Hassan's sublime ghazals and the hair-raising qawwalis of Nusrat Fateh Ali Khan.

I have always felt a karmic connection with Singapore, not only because Akshay was born there and his wife, Neha, is Singapore-bred. Kunal, having spent his early years there, found himself back in Singapore when he started working. Kunkun and I visit as often as we could, to spend time with our three grandchildren, and all our friends there, including Subhash Arora, who is now settled in Singapore.

HOMECOMING

The family had a hard time adjusting to Delhi, none of us more so than Kunkun. Accustomed as we were to taking basic services and the professionalism of domestic workers in Singapore for granted, dealing with power cuts, water supply issues and lackadaisical staff was frustrating. The 'chalta hai' culture proved to be immensely trying after Singapore's ease of living. I would go off to work and put these niggling problems out of my mind but for her, it was a daily struggle.

She may have found it easier if we'd had a home of our own. My brother Vijay was, in fact, supervising construction on a plot of land we had inherited from our father in South Delhi's Greater Kailash, but the building wouldn't be ready for at least a year. In the meantime, we moved into a rented accommodation in Defence Colony.

Kunal's transition was rather more difficult than Akshay's, who was only five years old and therefore more adaptable. For one thing, neither of my sons knew Hindi that well. We also hadn't anticipated how tough it would be to get them into a good school. I spoke with family and friends and finally, Kunkun's grandmother, Nainaji, came to our rescue. She spoke to the principal of Springdales School, who was kind enough to admit both our boys.

Mundane problems apart, I felt that I had taken the right decision professionally. It was clear to me that over the next three or four decades, India would witness consistent growth (the groundwork for economic liberalization was already underway). Besides, being in Delhi opened up a lot of avenues, and allowed me to make professional and personal connections, something I had not been able to do from overseas. A visit home during those years typically involved meeting family, particularly my mother and mother-in-law, and left no time at all for picking up old threads or meeting new people.

When I saw the HCL office at Nehru Place, though, I was tempted to bolt right back to Singapore. The interior of the Siddharth Building was grimy and smelt vile. The original colour of the walls was barely visible under successive coats of ugly red-brown stains; having been used as spittoons by pan-chewing office-goers.

One night, the electricity went out and I had to take the stairs, because the lift had no power backup. Gingerly making my way down flight after flight of stairs in the dark, I had almost reached the ground floor when I stepped into something squishy. It was cow dung. How on earth had it got there? The building had obviously become a sanctuary for stray cattle and dogs. I'd had enough. The next day, we launched a search for new premises and eventually moved to East of Kailash.

Initially, I was heading HCL's CAD/CAM division, and thoroughly enjoyed the process of developing and marketing new products. I had been handling our CAD/CAM strategy in Singapore, so I was familiar with the products and processes. In a few months, however, the head of our main profit-centre, the computer division, quit and joined our competition. I had to take over the reins and found that I had inherited a mixed legacy.

The computer segment in India was growing very quickly and the competition was intense, but we had the advantage of an excellent sales team. We certainly had momentum in terms of sales, but service—a critical aspect of our business—had failed to keep pace, and there were issues with delivery. It took me several months to identify and address the gaps.

Soon after, we were confronted with a shortage of dollars. A foreign exchange crisis was building in India, thanks to the twin deficit problem (by the end of 1990, the country would barely have enough reserves to finance three weeks of imports). Fortuitously for us, Hewlett Packard decided to enter into a joint venture with HCL to manufacture minicomputers and distribute PCs in India.

The previous year, HP had bought out Apollo and inherited the latter's relationship with us. HCL was its distributor for workstations in India, so I sought a meeting with HP's country head, Suresh Rajpal. We met at the Oberoi, a venue that had always proved lucky for HCL, and discussed the way forward. Suresh informed me that HP had decided to set up a subsidiary to manufacture its products in India.

'Suresh, you are starting a business in the commercial market from scratch. Is that wise? Bluestar took that route and it's sold maybe hundred computers in ten years,' I said.

He looked thoughtful, so I pressed ahead. 'You have the advantage of a relationship with us. Expand it, and we can give you a leg up. We already have a thriving commercial business and over a hundred people in sales teams across the country, not to mention a strong customer and services base,' I said.

Suresh said he'd think it over and get back to me. I had pressed the right buttons, but sensed that he would take a little more convincing. I suggested a meeting with Shiv, which took place the following week. At the end of it, Suresh agreed that HP should not go at it alone in India. A partnership with HCL would yield significantly better results. What's more, the JV would be called HCL-HP, because we were the bigger brand by far, and we would hold 74 per cent equity.

It proved to be a fruitful relationship. In fact, I would go so far as to say that it was a game-changer for HCL, because HP brought its top people to India and we learnt a tremendous amount from them. It was a masterclass in quality control and processes. We had made it thus far on the strength of sheer passion, but going forward, we needed to become a more process-oriented company. It was HP that helped us to 'think global'.

Alan Bickel was HP's point person on the deal. A warm and courteous individual, he made us feel valued as partners, and arranged for us to meet Lewis 'Lou' Platt, who had succeeded the legendary David Packard as chairperson of HP. We went to California, where Platt invited us home for dinner. There, I had the privilege of meeting Packard, who had cofounded the company with Bill Hewlett.

Tall and athletic, he shared some of the insights which would later appear in his book *The HP Way*. The HP culture was based on values of trust, teamwork and communication, and they were very partner-oriented.

Platt was an engineer, who had headed HP's computer services division and focused strongly on RISC/UNIX. Our deal with HP involved manufacturing RISC computers in India for the first time. We had also launched their Vectra PCs. Platt knew every single one of his products inside out. We had a long talk on technology and I was impressed by the range and depth of his knowledge. He was a great CEO, and an even better human being. He was known for his top-to-bottom connect with the HP staff and his trademark 'management by walking around' style, which I later put into practice.

BACK TO SCHOOL

The tie-up with HP had another effect. Our successes in hardware were many: we had been ahead of the field in developing the 8C microcomputer and in 1985, we introduced the UNIX-based computer, followed by a symmetric multiprocessor system known as Magnum. In the PC segment, our Busybees were an iconic product, as were the Beanstalks, created specifically for children. Infinity was our enterprise brand (later, we entered the tablet space with the 'ME' range).

McKinsey & Company was impressed with our track record and undertook a pro bono study of HCL's potential in the US market.

The findings were encouraging, so we set up HCL America to bring our hardware to the US market. Unexpected challenges cropped up, and we couldn't deliver, with the result that our finances took a major hit. Casting about for avenues to restore cash flow, we decided to capitalize on our UNIX strengths. This led to a pivot towards software.

HP had asked us to close down our RISC and UNIX R&D setup. To get around its caveat, we set up HCL Consulting, which later became HCL Technologies. So, parallel to hardware, Shiv was developing the software business, which was commanding all his time and attention.

In 1993, we won a deal to digitize the National Stock Exchange. As a space tech enthusiast, I kept a close watch on developments in satellite communications. The 1980s had seen the development of commercial VSATs (Very Small Aperture Terminals that access geostationary satellites to enable credit card transactions, access to high-speed internet, and distance education). When the government of India put out a tender for systems to connect all the brokers in real time, we bid for it, and won. HCL created the very first VSAT network for a stock exchange.

Around this time, Shiv told me I'd have to take over as president and CEO of HCL Infosystems. He suggested that before I formally took charge, I should undergo the executive programme at the University of Michigan, under the aegis of the legendary C.K. Prahalad, corporate strategist extraordinaire and distinguished professor at the university.

I was more than willing, given my love for learning. My reading habit had survived the increasing demands of work, and I continued to indulge my taste for thrillers. I read for pleasure, but also for work. The sheer pace of technological change demanded constant reading to stay abreast of the latest developments. Even so, the executive programme was far from easy.

Dr Prahalad was a tough taskmaster, and none of us dared show up for his class unprepared. His radar would zero in on slackers who hadn't read his case studies or weren't paying attention, and he would take them apart. His softer side surfaced only during the weekly get-togethers he hosted for students from India. His wife, Gayatri, would cook for us and he would throw open his well-stocked bar. As a whisky aficionado, he had an impressive collection of single malts. Needless to say, we had a great time and got to know his family well.

One day, he called on me in class.

'Ajai, please tell us, what is your vision for your company?'

I got to my feet and asked, 'C.K., would you really like me to share that? It's internal to our company.'

'No, there's nothing internal here. Please answer the question.'

'Well, we recently rewrote our vision statement. We want to be the largest software factory in the world,' I said.

No one reacted. I had made a startling statement, given that India had yet to become a global software power, but it didn't make an impression. For my peers, the idea of India as a software factory was beyond the realm of imagination.

I had made the statement with pride, backed by my belief in HCL and in India's capabilities, so I was a bit piqued at their indifference.

After class, I buttonholed Prahalad.

'C.K., why did you ask me that question?'

'Ajai, I wanted these chaps to know what India is capable of and where it is going.'

He had an unshakeable belief in India's potential, and a fierce desire to see the country transformed into an economic superpower.

Every year, he would hold a follow-on programme in Bangalore for those who had attended his course in Michigan. These sessions would, by and large, be devoted to economic developments in India. One of these get-togethers took place after India's software export boom. He summoned me and another gentleman from the hardware sector, and articulated his hope of 'world domination' by Indian digital hardware companies.

'Ajai, you should think of hardware in a big way, just like software,' Prahalad said.

'That's exactly what I'm doing, C.K.,' I replied.

'That's not what I mean. You should dominate the global market, in a specific product. For example, if you're designing and making disc drives, you should be the world's largest manufacturer.'

Prahalad passed away in 2010, having worked and lived abroad for most of his life. But he never lost his pride in being Indian. I can't help but think that Jai Krishna Chowdhry would have applauded his spirit!

GROWING, EVERY WHICH WAY

I returned from Michigan and became CEO of HCL Infosystems in 1994. It was a crucial phase for the company and the IT sector as a whole. In 1995, the internet—which had been introduced in India as early as 1986—became publicly available. Software technology parks were set up, cybercafés opened, online banking commenced and private internet service providers (ISPs) came into being. NASSCOM was established and a nationwide railway reservation system set up. By the end of the decade, IT revenues had grown over fifty times to 5.6 billion dollars, epitomizing the success of economic liberalization.

In 1997, we bought back our equity from HP. Empirically, the natural life of a joint venture is around seven years, and sure enough, a sense that we were pulling in different directions had set in. I was reminded of Prahalad's observation on joint ventures: 'Same bed, two dreams'. The relationship ended amicably.

A couple of years later, we encountered a prolonged spell of labour unrest. The progressive easing of regulatory restrictions had certainly enabled the rapid growth of certain sectors, particularly IT-enabled services, telecom and civil aviation, but governments continued to prove reluctant to take on powerful lobbies like trade unions.

This led to our shifting manufacturing out of Noida. As part of the National Capital Region, it was a good location, but it fell within the geographical boundaries of Uttar Pradesh, where labour unions patronized by influential politicians were causing repeated disruptions. Managers were often intimidated by belligerent workers. My driver, Mithilesh Mishra, an impressive personage universally addressed as 'Mishraji', took it upon himself to keep me safe.

One time, during an escalation in labour trouble, he was driving me home. I looked out the window and saw unfamiliar terrain. 'Where are we?' I asked. 'We are going home by a different route, just in case they block the road or attack the car,' he told me. It turned out that he had been altering our route every day, to avoid any trouble with the agitating HCL employees. I was deeply appreciative;

Mishraji was clearly more committed to my welfare than I was. We scouted various locations and eventually shifted our factory to Pondicherry (now Puducherry).

The family had moved as well. With two growing boys, we needed more space than the Greater Kailash house that we shared with Vijay's family. Besides, Kunkun and I were very keen on having an independent house, after having lived in apartments throughout our married life. I told friends that I was looking for a house, and one of them suggested that I put in a bid on a plot in Ishwar Nagar in South Delhi; a quiet, green locality not too far from Shiv's home. It was being auctioned off by the Income Tax department.

I asked Shiv to attend the auction with me, and he came along to give moral support. Mercifully, I didn't know that my main competitor was industrialist K.K. Modi, whose pockets were as deep as mine were shallow, otherwise I might have bolted. Even so, I looked at Shiv at one point and murmured, 'It's too much. I can't afford this.'

'Just go ahead and don't worry about the money,' he reassured me.

We won the bid. Two years later, our family moved into its very first independent house.

Shortly thereafter, the family fortunes improved dramatically, thanks to HCL Technologies' highly successful IPO of 2000. It was oversubscribed by a factor of 12.5, thereby making stock market history. For the first time, the Chowdhry family discovered the joys of a disposable income. It was a heady experience because so far, we had just about managed on my salary. After years of carefully balancing the household budget, we finally had money to spend.

Kunkun and I quickly expanded our social network. Returning to Delhi also allowed us to attend the musical evenings (baithaks) at Naina Devi's house, which continued until she passed away in 1993. Perhaps the most memorable musical experience we had was at Agra in 1997, when we were privileged to witness the spiritual grandeur of Yanni's show at the Taj Mahal.

I continued to sing at parties and my skills improved dramatically, thanks to a remarkable vocalist by the name of Inder Thakur. He was a prime favourite at our get-togethers and had the rare knack of getting an audience to sing along with him. Unlike most professional singers, who zealously guard the spotlight, Inder was only too happy to share it. We sang many a riotous song together. Nudging me towards the microphone, he would hand me the lyrics—he was aware of my lamentable inability to remember the words—and insist that I sing. Under his gentle tutelage, the depth and range of my vocals improved.

Kunal, meanwhile, graduated from school in 1996. He'd been a stellar student, serving as head boy and winning a whole raft of awards. From the beginning, he was mature beyond his years, with a rare poise and self-assurance. He was also academically brilliant. The kind of child parents wonder what they've done to deserve! His interests ranged far beyond his textbooks to world affairs. Even as a young boy, his general knowledge was so impressive that he would beat us all hollow in Trivial Pursuit. One time, he took the lead in a school project on South Africa and had the privilege of meeting President Nelson Mandela during his visit to India.

Akshay, on the other hand, was a fun-loving lad, very bright but easily distracted from studies, just as I had been at his age. He waltzed his way through school, displaying more interest in sports and music than in studying. He was a good cricketer and loved music so much that I bought him a guitar. 'I never learnt to play,' I told him. 'Why don't you give it a try?'

He became an accomplished guitarist, and much to the dismay of his teachers, formed a band in school.

Although my job was very demanding, I always made it a point to spend time with my sons. We did a variety of things together. I took them to Disneyland once, and they ran around like dervishes, from one ride to the next. I was so exhausted by the end of the day that I had to crawl into a jacuzzi to ease my aching limbs.

One time, when we were still based in Singapore, I decided to script a movie featuring the boys. On our visits home, we liked to spend time at their grandmother's farm in Ranchi, and one of their favourite activities was watching trains go by on the railway track behind the farm. I shot a whole lot of footage of the boys and the trains. I returned to Singapore, while the rest of the family vacationed in Delhi, and sat down to stitch the videos together into a movie. It was tough, because everything was shot on tapes and there was no editing software. It took me five weeks, but when I saw the delight on the boys' faces, it was worth it.

Growing up, my sons had a lot of interests in common. They both loved music and books and spent hours playing video games. I bought them a Nintendo and from their first taste of *Super Mario Bros.*, they were hooked. Every time I or anyone else went abroad, they would demand new games.

All through their school days, Sundays were sacred: our boys' day out. The three of us would head to Teksons bookstore in Delhi's South Extension, and spend many happy hours browsing and buying books. Then we would replenish our energies (mine, anyway) at a McDonald's, tucking into their trademark crispy golden fries. Often, we would round off the day with a movie.

Kunal's excellent marks in his board exams secured him a seat at St. Stephen's, arguably Delhi University's top college. That's where he met his future wife, Minakshi. He was going through an independent (or possibly socialist) phase, and insisted on taking a bus to college rather than the car. Somewhere along the way, he picked up a chronic infection.

For the next six months, we did endless rounds of doctors, but none of them could figure out what was wrong. Finally, we took him to a general physician in Mumbai, who diagnosed his ailment. The treatment involved a six-to-nine-month course of antibiotics, so Kunal lost a whole year of college. He continued to study at home and wound up topping the university in physics.

Kunal received a scholarship to Cambridge University. He would have gotten a full ride but, being incurably honest, he revealed that his parents could afford to pay his way, so his funding was limited to half. Minakshi eventually joined him at Cambridge. After they had settled in, we visited them, and all of us went to London. We had a wonderful time, taking in theatre shows and dining out.

In 1999, the year that Kunal left for the UK, I took over as chairperson of HCL Infosystems. The 1990s may have been a period of intense political and social churning, but it was clear that the economic reforms initiated in 1991 had acquired a life and momentum of their own. India was on the move.

It was an exciting time for the information and communications technology (ICT) sector, thanks partly to the 'Y2K boom'. The threat of the 'Millennium Bug' (the fear that computers would crash in 2000, unable to distinguish between 1900 and 2000, with a devastating impact on banking, finance, transportation, etc.) brought a lot of business to India. At the same time, technology was evolving so rapidly that policy was struggling to keep pace. The entire industry was gripped by a pervasive feeling that it was on the cusp of dramatic growth.

6

REVOLUTIONIZING MOBILE TELEPHONY

A ROUSING PARTY WAS UNDERWAY at the Belvedere on the rooftop of Delhi's Oberoi hotel. A balmy breeze had swept away the pollution haze; the city lights twinkled cheerily, reflected in champagne flutes and wine glasses as guests toasted the success of the HCL-Nokia partnership in India.

Away from all the hubbub and laughter, in a room adjoining the terrace, I—the host—was planning strategy.

HCL and Nokia had shaped a revolution in mobile telephony in India, making the handheld phone affordable and accessible to the masses. It was a game-changer in telecommunications, with a cascading effect across sectors. It was Nokia which enabled our entrée into the telecom sector; the first of two significant pieces of business that led to a quantum leap in HCL's size and revenues.

Nokia had a long track record in mobile telephony, starting with mobile radio phones. In the 1990s, Nokia was providing GSM (Global System for Mobile communication) services across the world. After Jorma Ollila became CEO in 1992, the company focused strongly on mobile telephones and telecom networks. The company entered India with the Nokia 2110 in 1994, and we partnered with it in the distribution of pagers and mobile phones, but the policy framework at the time was not conducive to the growth of mobile telephony, owing to high import tariffs on mobile phones and astronomical usage charges (Rs 16 per minute).

We had been in business with Nokia since 1995, and I had tried to persuade them to make their products more pocket-friendly in order to expand their consumer base, but failed. In any case, telecom represented a very small slice of our business in the 1990s. It was only when the regulatory environment changed in 2002, thanks partly to the efforts of the Indian Cellular Association, which we had cofounded, that I turned my attention to Nokia once again. ICA's Pankaj Mahendru and HCL's J.V. Ramamurthy had lobbied relentlessly with the government and finally managed to bring the policy-makers around.

The telecom sector was liberalized and licence fees for cellular service providers reduced, throwing the doors open to foreign investors. Service fees and call costs dropped sharply, enabling every middle-class Indian to afford a mobile phone. The market for handsets expanded exponentially.

I met with the Nokia team, determined to persuade them to change their pricing model. I argued with passion. Bringing the cost of a mobile phone down from Rs 16,000 to Rs 9,900, I said, would increase sales dramatically. I could guarantee the numbers. Three weeks later, Nokia got back to me and said it was on board. The success of the strategy was proven by the fact that we not only met the sales target, but exceeded it by a mile.

THE ODI STRATEGY

I called my sales heads and started what became known as the ODI model of sales (a reference to cricket's 'One Day International' format). Every manager and sales person was given targets, not just quarterly, monthly or weekly, but daily. Our performance skyrocketed, proving my philosophy that the more you measure performance, the better it becomes. From a few thousand units a month, we were selling the same number every day.

Also contributing to sales was the fact that the phone wasn't bundled with a service provider. So, the product and service were separate. We got the government to agree not to include the price of the phone in the AGR (Adjusted Gross Revenue). Nokia was suitably chuffed, and I deemed it appropriate to host a party for its people at our favourite hotel, the Oberoi.

After several mellowing rounds of drinks, I led them to a private room and launched into my pitch.

I said, 'Ok, what's next?'

Silence. Hesitantly, one of them said, 'What do you propose?'

'I think we need to rethink the price point. I would reduce it to Rs 6,999.'

This time, such was their faith in us that the Nokia people agreed without hesitation.

From then on, we never looked back. The eminently affordable Nokia 1100 handset, with a torch and an anti-slip grip, had been developed specifically for Indian conditions. Nokia had also acceded to our request for an ad campaign tailor-made for India. It featured a Nokia phone attached to the grill of a truck, to emphasize its dust-resistance and durability. The torch was a great selling point, and demand was through the roof. In effect, we managed to sell a high-end product in the smallest of towns.

In 2006, Nokia became the first mobile phone manufacturer to set up a facility in India. The idea emerged when I went to call on the IT minister, Dayanidhi Maran, and found him very receptive to boosting hardware in India. He was keen to bring electronics manufacturing to his home state, Tamil Nadu. This was music to my ears. HCL was equally keen for Nokia to start manufacturing in India. Maran moved quickly and cleared the way for Nokia to set up its unit in Tamil Nadu.

Nokia was an ideal partner, in that once it had made a commitment, it always delivered. Supportive, courteous and efficient, it never went back on its word. I learnt a lot about managing partnerships from the people at Nokia. Besides, for sheer hospitality, no one can beat the Finns, as we discovered when, as Nokia's largest customer, we were invited to visit their headquarters.

From the moment we landed in Helsinki, we were accorded royal treatment. We were met off the plane, swept into a VIP lounge and plied with drinks, while someone dealt with immigration and our baggage. A limousine whisked us off to the Nokia headquarters at Espoo, near Helsinki, to meet chairman Jorma Ollila. He told us about the history of the company, founded as a paper mill in 1865. It got into the electricity business in 1902 and moved into consumer electronics by 1967.

We delivered a presentation on Nokia in India and the chairperson declared himself delighted with our performance. At that point, Nokia's market share of 70 per cent was its highest in any country. Sustaining that momentum in the face of increasing competition was going to prove a tough challenge.

In 2006, Ollila was replaced by Olli-Pekka Kallasvuo. When the latter visited India, we warned him that new telecom players were offering products like dual SIM phones with a long battery life, as well as good deals and services. To retain its dominant position, Nokia would have to support us in developing a competitive product, or do so itself. In the meantime, it could pick up a product from an ODM in Taiwan and use either the Nokia or HCL-Nokia brand. He turned us down flat. Perhaps the Not Invented Here (NIH) syndrome had kicked in. As we had predicted, Nokia lost market share. The handset division was sold to Microsoft in 2014.

A REVOLUTION CALLED SYSTEMS INTEGRATION

The second significant piece of business we initiated was that of systems integration, which was to prove the biggest profit-centre of all. Going beyond hardware and office automation seemed a viable way forward to me, but first, I had to convince HCL's top management. I didn't believe in railroading people, and the manager in question, although a great performer, was chronically averse to change. We spent sixty minutes on a whiteboard, running the strategy and the numbers by him. He was still sceptical.

'Ajai, let's not do it,' he said.

'Why don't we discuss it tomorrow,' I replied affably.

It took me three days, but he eventually agreed. We went ahead with the launch and the venture proved a great success, creating Rs 8,000 crore worth of new business.

We created a strategy around following the money, by listing the sectors where the government was likely to invest heavily, like railways, roads, healthcare and e-governance. Each of these was potentially a different vertical. Sure enough, over the next few years, the money came in and we created large businesses in these verticals.

One of our targets was the government-owned behemoth BSNL, which was looking to roll out broadband internet across the country. The competition to get in on the action was fierce. Our competitors were of the view that HCL didn't have the capability to execute the project. We ignored them and got to work; if we didn't have it, we'd create it. We worked with multiple partners to devise a solution, which enabled us to offer the best technology at the best price. The deal was within our grasp.

The path of salesmanship never runs smooth, and there were many ups and downs. Our competitors raised all manner of questions and swamped the buyers with complaints. Perturbed, BSNL officials started toying with the idea of a re-tender. The deal was dying right before our eyes.

A.P.S. Bedi—my coworker and a brilliant salesperson—and I were positive that we could still save it. We turned to another colleague, J.V. Ramamurthy, who had excellent relationships in the telecom department. He knew everyone, top to bottom, and arranged a meeting with the minister. We made an impassioned presentation on the benefits of proceeding with the existing tender. It worked, and we brought the deal back from the dead.

We had also secured several other big pieces of business, including those for the Air Force Network (AFNet), a digital information grid, and the Commonwealth Games held in New Delhi in 2010. The latter was an incredibly challenging project because the deadline was unrealistically tight; we had to be up and running in two months. Our network had to deliver the results and if we failed, the Games would flop.

We picked a team of people who'd demonstrated passion for the job and threw the problem at them. The tech was new. They hadn't so much as seen the box that they were expected to install. But they downloaded and read up the manuals, and worked 24×7 right up to the last minute, undeterred by crises such as a rat nibbling its way through major cables. Pride in HCL and passion for the job translated into a spectacular performance.

The last big deal on my watch was Aadhaar. It involved a lot of software, and the competition was intense. The leading contender had been working on it for several years and believed it was a done deal. The entire industry shared that view.

HCL was not regarded as a credible rival, but then, no one outside the company knew that we had been working on it quietly. We were the proverbial dark horse and at the last minute, put in a bid around 50 per cent lower than that of the main contender. It was still a tall task, because the bids were being evaluated by a team of brilliant people, including Nandan Nilekani of Infosys—after all, we were going to take over what they had created. We won the Rs 2,200 crore UIDAI contract, the biggest IT deal ever done in India until that point.

PRIDE IN BEING INDIAN: THE 'MINDIA' CAMPAIGN

All through, we were competing with the biggest global brands in both the home and office markets. They were whales and by comparison, we were a minnow. We needed to differentiate ourselves somehow. Yes, we had the best sales force and support services in the country, but we needed to do more in order to stand apart.

I turned to my brother, who was something of a marketing guru. He suggested we bring on board a group of creative people who could help reposition our brand. They'd started an advertising venture of their own and were known for ingenious campaigns. After several rounds of brainstorming, we homed in on the notion of 'pride in being Indian'.

I loved the idea, because it accorded so beautifully with the deep respect for our cultural heritage that had been relentlessly drummed into me as a child. That sense of national pride informed many of my decisions and served as a constant inspiration. Recall that the company I cofounded incorporated 'Hindustan' in its name.

As an avid follower of sports, I am doubly excited if India is participating, be it cricket or tennis or badminton or the Olympics. An Indian victory has always been an occasion for celebration in our home, and this gave rise to a family tradition. Every time an Indian mounted the podium, the children—and later, grandchildren—would get a special gift from me.

In certain circles, nationalism is equated with xenophobia and nativism, and is therefore considered reactionary and unfashionable. For me, it translates simply into 'desh prem', love for one's country. I'm not in the least self-conscious or apologetic about it. Patriotism, to my mind, is a universal virtue and is expressed in different ways.

For instance, at the finals of the 2003 ICC World Cup in Johannesburg, I was enchanted to find a case of beer with the legend 'Proud to be South African' sitting in our box. It accorded beautifully with my own sentiments. I was naturally downcast when we lost, but those cans of beer, indigenously brewed and celebrating the fact, stuck in my mind.

Indigenous manufacture has always been an article of faith for me. At HCL, we created products by and for India. It was on the strength of brands designed, manufactured and marketed in India that we became the country's largest PC-maker. Our innovations were world-class and drew kudos from industry leaders like Intel.

The 'be Indian, buy Indian' slogan has a long history, beginning with the Swadeshi Movement. In 1991, the Rashtriya Swayamsevak Sangh (RSS) launched the Swadeshi Jagran Manch, with the stated objective of working towards a self-reliant India and an equitable world order. Rather than repackage that philosophy, we wanted to connect with people emotionally.

We asked ourselves, what distinguished Indians from the rest of the world? It occurred to us that Indian philosophy, thought systems, and modes of information processing have always been distinctive, and have historically shaped economic developments across the globe.

In the Vedic era, Baudhayana's *Sulba Sutra* stated the Pythagorean theorem; in the Buddhist age, Panini laid the foundations of linguistics; in pre-Gupta times, Aryabhata's table of sine differences initiated trigonometry; in the sixth century CE, Brahmagupta codified quadratic equations and square roots; in the fourteenth and fifteenth centuries CE, Madhava and Nilakantha developed what later became the fundamentals of calculus. The concept of zero and the decimal system is, of course, a seminal contribution of ancient Indian mathematicians.

The distinguishing factor, we realized, was the Indian mind. The idea was to subtly convey that the Indian mind was not just distinctive, but superior in many ways. The result was 'Mindia', spelled out in the colours of the national flag, and it had a powerful emotional appeal. To launch the brand, we turned to sports, to further hype its emotional content.

Cricket is often referred to as one of the three national obsessions of India, politics and Bollywood being the other two. Many companies have leveraged the preoccupation with cricket in brand-building, and I believe we were able to do so with panache.

I was inspired by the Great Indian Huddle, introduced at the 2003 World Cup by the captain of the national cricket team, Sourav Ganguly. The pre-match huddle was intended to sharpen the players' focus and infuse a winning spirit. It caught on and quickly became a trend. I admired Ganguly, not just as a cricketer, but as a dynamic captain and a proud Indian. His historic gesture at Lord's, the Mecca of cricket, in the 2002 NatWest tri-series final, is remembered to this day.

The Indian captain, standing in the balcony at Lord's, whipped off his T-shirt and waved it like a victory flag, in celebration of the winning runs by Mohammad Kaif and Zaheer Khan. It was a fitting reply to Andrew Flintoff who had done the same at Wankhede Stadium in Mumbai after beating India earlier that year. Ganguly's shirtlessness symbolized the Indian amour-propre, and counts as one of cricket's iconic moments.

For the Mindia launch in 2004, we decided to create a Ganguly-style HCL huddle as the signature theme for the audio-visual campaign. The subtext was 'pride in India'. We wanted to present an ascending India that had gone global and made its mark in several fields, notably software, space research and science.

For the campaign to be successful, the huddle had to be utterly convincing, which meant that our internal team had to fully buy into the concept. With that in mind, we created Mindia badges in glorious tricolour and made them mandatory for everyone, including me. We would attend client meetings proudly sporting our badges, and that would invariably pique their interest. When they asked what it was all about, we would give them our 'Indian Mind' spiel. At the end of it, we would walk away with a deal.

We travelled the country and made presentations on Mindia at virtually every major company. In effect, we took the huddle out of the stadium and to the customer.

The next step was the HCL Mind Conclaves, held in all the bigger cities and headlined by their brightest minds. The subject was, of course, perspectives on the Indian mind. In Bangalore, we had former chief justice of India M.N. Venkatachaliah. In Jaipur, it was Magsaysay award winner Rajendra Singh, speaking on the ingenuity of Indian water management. In Ahmedabad, it was National Institute of Design director Darlie O. Koshy.

The inaugural event was held in Delhi, with Ramesh Mashelkar, the world-renowned scientist and CSIR (Council for Scientific and Industrial Research) director general, as the principal speaker. Likewise, in Mumbai, we had the celebrated poet and screenwriter Javed Akhtar, as well as advertising doyen (and an old friend) Ranjan Kapur, then head of Ogilvy & Mather. Kapur eloquently described the ingenious innovations in advertising dreamed up by creative Indian minds, with a number of examples.

The audience, every one of whom was a customer, was spellbound. As they emerged mesmerized from the hall, I heard a lot of congratulatory comments along the lines of 'your company's amazing, you've done something so different' and 'what a great soft-sell'. That was, in fact, our strategy all along—subtly coaxing customers to engage with the concept of the superior Indian mind. The subliminal message was, 'if the Indian mind is so great, the product must be great as well'.

The conclaves created a huge momentum for HCL. Our people were visibly proud of the brand and the customers were delighted. We decided to extend the brand to the cultural realm. I had already started an HCL concert series in collaboration with the India Habitat Centre in Delhi. Every month, we would hold two or three dance recitals or music programmes. Among others, we featured Sonal Mansingh, Geeta Chandran, Madhavi Mudgal, Bharati Shivaji, Madhup Mudgal, Raja and Radha Reddy and Rita Ganguly.

We dovetailed that cultural connect with Mindia and called it 'Expressions of the Mind'. A big concert was held in January every year, with a major artiste performing. A top Government of India official was invited to inaugurate the event. The timing was strategic, as big purchase decisions by government agencies were usually taken in March, just before the end of the financial year.

We extended the drive internally as well, engaging the children of our employees through the 'Little Mindians' programme, at which we would hand out awards for performances. The 'pride of being Indian' campaign thus served as a major strategy for the company. It was a classic instance of deploying EQ (emotional quotient), as opposed to IQ.

HCL BPO

One of the parallel projects that Shiv got me involved in was the setting up of HCL's BPO (Business Process Outsourcing). India's BPO business got off the ground in the early 1990s with 'captives' set up by American Express and General Electric (GE), but the 'boom' came much later.

It was a new paradigm of salesmanship, different from face-to-face relationship-building that had been the norm. India, with its large English-speaking population and low labour cost, became a hub for remote selling. The so-called 'call centres' initially focused on selling products and handling customer queries over the phone.

Along with my colleague Sujit Baksi, I helped set up the HCL BPO. We had the requisite technology and language skills, but the challenge was communications. In those days, an uninterrupted power supply and connectivity simply weren't possible. So, we had to create backups—and back them up with another two layers of backup.

Our first customer was a telecom major. We were tasked with selling their internet packages to customers in the UK. The Telco's team wasn't convinced that we were up to the job, because our people didn't understand the British culture. For example, if our salesperson called an elderly woman suffering through a cold snap in the north of England and talked about upgrading her package, it wouldn't cut any ice with her. If you're selling in the UK, it is de rigueur to open a conversation by asking about the weather.

Ideally, the hypothetical conversation with the elderly customer should have gone like this:

Salesperson: 'How's the weather?'

Customer: 'Depressing. Cold and cloudy. Frost and freeze.'

Salesperson: 'That's too bad. Why don't you make yourself a nice hot cup of tea, while I hold? Then we can have a little chat.'

We addressed the problem of creating a rapport with customers by setting up an 'empathy lab'. Conversations with customers were taped, and the best, the medium-level and the worst were played back to teach our people how to empathize. A couple of months after we set up the lab, we saw tangible results. Our salespersons were able to make a connection with customers and the Telco was happy with the outcomes.

Apart from building a rapport, they were taught how to grab the prospect's attention, especially when making a cold call. A salesperson might use a 'hook' to reel in the customer by saying, 'Congratulations! You are one of the ten people to get an offer of a special package from us.'

SHAPING INDIA'S ELECTRONICS POLICY

Narasimhaiah Seshagiri, iconic founder-director of the National Informatics Centre (NIC) and father of India's IT revolution, was as delightful as his reputation was awe-inspiring. Behind square frames, his lively eyes spoke of a formidable intellect that might have been intimidating, but for his openness and amiability.

I had sought an urgent meeting with him, when the newly elected Atal Bihari Vajpayee government set up the National Task Force on IT and Software Development in 1999, helmed by Jaswant Singh, the then deputy chairman of the Planning Commission.

A couple of years earlier, I had realized that the ICT sector needed to interface much more closely with the government. India had joined the Information Technology Agreement signed at the WTO ministerial in Singapore in 1996, committing to a low-tariff regime for hardware products by 2005. Industry bodies like the Manufacturers' Association of Information Technology (MAIT) had not been taken into confidence.

The reduction of import duties on high-tech products was a blow to indigenous electronics hardware. Most companies that had created IT products from the ground up were now pushed towards cheap imports and trading rather than manufacturing. Domestic innovation was undermined and small- and medium-sized enterprises (SMEs) were badly hit. I decided that from then on, we would assiduously work on influencing policy in the electronics sector. Seshagiri was a member of the task force and had considerable clout in matters of policy.

I had just one question.

'Dr Seshagiri, why are you looking only at software? Why not hardware?'

'Well, that's what we've decided at the moment,' he replied. But he understood what I was getting at.

'Ajai, why don't you come to Bangalore for our next meeting and make a presentation to us on why we should look at hardware?' he asked.

I did as he requested, pointing out the excellent work India had done in hardware. My pitch went down well with the task force, which decided to constitute a separate team on hardware headed by Seshagiri. I was a member of his team. From that point on, I became a resource person on hardware policy.

The MAIT leadership, and especially Vinnie Mehta and other people from the industry, worked with me to create a report on preparing the industry for 2005. It was a path-breaking effort and we firmly believed it would change the future of India's electronics industry. Jaswant Singh was present when we handed over the report to the prime minister at his Race Course Road residence. He seemed positive about the exercise.

The report made its way up the bureaucratic pyramid, meeting with approval at all levels, until it landed on the desk of the finance minister, Yashwant Sinha. The Budget was imminent and my colleagues and I were hopeful that the measures we had suggested would find reflection in Sinha's budgetary proposals, especially as all the relevant people had signed off on it (I knew, because Seshagiri had shown me the file).

Only the FM's approval remained. However, the subsequent Budget proved to be hardware-unfriendly. The president of MAIT made a negative comment on the Budget, and that dealt a fatal blow to our proposals. I believe the FM received personal apologies from members of MAIT and a very senior industry veteran, but all our efforts to revive the report failed.

After Jaswant Singh became FM, the urban development minister and MP from Bangalore (South), Ananth Kumar, was asked by Intel to arrange a meeting for us. When we entered Singh's chamber, he gave me a penetrating look.

'Software or hardware?' he asked.

'Hardware,' I said.

'If you are from hardware, sit down. I do not want to discuss software.'

I told him about our report, which had come a cropper.

'Hardware has had a hard time. Software has had a soft time,' Singh observed in his characteristic gravelly voice.

He summoned a senior ministry bureaucrat and asked him, 'Have you read the hardware report?'

'No, sir.'

'You will read it now.'

The upshot of the meeting was that the 2004 Budget was very positive vis-à-vis hardware. Then the NDA lost the election and the UPA government was sworn in, which meant that we had to build bridges with the new dispensation.

RED-FLAGGING THE NEED FOR A SEMICONDUCTOR ECOSYSTEM

Dayanidhi Maran was a dynamic and hands-on IT minister. I went to him after Nokia's manufacturing facility in Tamil Nadu got underway to express my appreciation. He waved aside my thanks and got down to business.

'Tell me, what should we focus on next?'

'Semiconductors,' I replied.

'What about them?'

'We need a semiconductor and component ecosystem in India.'

I explained that the semiconductor chip, variously referred to as an integrated circuit (IC), microprocessor or system on chip (SoC), is the substrate of modern life, driving virtually every gadget you can think of, from smartphones to cars, LEDs to ATMs and toasters to medical devices. I pointed out that India was import-dependent for semiconductors, a big drain on the exchequer.

He promptly asked me to write a note on the subject. I called for pen and paper, and complied then and there. Those two scribbled pages on creating a semiconductor ecosystem in India found reflection in subsequent policy papers, but did not translate into action.

Maran was replaced in 2007 by A. Raja. The IT secretary, R. Chandrasekhar, called industry leaders for a discussion. In 2009, I was appointed chairperson of the task force on IT and hardware, with Kiran Karnik, former NASSCOM boss, as cochair. Bureaucrats were kept out of the task force, so I picked bright minds from within the industry.

We identified semiconductors as a key driver of the nation's economy, and predicted that India's electronics import bill would exceed that of oil in the near future (it hasn't yet, but it exceeded Rs 1.15 trillion in 2019-20). As an engineer, I thought in terms of the syllogism: 'India needs semiconductors. Semiconductors must be manufactured. Therefore, India must manufacture semiconductors.'

Our principal recommendations, apart from the semiconductor fab, were a National Electronics Mission reporting directly to the PM (much like the space programme), an incentive scheme for manufacturing, preferential market access for domestic products and an Electronics Development Fund to promote research and development. Most were implemented, but subsequently got bogged down in bureaucratic delays. I could only hope that at some point, the Indian government would grasp the importance of a robust electronics policy.

7

THE EYES OF WILLIAM HENRY GATES III, AND OTHER ENCOUNTERS

IF THE EYES ARE THE windows to the soul, Bill Gates's candid grey-blue gaze testifies to an inquiring spirit. I looked past the much-touted boy-next-door charm to the rare depth of intelligence in those luminous orbs. Probing the world from behind overlarge frames, they were endlessly questioning, seeking, evaluating.

Bill Gates is one of the living legends I was fortunate enough to meet, thanks to HCL Infosystems' strong relationships with global giants such as Microsoft, Intel and Apple. It also gave me the opportunity to work with and learn from some brilliant people.

From 1997 onwards, Bill Gates became a regular visitor to India. Given the strength of our partnership, I had the opportunity to meet him several times. But I will never forget that first encounter, a quarter-century ago.

I could see why he is often described as an INTP-type personality—Introverted, iNtuitive, Thinking, Perceiving. He appears to be driven by logic, constantly asking why. This is not to say he comes across as coldly calculating; quite the reverse. He is warm and friendly, albeit compulsively inquisitive.

It wasn't hard to be charmed by Bill. Here was the world's second-richest man (beaten to the top spot only by the Sultan of Brunei) and leading celebrity genius, sublimely unconscious of the prevailing Billmania, and endearingly nerdy. I found him courteous and easy-going, and of course, insatiably curious about India and its IT ecosystem.

He saw the potential of India, much like General Electric boss Jack Welch, who set the stage for the BPO revolution with the first in-house back office (GECIS, later Genpact, helmed by my friends Pramod Bhasin and Raman Roy). Gates observed that India had the capacity to 'be a leader in the digital economy of the twenty-first century' and a 'software superpower', with the right infrastructure. This was long before India had emerged as a leading software exporter.

HCL's relationship with Microsoft went back a long way. Both companies had been launched at around the same time. Even as we were setting up HCL's precursor, Microcomp, Bill Gates and Paul Allen had come up with their maiden product, the Altair BASIC interpreter.

In 1980, IBM contracted Microsoft to create an operating system (OS) for their open architecture-based PC. Microsoft had accepted the contract and while it did not have an OS in the works, it bought the 86-DOS from Seattle Computer Products and branded it as MS-DOS (IBM rebranded it as PC DOS, but it was licenced to other manufacturers as MS-DOS). The IBM PC became the industry standard, and Microsoft the leading OS vendor.

Meanwhile, HCL had launched its 8-bit microcomputer and set up Far East Computers in Singapore. In the early days, we designed everything from the ground up: hardware and software, including the OS and the interpreter and compiler (which translate programming language into machine code). We had no option, given the import curbs that were in place. Along came Rajiv Gandhi and liberalized the production and import of computers and other electronics.

This revolutionary step led us to Taiwan, where IBM lookalikes were manufactured on a large scale, bundled with MS-DOS. An HCL team landed in Singapore with the mandate to procure a PC and launch it in India in three weeks. I was closely involved in facilitating a tie-up in Taiwan. The machines were reverse-engineered, manufactured and marketed under the Busybee brand, and were wildly successful.

By 1986, HCL was the largest computer manufacturer in India, so Microsoft approached us in that year with a view to a partnership. It wanted to break into the Indian market, but realized that no one was actually paying for the OS. Nobody paid for software in those days. Unlike in the US, software piracy was an unheard-of concept; everyone copied. As the industry leader, HCL led the effort with the Department of Electronics to collectively negotiate a price for the Indian market. By that time, the demand for a graphic user interface had led to Windows, similar to the Apple OS, which was in turn inspired by the Xerox Alto. The early versions were clunky, with endless updates, but improved over time.

HOW MICROSOFT HELPED HCL SCRIPT A PC REVOLUTION

HCL was, thus, Microsoft's interface with the Indian IT industry. They were suitably grateful and the relationship prospered from there on. We also looked for special support from Microsoft when needed. A turning point came when we were challenged by Pertech Computers (PCL), who outsold us in the PC segment by the simple expedient of pricing their products cheaper.

To counter PCL with an even cheaper product, we created a team tasked with sourcing components from manufacturers at rates that would allow us to achieve the desired price point. Our purchase manager Rajinder Kumar led the effort and, after a month of intense bargaining, we pulled it off vis-à-vis the hardware. But we also needed Microsoft to licence its software to us at a lower price, even if that meant an older version.

We explained our rationale. The Indian PC market was poised to grow, with prices of hardware falling progressively owing to increasing global volumes. But the penetration of legal OS in the home and SOHO (small office, home office) segment was virtually nil because of Microsoft's high pricing. While anti-piracy measures may have been effective in the West, in India they were virtually unimplementable.

HCL's strategy in this scenario was to work on a very thin margin to sharply increase PC penetration. We were ready to bundle Windows with every PC provided they dropped their prices by 30 per cent. We also told them that with the launch of a non-Intel CPU-based PC, we would achieve the desired price point.

'No' was the unequivocal response from Microsoft.

Rajinder set about trying to find an alternative OS. After a bit of research, we determined that we could always opt for Linux. In 1991, Linus Torvalds had released the Linux kernel, and an OS could be built around it. Being open-source, it was free.

I decided to give Microsoft a last chance. After all, a new OS was a risky proposition and besides, we valued our relationship with Microsoft. I invited a team over and gave them our number.

'We need you to give us the OS at that price, otherwise we'll look elsewhere,' I told the team firmly.

Rajinder was shocked. 'What have you done?' he protested. 'How can you talk to them like that? They are our partners!'

'That's why I want to give them a chance,' I responded.

Microsoft obviously had to respond to the challenge.

'We'll have to talk to Redmond. We'll try and find a solution,' the team members said.

I was confident of my assessment, which was based on the fact that they had as much to gain from the deal as we did.

Microsoft came around, just as I had anticipated, and gave us a solution. Sure enough, the deal turned out to be a win-win. We lowered our price to Rs 19,990 and sold a lot more PCs, to our mutual advantage.

PCL had played on the strategy of taking full advance payment from customers at attractive pricing, offering them two to three months of delivery time. We took them head-on by not only beating their pricing, but providing a legal Microsoft operating system and ex-stock delivery. It pretty much decimated PCL's business. Incidentally, in 2003, we became the first company to sell 100,000 PCs. HCL then went on to create a PC revolution in India.

I'm sure Bill Gates was aware of it, because his regular visits to India were typically preceded by meticulous research and second-by-second planning. He was fully briefed on HCL and its operations. We were Microsoft's largest buyers, so HCL was his first stop in India. I enjoyed our chats over coffee, usually at the business centre at the Maurya Sheraton, where Microsoft—keeping the security of one of the world's richest men in view—would hire a whole floor. Bill always wanted to know more than his researchers had told him, and was open to ideas. We had in-depth discussions on the future of information technology, globally and in India.

During one of our meetings, I joked that he owed HCL a debt, because a former employee of ours was heading a division at Microsoft. He took it in good spirit, being a great believer in India's capacity to breed global talent. I also had the privilege of meeting Steve Ballmer, the then CEO of Microsoft. Schmoozing with the salesperson extraordinaire was a rewarding experience, given my own passion for sales.

XANADU 2.0

I had the opportunity to meet Bill Gates on his own turf when Microsoft held a convention of all its global partners at Redmond.

The hospitality team had pulled out all the stops. While we talked shop at the Redmond campus, our spouses toured the city. We were invited to dinner at 'Xanadu 2.0', as the Gates' 66,000-square-foot mansion at Medina, Washington state, came to be known. In the evening, everyone met up on the boat that would carry us there. I had read about the $147 million techno-home, with its gorgeous landscaping, sand imported from the Caribbean to create a lakefront beach, and the 60-foot swimming pool featuring an underwater music system, but the descriptions didn't even come close to the reality.

Bill and Melinda Gates were there to welcome us off the boat that had carried us across Lake Washington to Medina. Bill was his merry self, and the atmosphere was one of bonhomie. There were perhaps fifty guests, including Nandan Nilekani of Infosys, with whom I got along famously. He promised my wife, a coffee aficionado, choice roasts from Karnataka (he actually followed through).

As we walked through the house, Bill's technophilia was evident in the climate-control settings, music and lighting. Each room had a wall-mounted frame, with constantly changing, high-definition digital images of the great masters, to which he had the rights.

We admired his fabled 2,100-square foot library, stuffed with rare books and first editions, conserved in a pristine environment. And there, inscribed on the base of the dome that housed these literary treasures, was the much written-about quote from F. Scott Fitzgerald's *The Great Gatsby*: 'He had come a long way to this blue lawn and his dream must have seemed so close he could hardly fail to grasp it.'

Many writers have speculated whether Gates, with his house on the water and immense wealth, his restless intelligence and relentless optimism, bears comparison with Jay Gatsby. As for me, I doubt that Gates, unlike Gatsby, chases ultimately empty dreams. He is too much of a logician not to introspect on his own motivations, and has too much heart to limit himself to trivial aspirations.

FUTURE PERFECT

The visit to Medina afforded me the opportunity to meet one of my heroes: futurologist Ray Kurzweil. My passion for futurology developed early and has stayed with me since. I have always loved the idea of a limitless future, with infinite probabilities, some of which will coalesce into reality. Today's present is yesterday's tomorrow and many aspects of it were predicted long before they became fact: submarines, satellites, space travel, genetic engineering, artificial intelligence (AI), the internet … the list of actualized dreams goes on and on.

So, when I ran into Ray while gliding over Lake Washington en route to dinner at the Gates' mega-home, I was bowled over.

We were schmoozing with the other guests when I spotted a vaguely familiar-looking chap lounging solo in a corner. I went over to say hello.

'Ray Kurzweil,' he said, offering his hand.

'I've read your book, *The Singularity Is Near*!' I responded, delighted at the chance encounter.

I was in the presence of the rockstar among futurists, who had an astonishing record of accurate predictions. Ray was obviously a special guest. Gates, an admirer, famously described him as 'the best person I know at predicting the future of artificial intelligence'.

I had met him back in the 1980s while on a visit to the US, although neither of us had very clear memories of it, which accounted for my inability to recognize him at once. I knew of him, of course, as the inventor of the first optical character recognition system and reading machine, using a flatbed scanner and text-to-speech synthesizer. I knew that pattern-recognition was his bailiwick.

I could sense my wife bracing herself for boring sci-talk. As for me, I was lost. The lake, the boat and everyone in it faded away as we plunged into nanotechnology, transhumanism, human biochemistry and the future of AI. Ray is a soft-voiced but compelling speaker, absolutely focused on the subject at hand, and when he tells you that immortality is around the corner, you believe it.

He offered to share the manuscript of his next book with me, and he did. That's how I got a sneak preview of *Fantastic Voyage: Live Long Enough to Live Forever*. In it, he hypothesizes that customized diets, exercise and targeted supplements can maintain the body's chemical balance perfectly, thereby slowing human entropy. To this end, he took sixty pills a day and 'replaced' his blood every week. I couldn't help thinking that some of our sadhus, who seemed to have lived amazingly long lives on satvik diets, yoga and all manner of herbs, were on to something.

Kurzweil proposes that if individuals extend their lifespan long enough, advances in gene technology and bioengineering, including and especially biocompatible nanobots—microscopic robots introduced into the human body to repair DNA, fight infection, knock out tumours or deliver drugs—would allow them to live forever. I was enchanted; the prophet of tech had branched out into medicine. Collaborating with a friend who was an MD, he had brought his trademark intensity and vision to bear on human longevity.

I was to meet him again, at the 2012 India Today Conclave in New Delhi, where he was a speaker. I'd accepted an invitation to the conclave expressly to hear his speech; sitting through lectures is not my usual cup of tea! There were nine people at my table and Ray left eight of them utterly astonished. I found myself explaining his speech to the others, and to cut a long story short, I was asked to interview him by the organizers. That fifteen-minute discussion counts as one of the most exhilarating experiences of my life.

A KODAK MOMENT

I had my Kodak moment with the global photography company's CEO Antonio Pérez, when we entered into a deal to market their digital cameras in India. I asked about the brand name and he explained that it meant nothing. The founder, George Eastman, had made it up because he liked the letter 'K' and found it strong and incisive. 'Kodak' was short and snappy, and its two 'Ks' were memorable. It was a great lesson in branding.

I also learnt that Kodak had designed the first digital camera in 1975, but didn't introduce the product for the fear that it would impact sales of their cash-cow, photographic films. In the mid-1990s, it introduced a line of digicams, but it was only after sales of film dropped sharply in 2001 that Kodak made a big push in this segment. It did well for a while, but couldn't withstand Asian competitors. We sold Kodak digicams in India with some success, but the company itself filed for Chapter 11 (Bankruptcy) in 2012.

What impressed me most about Kodak was its phenomenal product development machinery. I took a tour of its museum, where the history of its technological evolution was displayed. Kodak had over a thousand patents, and these were eventually auctioned to buoy its finances. My big takeaway from Kodak was the importance of inculcating a culture of innovation.

One visionary I very much wanted to meet was Steve Jobs. Other than the fact that he was a living legend, I was prompted by a desire to build a relationship with Apple. We were already distributing the Apple iPod, with local content and good sales. I had great ideas for taking Apple forward in India, and suggested to its country head that I give a presentation to Jobs on the potential of, and strategies for, the domestic market.

Jobs had famously visited India in 1974 in search of spiritual insight. He went to Neem Karoli Baba's ashram in the Kumaon hills, and then met Haidakhan Baba. The late seer is regarded as an avatar of Mahavatar Baba, who was described in Paramhansa Yogananda's *Autobiography of a Yogi*, a much-acclaimed book that Jobs had read as a teenager. He downloaded it onto his iPad2 and reread it once a year.

Even so, he showed little interest in India, and in any event, he met very few people. So, I met Tim Cook, who was back then in-charge of worldwide operations. Steve Jobs was the visionary and Tim was the guy who translated his vision. He had a barrage of piercing questions, the first one being, 'What can we do in India?' He came across as a down-to-earth, solid businessperson well-versed in technology, marketing and distribution, and was very interested in the Indian market.

After he took over from Jobs as CEO, Cook confounded sceptics who believed Apple would go into decline. He successfully took the company forward, and opened up the market in India in a big way. On a visit in 2020, he declared that India was a top priority in Apple's scheme of things. Made-in-India iPhones now account for the bulk of Apple's domestic sales, and are priced in accordance with the Indian market.

Another memorable encounter was with Craig Barrett, CEO of Intel, a scholarly looking, wonderfully articulate man with a tremendous grasp of technology. Indeed, the engineer-turned-business executive has been said to have contributed significantly to Intel's technological prowess in the 1990s.

He had succeeded Intel CEO Andrew Grove, and I had no hesitation in telling Barrett that his predecessor was one of my icons. So was Intel cofounder, Gordon Moore, originator of the famous 'Moore's Law', to the effect that the number of transistors on an integrated circuit (IC) doubles every two years. A visionary statement, given that it was made in 1965, when there were only a few thousand transistors on a chip. Today, there are tens of billions.

I had read and loved Grove's *Only the Paranoid Survive*, in which he talks about the 'Strategic Inflection Point' at which a company must either adapt to massive changes, or fall by the wayside. I also read his account of how he beat prostate cancer. In the 1996 article in *Fortune* magazine, he wrote that he had taken it on as a 'project', with himself as the manager. When three of my friends were diagnosed with the 'emperor of all maladies', I sent Grove's article 'Taking on Prostate Cancer' to them.

I've mentioned a bare handful of the brilliant people I've met in the course of my career. Each encounter has underscored my belief that everyone you meet has something of value to impart. At HCL, we were open to learning, be it lessons in engineering, marketing, manufacturing, sales and services, or how to run a global company. We learnt from our associates, partners, customers and even our competitors, and used that knowledge to drive the growth of HCL.

From childhood onwards we learn from people around us, directly or indirectly. Call it social or observational learning, it shapes attitudes and behaviour and enhances skills. The unique human ability to learn from the experience of others applies to the workplace. Some of my most important learnings have come from my interaction with peers across companies, cultures and continents. I've benefitted from their wisdom and knowledge, in terms of what to do, what to avoid, what to change and so on.

I've had the privilege to work with leaders of global tech giants, as well as start-ups that were small in size but big on innovation. In each case, I gained insights that contributed to my clarity of thought, problem-solving and good judgment, helping me evolve as a manager and leader.

Isaac Newton famously wrote that he was able to see further because he stood on the shoulders of giants. In other words, progress is predicated on insights gained from pathfinders, and it is important to acknowledge their contributions.

8

TWO WEDDINGS, A FUNERAL AND AN AWARD

QUEEN HARISH HAD US ALL on the dance floor, jiving and laughing. In his colourful lehenga and blingy dupatta, the sinuous folk dancer from Jaisalmer swayed and spun, infusing the entire hall with his energy. His performance was the highlight of my son Akshay's wedding, held in Delhi in 2009.

As the father of the groom, I had to join the dance, which I did, to loud applause. Truth be told, I had been unsure how conservative Delhi would react to an artiste in drag. I need not have worried; so fluid and vibrant was his dance, so infectious his joie de vivre, that the guests were enchanted.

It was a truly memorable event. Not a big fat Indian wedding per se, but one with unconventional features that the guests would remember. We had avant garde music, an installation by artist Sumant Jayakrishnan, and the reigning Queen of Rajasthani folk dance to add 'chaar chaand' to the celebration.

The post-millennium decade was packed with landmark events in my life, personally as well as professionally. In 2002, I lost my mother. After my father had passed away in 1977, she was left on her own in Jabalpur. Eventually, she elected to live with my sister in Raipur. I often visited her there, and in later years, took my sons to see her, so that they could bond with their grandmother. Even during our sojourn in Singapore, I made it a point to go there at least once a year.

I first realized how physically and emotionally taxing eldercare can be when my mother fell ill. The task of looking after her fell on my sister and brother-in-law. As is often the case, my mother became very hard to manage as her condition deteriorated. My sister and her husband were both doctors, but that didn't make caring for her any easier. I saw how stressed they were and wanted to help. So, I called HCL's administrative manager in Nagpur and explained the situation. He was sympathetic, and took the trouble to find a trained eldercare attendant, who greatly relieved the burden on my sister.

My siblings and I were aware that it was only a matter of time before our mother succumbed, but foreknowledge does not prepare you for losing a parent. When I received the inevitable news from Raipur, I was deeply distressed. The challenges of work proved a welcome distraction.

The following year brought a happy family event. Kunal and Minakshi decided to get married. After graduating from Cambridge, Kunal had taken a job with Accenture. The dotcom bust delayed his joining by six months, so he took the time to backpack through Europe. He had always had a knack for languages and learnt Spanish before the tour. Two years after joining work, he felt settled enough in his career to move on to the next phase of his life.

Minakshi's family lived in Chennai, so the wedding was held there—the city of Kunal's birth. We also had an event in Delhi, for our extended family and friends. The stage was set for the next phase of my life: becoming a grandfather. My first grandchild was Aavienda, who is my absolute darling. From the day I set eyes on her at the Portland Hospital in London where she was born, Aavi has been my favourite person in the world.

The course of Akshay's academic career had never run quite as smooth as Kunal's. I had to coax him to study when he was in the twelfth grade, and after graduating from school, he wasn't quite clear about what he wanted to do.

'Where would you like to study?' I asked hopefully.

'I don't know,' he replied.

So, we set about researching programmes that might appeal to him. He applied to several good schools, including the University of Southern California in Los Angeles. The USC appealed to him because it covers the spectrum of the arts, technology, sciences and humanities, with schools of music, dance, cinema, law, architecture, medicine and communication. Plus, he wanted to be close to the centre of music. Akshay was so keen to get in that he slept with the USC brochure under his pillow until he heard from them.

USC is highly selective, but he made it. He chose to join the Annenberg School for Communication. That's where he met Neha, who was to become my daughter-in-law. He finished his studies by the end of 2006 and decided to get married two years later. As mentioned earlier, we already knew her parents, who were based in Singapore. So, when they got married, we naturally held an event there as well.

Kunal, meanwhile, had decided to go back to school. He had been with Accenture for seven years and it had proved to be a very demanding job. He often worked over the weekends, leaving Minakshi to manage on her own. They had acquired an apartment in London, and we stayed there when we visited. On one of our trips, he told me that he had applied to Harvard for an MBA.

I was delighted, because graduating from Harvard would not only allow him to write his own ticket anywhere in the world, but also make valuable lifelong connections. So, he went to Cambridge again, this time the one in Massachusetts! We visited him while he was there and were delighted to be able to sit in on a class and meet some of his professors. Kunkun and I were invited for his graduation. I still remember the date: 27 May 2010. We were incredibly proud.

He then picked up a job with DBS Bank in Singapore. After several successful years, his entrepreneurial genes kicked in and he started working with start-ups. He now manages his own investment fund and also helps me with my investments.

While Kunal was still at Harvard, the family suffered a major jolt; my mother-in-law fell gravely ill. She and I had become very close over the years. We had bonded over music, and when WorldSpace launched the first satellite-based radio network in 1999, I bought a receiver for her, with two large speakers to boot. I was among the first of some 4.5 lakh Indian subscribers to purchase the receiver, which gave us 24×7 access to broadcasts across the globe. I was very pleased with it. As for her, she was downright enchanted. We spent long hours listening to a variety of music programmes.

I loved spending time at my mother-in-law's farm in Ranchi. She had several beautiful dogs, and I would take them on long walks up the hill adjoining the farm. For many years, they were my canine 'fix', because Kunkun and I did not have an independent home of our own where we could keep pets. The dogs would invariably abandon me halfway up and run back to the farm. They knew where their priorities lay!

So, when Kunkun received a call late one night saying that her mother had been rushed to hospital with a serious gall bladder issue, I was rattled. We turned at once to a friend, Dr Dhiraj Bhatia, who was my cardiologist-cum-GP. He heard us out and said, 'She needs immediate attention.'

Abandoning his practice and cancelling all his appointments, he accompanied Kunkun to Ranchi. He called me from my mother-in-law's farmhouse.

'Ajai, matters are serious. The facilities here are not adequate. Let's get an air ambulance and take her to Delhi.'

In a matter of hours, he had arranged the flight. He had also organized an ambulance at Delhi airport, from where she was whisked to the hospital where I was waiting. She went into the ICU at once.

In three weeks, she was able to come home, and for the next twelve years she lived with us. The love and affection she showered on me during that time were gifts for which I will forever be grateful. Without Dhiraj, it would not have been possible. My mother-in-law was a stubborn soul, and I was the only one who could coax her into regular health checkups. I would march into her room and say 'Mummy, this test has to be done.' She never said no to me. For me, the first-hand experience of being a caregiver was a rewarding one. It calls for patience and resilience, and brings home the value of relationships and resources.

DAVOS TO DAR ES SALAAM

Shortly before Akshay got married, I attended the World Economic Forum at Davos. I have no hesitation in saying that the WEF is a heady experience for the uninitiated. It is possibly the greatest networking platform ever conceived, bringing together heads of state and global governance institutions, diplomats, titans of business, bankers, tech wizards, economists, public policy experts, scientists, mediapersons, academics and thought leaders.

The annual exercise is aimed at fostering public-private cooperation and finding ways of tackling the most pressing economic and social problems of the day. In 2005, Nicholas Negroponte, head of MIT's Media Laboratory had decided that one of these problems was the great digital divide—the inequality of internet access between demographics and regions.

Laptops in those days cost a thousand dollars or more; he wanted a hundred-dollar laptop to foster education in the developing world, primarily Africa and Asia. His project was dubbed One Laptop Per Child (OLPC) and one of its funders was Advanced Micro Devices Ltd (AMD), back then Intel's biggest competitor. Taiwan's Quanta was the designated ODM. The product, the OLPC XO-2, ran on AMD's Geode chip and was showcased at Davos in 2009.

h parents, Jai Krishna Chowdhry and Shakuntala, at Mt Abu, where they were posted, circa 1954.

Attempting my favourite actor Dev Anand's 'look', complete with dark glasses, scarf, bell-bottoms and dog-collared shirt in 1967.

s a five-year-old on my tricycle in Shahdol, Madhya Pradesh, escaping Sneh, in 1955.

The winsome Annie Veckens from France, my first pen friend, circa 1969.

The six techno dreamers who founded HCL in 1976: (front row, left to right) Subhash Arora, D.S. Puri, Shiv Nadar and Arjun Malhotra; (back row, right to left) Yogesh Vaidya and I.

Kunkun and I at our wedding in 1977, with Naina Devi (extreme left) and Kiran Nadar.

He wins Chinese deals but does not speak Mandarin at all

Face in the news

By NORA CHENG

VHEN the United Na-ions Development Pro-ramme put out a ten-er for a computer sys-em to conduct a census f China's population wo years ago, Mr Ajai Chowdhry's bid from ingapore was one of 40 eceived from the world ver.

He won it, and that $1.6 illion deal, also one of is first bids in the com-uter market, set Far ast Computers, of which e is the marketing direc-or, on the road to more hinese contracts.

A second deal worth 1.4 million followed that ame year. And just last veek, the Singapore ompany, which has its oots in New Delhi, an-ounced another two hina contracts, together vorth $3.5 million, making total of four computer ontracts with China vorth $6.5 million today.

More may be in the ipeline now that FEC is lso marketing The Apol-o, a CAD/CAM system uitable for companies of ll sizes, said Mr Chowd-ry, who, incidentally, loes not speak any Mandarin although his on and staff do.

"A lot of corporations are buying computers in China. To sell to the Chi-nese, you have to under-stand their buying psy-chology; they're out to buy the best technology there is, not yesterday's.

"They want to leapfrog into the world of informa-tion technology. The most obvious (way) is to go into education, where the young are taught the new-est technology," said Mr Chowdhry.

Thus, all four FEC deals with China were basically for educational purposes.

He attributes their suc-cess to a more aggressive strategy — FEC held their own exhibition on top of the computer fair held in China last year — and good references from their first Chinese users.

MR CHOWDHRY ... expecting a turnover of $20 m this year

"But we don't only sell computers, we're selling computerisation, which in-cludes a software solution package that is designed to meet the user's needs."

FEC intends to set up a branch office in China and already has branches in Malaysia, Australia and Thailand. In Indonesia, FEC uses a distributor.

The Australian branch has just started and is part of his plans to make FEC more export-orient-ed, a logical step for a company where sales has grown from a mere $1 million in 1980, when it started, to $12.5 million last year.

"We expect a turnover of $20 million this year and we're going to work very hard towards it."

But Mr Chowdhry, who still has time for bestsell-ers in between computer magazines and computer fairs, also sees immense potential for the personal computer and the CAD/CAM system here.

...s needed to boost ...cial centre status

earned by residents or non-residents, was tax-free, while in Singapore, the concessions only applied to non-residents.

Despite this, the bank has been gearing itself to become more involved in fund management in Singapore. Its merchant bank, Paribas South East Asia Ltd, has recently established an investment arm to initially provide advice on Singaporean and Malaysian stocks to the bank's Luxembourg-based fund management subsidiary.

Later, it hopes to man-age some of the bank's funds in Singapore before establishing a separate fund management centre here in about "two or three years" to manage other clients' money.

However, the recent moves by the government to promote fee-based banking business would contribute to the increas-ing sophistication of Singapore as a financial centre.

Mr Haberer, who was formerly Head of the French Treasury, said that merchant banks could be involved in four types of fee-based activi-ties:

- CORPORATE fi-nance such as share underwriting, share place-ment, mergers and acqui-sitions and advisory roles in public listings;
- CLUB deals or loan syndications;
- FUND management and venture capital funds and;
- MISCELLANEOUS advisory services.

The Strait Times takes note of Singapore-based HCL subsidiary Far East Computers' success in securing 6.5 million dollars' worth of deals in China, in 1985.

Doting dad with his sons Kunal and Akshay, in 1988.

With Bill Gates during his visit to India, in 2000, marking twenty-five years of Microsoft.

Singing at a party to celebrate twenty-five years of HCL at Shiv Nadar's home in 2001.

Good enough to eat: a cake shaped like our very first product, the Micro 2200 computer, to mark twenty-five years of HCL at Shiv Nadar's home in 2001.

With Dr Selot, my professor at Jabalpur Engineering College, and my friends from college, in 2003.

The famous four: a get-together with my college buddies (left to right) Sharat Saxena, Suresh Sundaram and Chintan Sagreiya, in 2003.

With my mother-in-law June (left) and Billy Maasi in 2008.

Receiving the Padma Bhushan, India's second highest civilian award, in 2011, from the then President of India, Pratibha Patil.

At Rashtrapati Bhawan after receiving the Padma Bhushan, with (left to right) daughter-in-law Neha, Kunkun, son Akshay, daughter-in-law Minakshi and son Kunal.

Jashan, the state-of-the-art auditorium at Jabalpur Engineering College named after my parents, Jai Krishna and Shakuntala, in 2012.

The verdant campus of the Indian Institute of Information Technology (IIIT) at Naya Raipur, Chhattisgarh, of which I was the first chairman in 2014.

With my oldest grandchild, Aavienda, in 2014.

At the launch of the TV serial *Main Kuchh Bhi Kar Sakti Hoon* in 2014, with (left to right) Poonam Muttreja, Tripurari Sharan, Sharmila Tagore, Naina Lal Kidwai, Feroz Abbas Khan and Sam Sharpe.

Receiving the Cybermedia Business ICT Lifetime Achievement award in 2014 from the then chief minister of Gujarat, Narendra Modi.

Teaching a programme in entrepreneurship at IIT Hyderabad in 2015.

Let there be light: with Rajnikant Yadav the inauguration of a solar power projec sponsored by Swayam in Khamkhera village, near Jabalpur, in 2015.

The Chowdhry siblings at the launch of *Habib ke Naghme*, a musical rendition of Jai Krishna Chowdhry's poems, in 2016: (from left to right) Sneh, Pammi, Raji, Indu, Vijay and I.

At my alma mater, Christ Church Boys' Senior Secondary School, in 2019, speaking to students on the future of jobs.

With my grandson, Raahil, in Singapore in 2019.

My grandson, Rishaan, in Singapore in 2019.

Dexter, the Shar Pei who stole my heart and became my most constant companion, circa 2019.

With my grandsons Arhan (left) and Ronen at a park in London in 2019.

At the launch of EPIC in 2022, with V.K. Saraswat, Jasmine Shah, Arjun Malhotra, Abhay Karandikar, Dr Phatak, Nitin Kunkolienker, Vinod Sharma, Abhilasha Gaur and others.

AMD was working with HCL on a small notebook—a netbook—along the lines of OLPC at the time, and was planning to display it at Davos. AMD requested us to attend the launch. The decision was taken at the last minute, less than a fortnight before the WEF. We had to scramble to get our paperwork ready. I told Kunkun that spouses of attendees were very much a part of the scene at Davos, so she agreed to come along on the trip.

The little Alpine resort (population: 10,000) combines a charming village ambience with urban infrastructure. It was draped in white when we arrived; the snowflakes came down, gently but relentlessly, blanketing the streets, rooftops and cars. It was bitterly cold, so buying heavy winter gear was clearly a priority.

As it turned out, our biggest problem was not the cold; it was accommodation. To our dismay, there wasn't a single room available in Davos. The town itself has just about ten hotels, with a few dozen more in the neighbouring areas. Eventually, we managed to find a room in a hotel some two hours away from the Davos Congress Centre.

In contrast to the peaceful, laidback atmosphere of the town, the centre was a beehive of activity. We found ourselves in a maze of lounges, lobbies, cafés, juice bars and lecture halls, all teeming with people. Designer suits in conservative colours were interspersed with sweaters, bomber jackets and even saffron robes.

The centre was designed to facilitate interaction: we could drift from one session to another, hold meetings, or have one-to-one conversations with people we encountered by chance or design. We heard the charismatic Bill Clinton's speech, hobnobbed with political and business leaders, and met global Indians. Rahul Bajaj was there, and when I heard about his passing in 2022, my memory flashed back to sharing a cab with him at Davos.

Shortly thereafter, while I was representing the Confederation of Indian Industries (CII), I was asked to cochair the World Economic Forum on Africa at Dar es Salaam in Tanzania. Among the heads of state who graced the event was the then president of South Africa, the colourful Jacob Zuma.

My speech emphasized the necessity of a big push towards ICT in the African context. Taking a quantum leap forward in broadband and hardware would yield faster and more enduring developmental gains than roads or multimodal transport hubs, I observed.

In Africa, as in India, connectivity would provide the means to address infrastructure, education and health issues. I pointed out that HCL had helped connect 53 heads of state in Africa through video-conferencing. My suggestions were very well received. Today, Africa's rapid strides in internet connectivity are acknowledged as a key driver of growth.

All in all, it was an enriching experience and gave HCL a lot of international exposure. I met people from all over the world, including my fellow cochairs. There was Pat Davies, CEO of Sasol, South Africa; Joergen Haslestad, CEO of Yara International, Norway; and of course, Klaus Schwab, the founder of WEF. I gave a bunch of interviews, in which I reiterated the importance of a broadband/hardware focus, drawing on India's example. I also wrote about Africa and its tremendous potential in terms of partnerships with India.

Jacob Zuma and I had a moment, when he proudly told me how one incident in Africa converted Barrister Gandhi to Mahatma Gandhi. As I recounted in a subsequent article for a newspaper, I found that India's soft power in Africa was not limited to Gandhi. I heard A.R. Rahman's 'Jai Ho' (from *Slumdog Millionaire*) being played at a WEF soirée. At the State House in Dar es Salaam, we witnessed a Bharatanatyam recital.

The president of Tanzania, Jakaya Kikwete, invited us for dinner. We turned up, suited and booted, as protocol demanded. As cochairs, we were seated in the front row. It was quite hot, so after a few minutes, we were melting in our suits. President Kikwete came in, started his speech, and then stopped short. He cast a knowing look at us and said, 'It is rather warm. I can see some discomfort. You can remove your coats, if you like.' Smiling in sheer relief, we immediately shed our jackets.

AWARDED!

Around the turn of the decade, I had begun feeling restless at work. I had helped script a phenomenal phase of growth for the company, which had resulted in revolutionary leaps forward, not just for HCL, but for India's ICT sector as a whole. After the PC revolution came mobile telephony and then, the systems integration business which proved to be a game-changer. During this time, our revenues increased by a factor of thirty.

I had also served as adviser to governments, been a member of various committees and achieved significant recognition. But I had fallen prey to the 'lonely at the top' syndrome. Shiv had always been a sounding board, but was now tied up with other ventures and was not available for the most part.

I also found myself increasingly impatient with the challenges of running a listed company. It's something of a treadmill, with a relentless focus on quarter-on-quarter profits. Not to mention the annoyance of having to deal with youngsters from financial consultancy firms, who knew very little about the business but were addicted to endless inventorizing!

Never one to shy away from honest introspection, I asked myself if my increasing disquiet was a sign that I needed to move on. The answer was yes. I wanted to get off the treadmill, and do something creative.

There was a second factor at play. Having turned sixty in August 2010, I realized that the industry had began to look at me as some sort of elder statesman. For me, the descriptor 'the father of Indian hardware' was a red flag. Was I over the hill? I certainly didn't feel like it, but perhaps it was time to take on an advisory rather than a hands-on role. I put plans for my departure in motion at once, knowing that the transition would take at least a year.

The question I kept asking myself was whether I had done enough, in the course of my long career, for the industry? Apparently, many people thought I had.

On the night of 25 January 2011, I was working late. My colleague and our COO, J.V. Ramamurthy, walked into my office, grinning ear to ear. 'Congratulations, sir! You are going to get the Padma Bhushan. I've just seen the list.' I was speechless. To be selected for India's third-highest civilian award, given to just about a thousand people before me, was overwhelming.

A few months earlier, a senior bureaucrat, with whom I was on excellent terms, had told me, 'I'm going to propose your name for a Padma award'. I was surprised, and a little gratified, but didn't take it very seriously. I didn't lack appreciation, but the fact was that no one from the hardware industry had ever received a national award. A few days later, another senior bureaucrat informed me, 'I'm going to do my best to put you on the Padma awards list this year'. I thanked him, and put it out of my mind.

When the award was announced, the whole office, the entire company, was thrilled. The general sentiment was that HCL Infosystems had been honoured, not just me. My family, needless to say, was over the moon. To me, it all seemed a bit surreal, until I received a telegram from home minister P. Chidambaram, followed by a letter from home secretary Gopal Krishna Pillai.

In all the years of working towards building India's ICT industry, I had never sought or expected accolades. Of course, it was always nice to get one, like Skoch Consultancy's 'IT Man of the Year' award in 2004 and Dataquest's 'IT Person of the Year' award for 2007.

Having received more than my fair share of industry recognition, I can safely say there is no experience more humbling than receiving a national award. Standing before the President of India, the embodiment of the Republic you have been privileged to serve, you are conscious of having done no more than your duty. Of a billion-plus citizens, each playing their part, you have been singled out for extraordinary recognition. I was reminded of Swami Vivekananda's words: 'Let us work on, doing as we go whatever happens to be our duty, and being ever ready to put our shoulders to the wheel. Then surely shall we see the Light!'

I was given a choice of two dates for the presentation ceremony. I selected 1 April 2011, because it was my wife's birthday. I was summoned to Rashtrapati Bhavan for a rehearsal. The ceremony is carefully orchestrated and you can't put a foot wrong as you step forward to receive your award.

On the day, weighed down by emotion and the gravitas of the occasion, I could barely take in the splendour of Rashtrapati Bhavan. As I walked up to receive a medal and a citation from President Pratibha Patil, I was conscious of PM Manmohan Singh, Congress president Sonia Gandhi and other notable figures in the audience. My family—Kunkun and both our sons and our daughters-in-law—were there as well.

After the ceremony, we met the other award winners, among them thespian Shashi Kapoor, philanthropist Rajshree Birla and ITC chief Yogesh Deveshwar. Shashi was accompanied by his sons, and we reminded him that he had been present at the Oberoi when Kunkun and I were celebrating our engagement.

That evening, we celebrated with a dinner for family and friends. Hans Raj Hans was invited to sing, and we had a wonderful time. Later, the company insisted on marking the occasion with a dinner, where several colleagues found rather nice things to say about me.

Coincidentally, from the moment I made up my mind to quit the company I'd founded, it was raining awards. I was specially chuffed to get an Honoris Causa Doctorate of Science (D.Sc.) from the Indian Institute of Technology (IIT) Roorkee. I received CNBC's India Innovator of the Year award from finance minister Pranab Mukherjee, as well its Asia Business award in the Viewers' Choice category. I was also dubbed 'Electronics Man of the Year' by ELCINA-EFY.

I went on to receive the Cybermedia Business ICT Lifetime Achievement award from Narendra Modi in 2014. In that same year,

I was also honoured with an Honoris Causa (D.Sc.) by the Indian Institute of Information Technology, Jabalpur.

Awards are meaningful to the extent that they affirm your contribution to the common good. They do not set your achievements up above those of your fellows, because each of us follows what happens to be our particular duty, or dharma. To cite Swami Vivekananda again, 'devotion to duty is the highest form of worship'.

EXIT STAGE LEFT

In 2012, it was time to move on from HCL, and in June of that year, I stepped down as chairperson. Harsh Chitale had taken over as CEO in 2010 and moved into an office next to mine. As I told journalists at the time, from the moment he joined, my job had changed from leading to mentoring. That role, I felt, had been accomplished satisfactorily and I could now exit stage left with a clear conscience.

When I left HCL—and I made it clear that the connect would stay alive—I took only one person with me. Her name is Lalita Gurnani and she deserves special mention, because she has orchestrated my various companies, investments and variegated activities over the last decade like a maestro.

I first met Lalita when she was working with another member of the HCL board, who appreciated how brilliant she was. Her education had been cut short because of troubles in her family, and she had joined HCL as a receptionist. Her amazing ability to handle just about anything brought her to her boss' attention.

We had her trained in Quality Standards Management (QSM) and pretty soon, she was taking care of our customer complaints. She was taught the concept of 'complaint is a gift'. She delivered on that! She became my assistant and later, my executive secretary. So efficient was she that I wondered how I had ever managed without her. She has been there for me 24×7, consistently going above and beyond the call of duty. Once, Kunkun lost her credit card in London and called Lalita in a flap late at night. It was sorted out in no time.

I am impressed not only by her commitment, but also her largeheartedness and empathy. I have no hesitation in saying she is one of the finest human beings I have ever known. After she quit HCL to join me, I had her trained in managing investments, and made her a part of my companies. She became a senior manager and subsequently, the general manager.

At the time I retired from HCL, I was 62. In good health physically and financially, I was happy to escape from the daily grind and enjoy the luxury of being able to switch off from the demands of leading a company. But it was clear to me and to my family that while I had retired from HCL, I was not about to retire from work.

I certainly wanted to spend more time with my family, and to pursue my hobbies, but I also had multiple new projects in mind that would need a great deal of time and attention. That's why I needed Lalita to serve as the point person on all my new ventures. I felt mentally rejuvenated and impatient to begin the next phase of my life.

For one thing, I was already serving as chairperson of the board of governors of Indian Institute of Technology Hyderabad (IITH), which was then in its formative phase. It was not an empty title for me, but a responsibility I took very seriously. Technical education was an area of interest and I was determined to do it right.

For another, I had planned a range of philanthropic efforts, some of which were centred around my hometown, Jabalpur. I had also wanted to keep my father's memory and his musical and literary contributions alive, but had never found the time.

Most of all, I had a dream, of India becoming the world's electronics hub. There were three ways in which I could contribute. First, I could serve as an enabler through various industry bodies and government committees, towards ushering in a hardware-friendly policy environment. Second, I could play a more direct role by promoting tech entrepreneurship, both as an investor and mentor. And third, to ensure that talent was available to scale indigenous electronics manufacturing, I could foster technical education in India.

9

BUILDING INSTITUTIONS

AT THE PLATINUM JUBILEE CELEBRATIONS of my alma mater, Jabalpur Engineering College, Madhya Pradesh chief minister Shivraj Singh Chouhan observed that the institution had the potential to become one of the best in the country. We all clapped dutifully, all too aware that the college stood nowhere in the institutional rankings.

Once a pioneer in several fields, JEC had slid from its position of eminence, a sad commentary on the state of mainstream technical education in India. Our IITs and IIMs, the Indian Institute of Science (IISC) and a handful of other institutions are centres of excellence in an otherwise mediocre landscape. Small wonder the 'shadow education' industry is booming; aspiring engineers spend years in coaching classes to prepare for the IIT entrance examination, as depicted in the web series *Kota Factory*.

Building (or rebuilding) institutions with a culture of excellence is vital for facilitating economic development and bringing about social transformation. Indeed, it is a form of social engineering, in that it makes our youth globally competitive and self-reliant. This is particularly true in the context of the knowledge economy.

My experiments in institution-building began in 2009, when I was appointed chairperson of the Indian Institute of Technology Hyderabad. It had been set up in 2008, with IIT Bombay professor Uday B. Desai as founding director, but was still functioning out of temporary premises at the Ordnance Factory Medak. Our job was to get an independent campus up and running. It was challenging, to say the least, but I had the advantage of working with Uday.

A chance encounter with the former head of CSIR (Council of Scientific and Industrial Research), R.A. Mashelkar on a flight to Hyderabad also proved useful. He suggested I read *The Innovative University* by the eminent American academic Clayton Christensen. The author, who developed the theory of 'disruptive innovation', holds that educational institutions must innovate and develop functional strategies in response to the demands of the society.

The book examines how the German university system pioneered an emphasis on new knowledge (that is, research and development) rather than mere transmission of learning. It offers insights on new approaches to curricula, faculty, enrolment and retention of students, campus infrastructure and so on. I absorbed the book, learning key passages by heart.

The first task was designing the campus and its buildings. Keeping resource-efficiency in mind, we worked on a vertical layout, rather than the horizontal one that is the norm at most IITs. Christopher Benninger, the eminent architect, designed clusters of environment-friendly buildings scattered over the 546-acre campus. Work began in earnest in 2011.

The infrastructure was being funded in part by the Japanese government. The collaboration had started with a working group for setting up a new IIT in August 2007, as per an agreement between the prime ministers of Japan and India. The IITH consortium of Japan was set up in August 2009 as the umbrella organization of government, academia and industry from Japan, aiming at promoting collaboration with IITH.

We had to take the team representing the Japanese consortium into confidence at each step. Prof. Desai told me that they were not happy with our mode of functioning, and this was holding up the execution of the project. I realized that they were accustomed to detailed reports at each stage, and found our methods a bit ad hoc.

I called a meeting with them in Delhi to sort out the matter, and suggested that we appoint a project manager to oversee the work and provide constant feedback. The Japanese team concurred, and it worked out very well. They ended up contributing a generous amount over three years and were pleased with the outcome.

THE TRAINING OF MINDS

Implementing learnings from Christensen's book, I held workshops with the faculty members. The idea, I said, was not merely to turn out engineers, but well-rounded human beings. We didn't want pure nerds. To that end, we introduced fractional courses in humanities and other subjects that carried half the credits of the regular ones. Attending classes in humanities subjects, the students were told, would have a direct bearing on their personal and professional lives.

We placed a lot of emphasis on R&D and entrepreneurship. To my mind, an institute of higher learning should lead the way in innovation and technological breakthroughs. That's what puts it on the map. So, each student was given a research project. We also had a programme to help the students improve their English language skills. Many of them came from small towns, and both their spoken and written English was very poor. When I asked one of my ex-HCL colleagues, Sandeep Madan, to test the students entering the institute, we discovered their weak grasp of English. When asked, 'How do you find IITH', the top answer was 'Google'.

Courses outside the realm of the pure sciences were a new concept for an IIT. The credit for the success of the initiative goes to Prof. Desai, an open-minded and innovative educationist. In this context, a recent observation by the director of IIT Delhi is relevant. He said that if the IITs are to maintain their global standing, they would have to promote interdisciplinary education at all levels.

We also introduced a minor in entrepreneurship. Our premise was that IITians should see themselves as job creators, not merely job seekers. The programme carried credits and ran parallel to the main course in the last two years of the four- to five-year programme. Keeping time constraints in view, classes were flexible and could be held even on a Sunday.

The courseware was created keeping practical aspects in mind. Sales, marketing and accounts were taught by professors from IIM Bangalore, and the rest by practitioners. Drawing on the innovative approach adopted by Babson College, Massachusetts, we emphasized practical knowledge, aimed at recognizing opportunities and building viable business models. I taught the introductory programme, which involved some eighteen hours of lectures.

To create the courseware, I drew on several books on entrepreneurship and added my own learnings to the mix. I made it a point to use audio-visual aids, notably episodes of *Dragons' Den*, the British reality TV business programme where budding entrepreneurs pitch their ideas to investors.

I also introduced them to two films, *Rocket Singh: Salesman of the Year* and *Jerry Maguire*, which discuss good salesmanship and emphasize the value of customer service and satisfaction. The latter spawned two popular quotations: 'show me the money' and 'help me help you'. The students had to make presentations on the key takeaways from the films, based on the concepts that had been taught, so that I could evaluate their learnings. I taught the programme for seven years.

The thrust, and the central message of my first convocation address, was the importance of producing fully developed individuals. In his book, Christensen echoed Harvard professor Harry Lewis's indictment of the education system: 'Universities have forgotten their larger role for college students ... Rarely will you hear more than bromides about their personal strength, integrity, kindness, cooperation, compassion, and how to leave the world a better place than you found it.'

Top universities are in competition for grants, rankings, big name faculty and students who can bring recognition, Christensen points out. The more involved they are in the rat race, the less likely to invest in character-building. To drive this message home, we asked the former president of India, A.P.J. Abdul Kalam, to deliver some of his inspirational lectures.

A CASE FOR HYBRID LEARNING

One of the measures I would have liked to introduce was hybrid teaching and learning, which combines on-campus activities and online education. The DeVry College of New York went online a decade ago, and several universities in the US have followed suit. The COVID-19 pandemic certainly expedited the process, but the trend was already underway.

I made a concerted effort in this direction at IIT Patna, which was my next assignment. I took over as chairperson of the board of governors in October 2012, and went on to serve a six-year term. During that time, I managed to introduce a platform for online learning, called Aurus, developed by a student of IIT Kanpur. I could see that digital learning was the wave of the future. In effect, my efforts foreshadowed Byju's, currently the world's most valued ed-tech company.

I also mentored an ed-tech company, Talentedge. They combined online learning with in-person classes at a number of centres, along the lines of NIIT. A friend of mine was on their board and I remember asking him why they bothered with the centres at all. It would have been far more cost-effective to focus on the digital aspect of the business. Eventually, Talentedge was acquired by upGrad, for some Rs 350 crore, and they went totally digital.

One can take technology to people, but one can't make them adopt it. Gaining acceptance for hybrid learning at IIT Patna was a challenge, because the faculty members were resistant to change. It took a lot of persuasion to get them to record their lectures, so that they could be put on the central website, enabling students who had missed classes to catch up. Even after two years of relentless effort, only 50 per cent of the professors were on board.

In the six years that I spent at IIT Patna, I was more successful in pushing the rest of my agenda, namely an emphasis on research and entrepreneurship and an incubator for hardware, focusing on Electronics System Design and Manufacturing (ESDM) and medical electronics.

With the expansion in the number of IITs and a concomitant decline in international rankings, I strongly felt that the institutions needed to market themselves better. I raised the subject at a meeting of the IIT Council, comprising the chairpersons and directors of the institutes and headed ex-officio by the Union Minister for Human Resource Development (now the Minister of Education).

At one stage, when Kapil Sibal was HRD minister, he decided to have an off-site. He asked for a list of ideas to improve the IITs, from which he picked the top six. We spent an hour discussing each of them. It afforded me the opportunity to point out that the IITs have absolutely no mechanism for marketing. My stint at the University of Michigan had given me an insight into the importance accorded to promotional activities by institutions in the US. The professor who taught marketing and sales also led the university's efforts in this regard.

While universities in the US build their reputations on high academic standards, crack faculty and top-quality students, they also make concerted efforts towards outreach, transnational collaborations and self-promotion. There's no question of resting on one's laurels.

By contrast, the IITs are insular and the prevailing attitude is one of self-satisfaction. This is understandable, given that only the best and brightest gain admission. Over a million aspirants compete for the 16,000-odd seats available every year, and a tiny fraction make it to a coveted course in one of the top IITs. Every year, several graduates are recruited by top international and domestic companies, at hefty salary packages. This creates a certain sense of complacency.

I was asked to prepare a note on the subject. Drawing on developments in educational institutions all over the world, I submitted a comprehensive report, with suggestions on how the IITs could position themselves globally. As is often the case with government, it remained on paper.

A 'NAYA' BRAND

My next project was in Chhattisgarh. B.K. Gairola, former Head of the National Informatics Centre (NIC), rang me up. 'I want you to meet with a very senior official from Chhattisgarh. It has to do with an IIIT they have set up,' he said.

I learnt that the International Institute of Information Technology (IIIT) was an autonomous university focused on research and development in IT, a joint venture between the state government and NTPC (National Thermal Power Corporation). It turned out that they were very keen to have me on board as chairperson.

I agreed, because the idea of applying my learnings at IITH to shape a tech-ed institution was quite exciting. I joined in June 2014. The immediate challenges were to complete the infrastructure and appoint a director of suitable eminence. The first step was to form a board. I assembled a high-profile team, including A.J. Paulraj of Stanford University, Sujit Baksi of Tech Mahindra, Steven A. Pinto, the well-known banker, and Gairola.

We set up a selection committee tasked with finding a director. 'Let's aim high as we need to build the brand,' I told the board. They concurred, and an agency was hired to create and place ads for the director's position in India and the US. I personally wrote to some three hundred professors, but realized that the best people would be reluctant to move to what was perceived as a backwater. So, we launched a website, positioning Naya Raipur as India's first 'smart city'.

With the support of the state government, we initiated a brand-building exercise. The consensus on the name of the institute was to call it 'IIIT Naya Raipur'. We ran our marketing and public relations campaign like a private company, and engaged aggressively on social media. The objective was to position IIIT-NR as a new-era institution that fostered quality education as well as research and innovation.

We homed in on a suitable candidate in our first round of selection, but he turned us down. The second round was successful; we offered the position to Pradeep K. Sinha, formerly of C-DAC, where he had led programmes in supercomputing, grid computing, and health informatics. He had also authored several textbooks on computer science. I insisted that as part of the branding exercise, he be appointed vice-chancellor as well as director.

In terms of the syllabus and curriculum, S. Sadagopan, the director of IIIT Bangalore, gave us valuable inputs. Kiran Karnik, who was chairperson of IIIT Delhi, was also helpful. We started at an off-site location in IIIT Delhi and launched two courses, in computer science and electronics, with sixty students. Later, we introduced courses in artificial intelligence and data science.

I wanted to make the institution world-class, so we reached out to academics overseas and got them to teach remotely. As I had done during my stint at the IITs, I placed a lot of emphasis on hybrid learning, which ensured that IIIT-NR was well-prepared to handle the pandemic, and the students did not fall behind. We also initiated a lab where students could enhance their language and communications skills.

I remained chairperson for seven years. A friend of mine, Saurabh Srivastava, cofounder and former chairperson of NASSCOM, took over from me. I explained my vision for the institute to him, and was pleased to see that he retained the same board, which had been so supportive of all my initiatives. Each one had brought something to the table, whether in terms of funding, or an industry connect, or an international perspective.

Our branding exercise yielded excellent results. IIIT-NR was ranked among the top seven tech-enabled engineering institutes by

Dataquest in 2020. The first batch, which graduated five years ago, achieved 100 per cent placement. We had created, innovated and succeeded.

After having helped build three technology-oriented institutions, I was presented with a rather more challenging assignment in 2018: the chairpersonship of the National Institute of Forge and Foundry Technology (NIFFT) in Ranchi. Set up in 1966 in collaboration with UNDP-UNESCO to train engineers and technicians for the forge and foundry industry, it was hopelessly behind the times.

I decided that the old-fashioned institute needed a complete overhaul. I was fortunate to have a pro-active director, and we set about implementing my agenda of transforming NIFFT to serve the needs of 'Industry 4.0', a blanket term for smart automation and the use of Internet of Things (IoT) platforms for manufacturing. We approached the HRD ministry and appointed a committee to create a strategy based on my ideas. It was approved and a budget of Rs 100 crore allocated.

The institute was rebranded as the National Institute of Advanced Manufacturing Technology (NIAMT). I suggested new courses in mechanical engineering, electronics and computer engineering. I also initiated an agreement with the Software Technology Parks of India (STPI) to create a centre of excellence. When I left in 2020, it was with the satisfaction of knowing that my stint had been transformative.

SKILLING INDIA'S ELECTRONICS SECTOR

In 2011, on the cusp of leaving HCL, I got a call from Rajoo Goel, secretary general of the first industry body for hardware, Electronic Industries Association of India (ELCINA). He wanted to discuss a recent decision by the central government to set up sector-wise skill councils, geared toward particular industries. The National Skill Development Corporation (NSDC) had earmarked funds to that end.

Rajoo told me that six of the industry associations had decided to seize the opportunity and establish an electronics sector skills council, tasked with creating skilled manpower. Their training would cover the spectrum from consumer electronics to automation and semiconductors. 'We would like you to be chairperson, because yours is the one name that everyone will agree to without hesitation,' he said.

The Electronic Sector Skills Council of India (ESSCI) came into being, as a not-for-profit start-up. At the outset, we set standards for training, developed infrastructure and equipment, and engaged with the electronics industry to better understand their requirements. In the next decade, we would facilitate the training of some 16.5 million people in the manufacture, installation and repair of computers, mobile phones, TVs, solar power systems, surveillance cameras and so on.

By the time I relinquished my chairpersonship of ESSCI, we had over 4,500 training centres, as well as 1,200 industry partners, and had managed to place over nine lakh trainees through our job portal.

JASHAN: THE JABALPUR CONNECT

What about my alma mater, you might ask? My efforts in the field of education have naturally included JEC, and I have served as chairperson of its Institute Management Council (IMC). It all started with my desire to give back to JEC is some shape or form. Having lost touch over the years, I had no idea what was going on at the college and how I might contribute.

I spoke with M. Selot, one of the professors who had taught me at JEC, about what I could do for the institution. We'd kept in touch over the years and the teacher-student relationship had evolved into a warm friendship. He'd attended the weddings of both my sons and dropped in on me whenever he was in Delhi.

'I want to do something special for the college. Could you find out what they really need?' I asked.

'I'll have a discussion with the principal, Prof. P.K. Jhinge, and the rest of the faculty,' he replied.

He got back to me with a proposal. 'What JEC needs is a state-of-the-art auditorium. The one we have is shabby, with no air-conditioning or amenities,' he said.

We got to work, and by July 2012, JEC's new auditorium was ready.

With a seating capacity of 280, audio-visual surround sound, central air-conditioning, aesthetically designed spaces and a green room, it provides an ideal ambience for conventions, workshops and cultural events. It is called 'Jashan', a combination of my parent's names, Jai Krishna and Shakuntala. The college was kind enough to put up a plaque in their memory.

The day before the inauguration, I got my college mates together and hosted a dinner, so that we could all share the moment. The mayor of Jabalpur did the honours, at a function attended by the district commissioner and several eminent people from the city.

I continued to be an active member of the JEC Alumni Association and, out of the blue, was invited to a meeting with Yashodhara Raje Scindia, Madhya Pradesh's minister for technical education and chairperson of the JEC board. A batchmate of mine, Romesh Sobti, had told her that JEC's platinum jubilee celebrations, of which I was the chair, were coming up in mid-2021. He also mentioned that the college board hadn't met for quite some time.

So, she invited Romesh and me to a meeting of the board. We discussed the jubilee event, after which she appointed the IMC and asked me to chair it. The celebrations got off to a great start, a year ahead of the platinum jubilee. An alumnus, Abhijit Srivastava, had created a portal for the college and livestreamed the event for the benefit of JEC alumni scattered across the globe. The CM was the chief guest, and several ministers attended.

The laudable objective of restoring JEC's position of eminence calls for a significant upgrade of its infrastructure. Funds have been allocated towards that end, and at my suggestion, two new courses have been introduced: one in artificial intelligence and data science and the other in mechatronics. Various friends in the IITs have helped by furnishing the full course content. Another initiative we have sponsored is a collegiate club to promote designing and manufacturing of off-road vehicles.

As a nation in transition in the midst of a great technological revolution, India needs world-class institutions, capable of producing Nobel laureates and racking up patents. We must have a mix of applied and basic research, and orient technical education towards the needs of the industry, so that we can emerge as exporters rather than importers of high value-added products and services. This calls for consistent and deep innovations in higher education, towards which my humble efforts have been directed.

As chairperson of several institutions, and as a teacher and mentor, I have imparted my learnings under three broad heads: entrepreneurship, salesmanship and people management. I have summarized them in the subsequent chapters.

10

START-UPS, WHERE ANGELS LOVE TO TREAD

MY VIEW OF ENTREPRENEURSHIP IS summed up by the inequality 'A>R'; that is, aspiration is greater than resources. I owe this formulation to the late C.K. Prahalad. The full quote being, 'If you have the aspiration, resources will happen.' The point is that passion, self-belief and courage of conviction are critical for entrepreneurship.

India has nurtured free enterprise all through her turbulent history. Consider the unicorn seals found in the Harappan archaeological sites. These intriguing remnants of India's earliest civilization were probably used in overseas trade, testifying to an entrepreneurial zeal among its inhabitants.

Economist Angus Maddison (*The World Economy: Historical Statistics*) notes that in the first century CE, India accounted for a third of the global GDP. As recently as the eighteenth century, it was a quarter of the world GDP. Knowledge-based innovations, supported by a structured education system, led to such marvels as Wootz steel, the corrosion-proof Ashokan Pillar located at the Qutub Minar in Delhi, the Sultanganj Buddha and the paisley shawls coveted by the European nobility.

In the early modern period, the seventeenth century Surat-based entrepreneur Virji Vora was the richest merchant in the world. He was later followed by the Birlas, Goenkas, Shri Rams and changemakers like J.R.D. Tata, M.S. Oberoi and Jamnalal Bajaj.

Some four millennia after the unicorn seals made their way to Mesopotamia, the Indian entrepreneurial spirit is alive and evolving, and more than a hundred Indian companies bear the 'unicorn' stamp. Quite as elusive as the mythical creatures after whom they are named, these privately-held start-ups (with a minimum one-billion-dollar valuation) are every entrepreneur's dream.

The quest for the unicorn is fraught with risk and hazard. Ninety per cent of start-ups are slain on the perilous journey. Among those that survive, unicorns are rare and decacorns (with a ten-billion-dollar valuation) even rarer. Undaunted by these odds, thousands take up the challenge of entrepreneurship every year. To succeed, they need courage, confidence, commitment, creativity and above all, passion.

Entrepreneurs have acquired a certain mystique in recent years. They are seen as innovators, agents of change and harbingers of development. The last four decades have seen successive waves of entrepreneurship, coterminous with the growth of the IT industry. HCL, Wipro and Infosys were among the first tech start-ups to go global. In the late 1990s, the advent of internet services led to consumer start-ups known as dotcoms (Shaadi.com, Naukri.com, etc.). Thereafter, the mobile and broadband boom powered a diverse range of start-ups, from e-commerce and logistics to fintech, edtech, spacetech, etc.

IT had the potential to create numbers, so it quickly overtook pharma, and had a catalytic effect on parallel sectors. The experience of entrepreneurship-led economic growth in the last two decades has demonstrated that it promotes inclusion, generates employment and triggers a chain-reaction of development.

The scenario for entrepreneurs has changed drastically since the 1980s. Funds are available, investors are accessible, and the regulatory system is no longer impenetrable. The government's 'Startup India' initiative got off to a slow start, but as of March 2022, recognized start-ups numbered around 65,861, of which 35,000 were added after 1 April 2020. Still a very small number, given India's size and potential, but the trend is encouraging.

PASSION: THE SINE QUA NON OF ENTREPRENEURSHIP

The ecosystem for start-ups has certainly improved. However, to capitalize on it, a would-be entrepreneur needs two things. The first is passion, an unshakeable belief in your idea and a determination to deliver it to the world. Any investor—and I'm speaking for myself and others I know—will first assess how passionate you are about your venture. It is the sine qua non, the essential condition, for entrepreneurship.

The second is the requisite know-how. Do entrepreneurial hopefuls have the appropriate guidance? Do they have the training to find funding, navigate dynamic markets and 'swim with the sharks'? I once asked a would-be entrepreneur, after a terrific technical presentation, to take me through his financials. The answer: 'I haven't worked it out yet'!

Therein, to my mind, lies the gap. Entrepreneurs are ideas people. All too often, they are so consumed by the 'big idea' that the finance and accounting, sales and marketing, and human resources aspects of the business plan don't get the attention they deserve. A lot of projects go bust at the development stage because of a lack of clarity and an inadequate execution strategy.

That's where incubators come in, to help entrepreneurs develop their businesses by providing physical infrastructure, training, seed money and access to venture capital financing. But most are located in educational institutions, where the accent is on technical mentorship. This is valuable, but not more so than business mentorship. It was to that end that we introduced a minor in entrepreneurship at IITH and a course at IITP, because entrepreneurs are made, not born.

One of my favourite mantras while teaching was, 'failure is not an option'. Unanticipated setbacks are part of the game, but if you are absolutely committed to the success of your venture, you will find solutions. Abandon the 'safety net' mentality. If you stake your future on something, you will make it work. A nuclear power plant can't afford to fail; nor can you. The question is not what happens if you fail but, to quote American businessperson Regina Dugan, 'what would you attempt to do if you knew you wouldn't fail'?

Fear of failure undermines the very premise of entrepreneurship. As HCL's first print campaign, consciously targeted at the youth, declared, 'you don't have more courage when you are young; you have less fear'. So, recapture that youthful spark and unlearn fear. To quote psychologist Karl Menninger, 'fears are educated into us, and can, if we wish, be educated out'. When you are driven by passion to realize your purpose, you will conquer fear. In other words, your passion for the venture must be greater than the sum of all your fears.

What-ifs are a waste of energy and mind space. What if you're not good enough, what if the customer or investor rejects you, what if disaster strikes? The hard part is convincing yourself. Only then can you win over the customer, investor, mentor or partner. To do that, you need to be relentlessly optimistic. More important than having robust recovery systems in place is an enabling geist, or spirit, within the organization.

As an investor, passion is the determining factor for me. As an entrepreneur, how passionate are you? Passion fuels the venture and engenders creativity, persistence and performance. At the same time, it makes you appear more authentic and interesting to the investor.

NOISE TO SIGNAL

Opportunities for entrepreneurship in India have multiplied with the changes in its demographics. A high working-age percentage, nuclearization of families, dual-wage households and the emergence of Tier II and III urban centres, has created a market for all manner of products and services. Tech penetration has likewise created new demands.

E-commerce and e-learning platforms are exploding and there's scope for innovation, and value addition in existing products and services, from the medical and security needs of the elderly to new apps, games and devices. Government projects, too, offer space for products: digitization, smart grids, transport and so on.

Entrepreneurship is about innovation. It can be disruptive, radically altering the existing order, or incremental, involving a new approach to or an improvement of a process. Either way, it takes both creativity—a big idea—and implementation. The first step is to look for a gap in the market, not necessarily a whole new product. Facebook didn't reinvent the wheel; it took an existing service and made it more appealing by addressing gaps. The same applies to the iPod.

Pranav Mistry's SixthSense is another example I like to cite. He figured out how everyday objects can be integrated with the digital world. Hence, 'Mouseless', the invisible computer mouse; Sparsh, which allows copying and pasting of data between digital devices; and Quickies, which are intelligent sticky notes that can be retrieved and can set reminders.

Entrepreneurial youngsters typically have a plethora of half-formed notions buzzing around in their heads. That fuzzy cloud needs to be coalesced into a clearly developed big idea. In engineering parlance, the 'noise' must be converted into a 'signal'.

When screening ideas, scalability should be a prime consideration. The 'wow' or novelty factor for the customer must translate into a market-size large enough to attract investors. So, keep that in mind while designing a product or service.

During my lectures, I would introduce the concept of 'the 86 per cent opportunity', derived from Vijay Mahajan and Kamini Banga's seminal *The 86% Solution: How to Succeed in the*

Biggest Market Opportunity of the Next 50 Years. In brief, most entrepreneurs look at a 14 per cent slice of the global market, ignoring the 86 per cent represented by India, China and, increasingly, Africa. General Electric was one of the few companies that saw the potential in developing India-specific products.

Another useful tip is to put yourself in the customer's shoes, so that you can customize your product. A prime example is Intuit's home accounting software for personal finance, widely used by homemakers to keep track of grocery bills, medical expenses, savings, college funds and so on. Realizing that the end-user simply would not be able to deal with bugs in the system, or pay ongoing maintenance charges, Intuit ensured that its software was bug-free.

The time and timing of your product are critical. Be aware not only of the time to market—how long it takes to convert your idea to a product—but of the contextual validity of the idea. Say, in the midst of the COVID-19 pandemic, you've come up with a designer range of temperature-monitoring jewellery. If you get to market when the pandemic is over, there's not much point to that exercise.

The trouble with techies, as a friend of mine once said, is that they are always polishing the apple. Keeping a product in development costs money and risks losing out on market share. In the early days of our start-up, we had barely eight months to deliver our first product, and we did.

A new idea is at the heart of a start-up. Innovation is the process of delivering that something new. To quote Peter Drucker, 'innovation is the specific function of entrepreneurship, the act that endows resources with a new capacity to create wealth'. Or, of course, to give old ones more potential for creating wealth. The idea is essential, but not enough in itself. An entrepreneur needs mentors and investors to help refine it into an innovative business model.

Mentorship can be critical in getting off the ground. A mentor who can open doors, help you build your business, hone your strategy and navigate challenges will make all the difference. I firmly believe that mentorship must be a formal process to prove beneficial, with clarity of goals and requirements at both ends.

A start-up must determine what kind of mentoring it needs, whether it is expertise in a particular industry or in finance or marketing, or simply a high-profile, influential individual. Preferably, it should be someone the entrepreneur holds in high esteem. Conversely, the mentee must be 'mentorable'; that is, open to advice, with a coherent vision, realistic goals, discipline, focus and commitment.

A mentorship cannot be haphazard, with the mentor stepping in only when the mentee hits a roadblock. Regular meetings, defined objectives and timeframes, and a system of performance and progress review are necessary for course correction, refining business strategy and boosting networking skills. It is a two-way street of information sharing, involving time commitment and mutual trust.

Mentors can help in finding the money. Start-ups can access small funding from incubators, or family and friends. Most will look to angel investors ('angels'), who invest at the nascent stage and can also serve as mentors. Typically, in India, a consortium of twenty-five to thirty individuals puts up the initial funding of five to seven crore rupees, with valuations based on the uniqueness and scalability of the idea.

For the next round of funding, the entrepreneur will look at venture capitalists (VCs)—professionals who manage the capital of wealthy individuals, pension funds or endowments. With a capacity of rupees twenty crore or more, they specialize in certain sectors and look for a good return on investment. Apart from an innovative product, they want to see leadership, a quality team, a clearly defendable market positioning and scalability.

MAKING YOUR PITCH

Don't confuse an angel (or a VC) for a fairy godmother. Investors want the maximum return on investment and will look for sectors with growth potential, be it consumer, health, education, mobile or internet. The angel must see your idea as not just catering to the current, but the future needs of the market. Since they put in their own money, they are bound to be interested in how it's used and could very well become your best ambassadors.

When looking for an angel, it's best to research their investment record, because they prefer ventures that complement their portfolio. For the entrepreneur, likewise, it is preferrable to find someone who has knowledge of the industry and can act as a mentor.

In 2010, I became a member of the Indian Angel Network, which connects investors to start-ups. It comprises individuals with a strong entrepreneurial or operational background, who are willing to invest time and money in creating scale and value for start-ups. I'm personally invested in fifty.

Before making a pitch, be sure to have a solid business plan in place. 'Business has only two functions, marketing and innovation,' Milan Kundera observed. The importance of a sound marketing strategy can't be overstated. Nothing sells on its own. Steve Jobs may have given market research the go-by on the premise that customers have to be told what they want, but that's unconventional thinking.

Do your market research and suss out customer preferences and spending patterns. Know your market and your competition. Does your product compare with others in the same space? How can it be differentiated? Be clear about your positioning and platform for marketing. If it's business-to-business (B2B), you are looking at salespeople and distributors. If it's business-to-consumer (B2C), then internet and retailers. Digital marketing is generally cheaper than other options, in that it can be targeted to a specific customer base. But you definitely need to look at the cost of acquiring a customer (CAC).

Moving on to financials, a forecast of operating costs, revenue, cash flow and burn rate is helpful. Familiarize yourself with the legal scenario, specifically trademark and copyright laws. Be aware that you have just the one shot with the angel or VC, so make it convincing. Communicate clearly and professionally.

TEAMWORK

Also, bear in mind that entrepreneurs are no longer seen as lone visionaries; teams, divisions and even whole enterprises are striving to be more entrepreneurial. '*Ekla chalo re*' (go for it alone) doesn't cut it anymore. Having a quality team multiplies funds, talent, ideas and passion.

When receiving your pitch, given that the only thing you have on the table is an idea, the angel is more likely to assess your team. What should be visible is a hunger for success, a strong technical foundation and business acumen. Team members should complement each other. Subject matter expertise should be supplemented with skills in accounting and finance, marketing and sales. Speaking for myself, I'd go with the better team rather than the better idea, every time.

On the flip side, having a team implies potential ego clashes and fuzzy or delayed decision-making, because one person doesn't have absolute control. To avoid these pitfalls, crucial aspects of team-building must be kept in mind.

First, every member of the team must add value, and their skills should be complementary. Second, one person must be nominated to captain the ship; it is their job to actualize the start-up's vision. Third, the ownership pattern should be clear from the outset and shared among founders, keeping open a provision for employee stock options. Offering a stake to high-quality advisers and key people can be useful. Fourth, don't bring friends on board simply to create a comfort zone for yourself; it can be a slippery slope. Personally, I'm never keen on husband-wife teams, because I'm never sure if both partners add value.

Get the best people you can, and groom them, so that they become a part of your venture, even if that means paying them more than you pay yourself. If you can, rope in an experienced business development manager as a cofounder. Don't stint on a good sales force and empower them with the right tools: appealing presentations and brochures, and an eye-catching website. Preferably avoid part-time salespeople as they tend to move on and you can't count on their loyalty.

Within a set-up, designations can be tricky, a constant source of bruised egos. To underline the hollowness of job titles, I fall back on a favourite anecdote. It goes like this:

A man was struggling up a hill. En route, he spots a house and decides to ask for a glass of water. As he lifts the latch of the gate, a large dog erupts from behind the house, barking and snarling ferociously. The din summons the owner, who provides water. The man compliments him on the dog's alertness and carries on up the hill. On his way back, he stops at the house again. All is silent, so he opens the gate and hails the owner.

'Where's the dog?' he asks.

'He's around, but he doesn't bark any more'.

'How come?'

'Well, after you complimented him, I changed his name to Director. Since then, he just lolls around and does nothing.'

COVID INNOVATION

Nothing testifies to the spirit of entrepreneurship like the wave of urgent innovation triggered by the COVID-19 pandemic. In the face of a time crunch, limited resources and the need for quick scaling, technovators in India—and across the globe—came up with creative solutions to the worst global crisis since World War II.

India was woefully underprepared when the first wave hit, heavily dependent on imports for essentials such as sanitizers, masks, PPE kits, pharmaceuticals and medical devices. As the country went into lockdown on 25 March 2020, the central and state governments began ramping up public health infrastructure.

Nobody had anticipated the sheer scale of the challenge, but a combination of time pressure and focus, achieved a near-miracle. The government announced the 'COVID-19 Solution Challenge' on 16 March 2020 (when India had just sixty cases). By December of that year, India had created the capacity to produce half-a-million PPE kits daily, was more than self-sufficient in producing masks and sanitizers and was manufacturing sophisticated ICU ventilators.

Small and medium enterprises, and start-ups, responded to the call for 'atmanirbharta' (self-reliance) by revamping or setting up assembly lines to make COVID-related products. Pop-up hospitals such as those in repurposed train wagons mushroomed, and biotech companies stockpiled enough vaccine doses not only for the domestic vaccination programme, but for export to our neighbours and countries in need. All in a matter of months.

I had a ringside view to these developments, having been drawn into three separate COVID-related ventures. The first is now the subject of a book called *The Ventilator Project*. The title is self-explanatory, so suffice it to say that the direct correlation between Acute Respiratory Distress Syndrome (ARDS) and COVID-19 underlined the desperate need for indigenous invasive ICU ventilators.

Anyone who has seen a medical drama series on TV knows what a ventilator is—a device that pumps air into a patient's lungs, usually by means of an inflatable ambu-bag. A non-invasive ventilator delivers air through a mask placed over the nose or face, and works well for patients in mild to moderate respiratory distress. In severe cases, the patient needs an invasive ICU ventilator, where a mix of air and oxygen is delivered through an endotracheal tube.

Several Indian companies announced plans to manufacture ventilators when the pandemic hit, but these were inadequate for patients suffering from ARDS.

The Ninety-Day Countdown: In late March 2020, I got a call from Saurabh Srivastava, cofounder and former chairperson of NASSCOM and a member of the board of IIT Kanpur. He told me that IIT Kanpur's incubator—the Startup Incubation and Innovation Centre (SIIC)—had taken up the formidable challenge of creating an invasive ICU ventilator.

Prior to the pandemic, only large hospitals could afford such ventilators, because they were expensive and tough to operate. The challenge was to come up with a low-cost, world-class, easily manufacturable invasive ICU ventilator. Nocca Robotics, a start-up incubated at IITK, had pitched its concept to SIIC head Amitabha Bandyopadhyay.

Originally in the business of waterless, solar-panel cleaning robots, Nocca pivoted to the ventilator project as soon as they heard about the COVID-19 challenge. The promoters, IITK graduates Nikhil Kurele and Harshit Rathore, with help from their batchmate Abhishek Kulkarni and junior Tushar Agarwal, came up with an ingenious prototype by repurposing electronic circuits from the solar-panel cleaning robot, a pressure pump from a fish tank and sensors from a toy drone!

IITK introduced the Nocca team to Dr Govind Rajan, critical care specialist and professor at the University of California, who validated their concept. It also led the effort to raise Corporate Social Responsibility (CSR) funds for developing, designing and scaling the product.

Nocca planned to bid for a tender announced by HLL, a public-sector undertaking tasked with procuring 70,000 ventilators. But the timeframe was very tight; in effect, the ventilator had to be ready and certified within three months, because these machines would make the difference between life and death.

Saurabh said my expertise in hardware was urgently needed, and asked me to join the taskforce that would oversee and guide the IIT Ventilator Consortium. He pointed out that none of the others on board had experience in designing and manufacturing hardware. I agreed, but foresaw a host of problems, given the exigencies of lockdown and likely disruption in global supply chains.

I suggested that Rajesh Raizada, my former colleague at HCL and the best procurement manager I have ever known, be brought on board. If anyone could source components and raw materials at viable prices during these difficult times, it would be Rajesh. 'Give him a bill of materials. Let's get to work right away,' I said.

On 29 March 2020, the Consortium had its first Zoom meeting. For the next ninety days, the ninety-minute meetings would be held at noon every single day. We would home in on a particular aspect of the project and discuss it threadbare. Our agenda spanned the spectrum of product development, from design to manufacture to sales and service.

While the Nocca team worked on the design, I focused on the logistics. With imports at a standstill and air freight and travel shutting down, I had to leverage my contacts in the government and abroad to source components. For one particular part, a friend in Invest India—the national investment promotion and facilitation agency—reached out to our ambassador in Singapore, who then arranged for transport. Likewise, I asked a former HCL colleague based in Dubai to send components from there.

The first two iterations of the ventilator were submitted in the bid to the HLL, but the government changed the specifications, so we went back with a third one in mid-May. After the award of the first HLL tender, the business news portal The Ken alleged fake certification of ventilators already ordered by the Indian government. Hastily, a committee of experts was set up under the Director General of Health Services (DGHS) to evaluate the ventilators.

By June, the Noccarc V310 passed the IEC 60601-1 standard compliance test at the Swen Konformity Lab in Pune as well as the DGHS hurdle. Next, Dr Prachee Sathe, director of the ICU at the Ruby Hall Clinic, subjected it to rigorous testing on actual patients and certified the product. A couple of days later, the Medanta and Artemis hospitals, as well as the Army Base Hospital in Delhi also gave it positive reviews.

In ninety days, despite numerous roadblocks, the ventilator project had come to a successful conclusion. It was a stunning achievement. In ordinary circumstances, it would have taken at least a couple of years.

Meanwhile, Nocca received offers of manufacturing partnerships and signed memoranda of understanding (MoUs) with AVI Healthcare and Bharat Dynamics Limited (BDL). The latter was a defence PSU and its interest was piqued by a tweet from the Defence Secretary, to the effect that one of the best examples of COVID-related innovation was the 'Rs 50k ventilator by #NoccaRobotics'. BDL wanted to partner with Nocca for the second tender, but the partnership floundered and did not progress past the MoU stage. In any case, once the first wave of COVID-19 had receded, the government was disinclined to purchase more ventilators.

Nocca entered into a licencing agreement with AVI Healthcare. We helped it develop distribution, branding, sales and service strategies. Orders were obtained and manufacturing began. By mid-July, the first Noccarc V310s had been dispatched.

Decontamination Devices: Critical care devices like ventilators are one end of the med-tech spectrum. Preventive devices are the other. The one that caught my attention was the Scalene Hypercharge Corona Canon (SHYCOCAN). Unlike most virus-killing contraptions, which involve UV irradiation, ionization or sanitizing sprays, it uses light particles. Or in technical terminology, 'photon mediated electron emission', also known as the photoelectric effect.

The mechanism is relatively simple. It produces high intensity photons, which strike solids in a confined space, causing them to emit electrons. The negatively charged electrons then attach themselves to the positively charged spike protein of the SARS-CoV-2 virus. This neutralizes the spike protein, rendering it incapable of attaching to the negatively charged human cell receptor.

I first heard about Rajah Vijay Kumar, the scientist who came up with the concept, from Alok Sharma, former MD of Apple India. 'Come to Bangalore. There's a scientist you should meet,' he said. It turned out that Kumar had created a form of cancer therapy called the 'cytotron', a machine that uses fast radio bursts (FRB) to prevent proliferation of tumours.

It looks something like an MRI, and targets specific proteins in cancer cells, thereby preventing them from multiplying. Once the cancer is arrested, the patient can go in for conventional treatments. Kumar spent decades developing his machine, and the US FDA recognized it as a 'breakthrough device' for cancer therapy in 2019, but it faced a lot of opposition from the scientific community.

The affable scientist gave me a tour of his lab, and I asked him how the cytotron was linked to the Shycocan. Dr Kumar said that he'd stumbled on the concept by accident. He noticed that staff members who worked in the cytotron room rarely fell sick. Surmising that emissions from the machine were killing viruses in ambient air, he wondered whether it would be effective against SARS-CoV-2. He created a photon gun based on his theory and had it evaluated at several laboratories in India and abroad. It was found to be effective against a variety of coronaviruses.

Alok had the rights to commercialize the Shycocan, and sought my help. I crafted a sales strategy and introduced him to several people in government. He was met with widespread scepticism. Many scientists questioned the premise and efficacy of the device, and a negative article in a popular daily didn't help. The product began to move through e-retail, but the numbers remained low. According to Shycocan, some 15,000 machines are currently in use, and a couple of hospitals have furnished testimonials.

Personally, I found the device effective, in that no member of my family who installed it in their rooms fell prey to COVID. Even though our domestic staff was infected and interacted with us on a daily basis, we remained COVID-free. That said, the jury is still out on the Shycocan.

Recently, I came across an online review of a pocket-sized contraption for disinfecting face masks. It was intriguing, because I had been associated with the development of a similar device. An IIT Delhi-incubated start-up that I was mentoring had approached me with the idea of reusable PPE kits and surgical masks.

The company, Chakr Innovation, had developed a product that could reduce emissions from a diesel generator by as much as 70 per cent. Like many others, Chakr shifted its focus to the national effort against COVID-19. In any case, its factory had closed down and demand had fallen off.

Chakr pointed out that disposable PPE kits and masks posed a threat to the environment, given the challenges of safe waste disposal. Besides, PPEs were in short supply, so it made sense to reuse them. It proposed two disinfecting devices that would render protective gear reusable: a small box for masks and a chamber for PPEs.

I liked the presentation, and suggested that we create a taskforce to take the project forward. We brought in colleagues from the Indian Angel Network and they, in turn, inducted doctors and professors from IIT Delhi. For the next sixty days, we met at 5 p.m. every day.

The product was unique, so it presented a challenge both in terms of development and evaluation. Among the major problems we encountered were sourcing materials and reducing the weight of the devices, so that they could be shipped. We decided to focus on an N-95-specific mask disinfection device—the Chakr DeCov—as the PPE chamber was too heavy.

Testing the product necessitated a very secure lab. We first tested it against SARS-CoV-2 equivalents, and the third iteration passed with flying colours. To test against SARS-CoV-2 itself, we needed to get a time slot in an accredited virology lab. We approached the Ahmedabad Textile Industry Research Association (ATIRA) lab and managed to get it tested there. Buoyed by a successful test, we approached the National Institute of Virology (NIV) in Pune. As I had half-expected, it simply didn't have a time slot available. We tried several routes, including the Science & Technology Secretary, but drew a blank.

Having exhausted all options, I wrote an impassioned mail to the director of the NIV, pointing out that our technology was literally lifesaving. For health workers exposed to COVID-19 day in and day out, pristine N-95 masks were an imperative. The director relented and gave us a time slot.

In the meantime, I had already arranged for sales and service partners. But it turned out that the price was higher than the market could bear. I drafted in Rajesh's services, and between the two of us, we reduced the bill of materials by 40 per cent. Even so, it was too expensive. In any event, the first wave of COVID had receded and demand dropped off sharply. I bought the first machine and donated it to the Goa Medical College.

The response to the pandemic was informed not just by entrepreneurship, but a surge of civic nationalism. For the first time, the government, private sector, academics and researchers worked together. Regular meetings were held with officials from multiple agencies and eminent scientists to resolve the problems being faced by companies, be it sourcing, travel restrictions, regulatory hurdles, or just guidance.

SOCIAL ENTREPRENEURSHIP

Generating profit is the business of business. Social entrepreneurship, however, has different objectives and rules. It is a process of bringing about social change, with deeper, more broad-based and long-term impact than traditional NGOs or the state, and sees people as active participants in problem-solving, rather than as passive beneficiaries dependent on a 'maai-baap' (all-powerful) entity.

Of late, India has developed advanced and innovative social entrepreneurship models, aimed at improving public delivery systems, bringing jobs to rural areas, and bridging the digital divide. For instance, there are business models built around innovating low-cost products and services, aimed at resolving social problems.

Increasingly, social entrepreneurs are leveraging technology to zero in on and cater to beneficiaries. Many companies are now promoting social entrepreneurship through initiatives such as the

Sankalp Forum, Dell Social Innovation Challenge, Ashoka, Unlimited India, etc.

The extent to which social entrepreneurs focus on social impact rather than profitability varies, but to make a lasting difference, the venture must be financially sustainable. Is it even possible to profit while working for a social cause? Going by the Amul example, the answer is an unqualified 'yes'. Set up in 1946 to combat unfair milk trade practices, through cooperatives independent of cartels, Amul has proved to be an income generator for farmers, as well as a job creator.

Whatever your vision or goal, whether it's transforming society, changing the world or simply adding to the happiness quotient of a community, go after it with a sense of mission. If you have a great idea, but are fearful or risk-averse, entrepreneurship is not for you. Self-belief is the soul of the start-up. As Walt Disney is believed to have said, 'if you can dream it, you can do it'.

11

GROWING A PEOPLE TREE

On my desk is a chunk of rock from the Australian Blue Mountains, about the size of my palm. It sits on its one flat plane, so what I see is a rough, shapeless, lacklustre mass. 'That's how most people are,' said my friend Peter Purushottama when he gave it to me. 'All irregular and bumpy with jagged edges. What we need to do is to sandpaper them smooth, then polish them to a high shine.'

People are a company's greatest asset, it's often said. A useful maxim, provided you hire the right people, keeping in mind the company's culture, and train them well. A company doesn't spring into existence overnight. It is an organic entity that evolves over time, and people grow along with it.

Polishing people takes time, effort and patience. 'Why not hire polished people in the first place and save yourself the trouble?' you might ask. First of all, you don't normally get a finished person, and if they are, there's very little scope for training. Second, a company is not a jigsaw puzzle, with pre-cut pieces conforming to a pattern. It's a community, where people constantly rub up against each other while integrating, reciprocally smoothening rough edges until they fit together.

As a manager, the best investment you can make is in people. To cite management guru and former General Electric boss Jack Welch, 'when you were made a leader, you weren't given a crown, you were given the responsibility to bring out the best in others'.

It helps if you genuinely like people. Fortunately for me, I'm a people person. I strongly believe in the basic goodness of human beings, and tend to see the best in them. My approach is never sceptical, nor am I judgmental. If a person has a flaw, it's usually the result of negative experiences rather than an inherent defect. I want every individual to become the best version of themselves, and am more than willing to help them along in that journey.

Time invested in talking to and mentoring people is never wasted, because it gives them a sense of having been heard and appreciated. This translates into a feeling that their role is important, and they must discharge it to the best of their ability. Happy and fulfilled people make for an effective workforce.

My people management skills are a result of decades of experience and my learnings at the University of Michigan, where Jack Welch was freely quoted. 'Before you are a leader, success is all about growing yourself. When you become a leader, success is all about growing others,' he has said. Welch famously spent 70 per cent of his time on people issues. As CEO, I tried to follow suit.

If an employee had a problem, I would drop everything else to address their concerns. Every person wants to feel valued, not ignored. A scene from the sitcom *Friends* illustrates my point. An office manager, Earl, declares that he's going to kill himself, because he is in a dead-end job and none of his coworkers even knows that he exists. 'I wish they'd care just a little bit,' he says.

Employees must feel that the company cares about them. Every person is significant, so no matter how pressing sales and revenue reports or business calls might seem, make time for them. This is particularly true if someone wants to quit. 'A company is only as good as the people it keeps,' American businessperson Mary Kay

Ash has observed. So, find out why they want to leave, coax them to talk about their grievances, and assess whether these can be rectified. Often, just airing a problem can throw up a solution.

An unhappy or underperforming individual reflects poorly on their boss, and by extension, the company. Putting the onus of employee satisfaction on the human resources department is not acceptable. Often, a manager would mention someone was leaving and add, 'HR doesn't care'.

My response would be, 'Who's the HR manager?'

'So and so,' they'd reply.

'Who does the employee report to?'

'To me.'

'Then who is their HR manager? In effect, it's you.'

The point is that the HR department does the background work, like disbursement of salaries, administration, formulating policies, training programmes and so on. Managing a team day in and day out is not the HR's job. It is the manager or team leader who must take responsibility if a member wants to quit.

It's said that employees don't leave companies, they leave managers. Numerous surveys have identified disenchantment with bosses as the main cause of attrition. If employees don't respect and get along with their supervisor, they will quit regardless of high salaries. A 2012 ASSOCHAM study found a high proportion of job-leavers who cited their bosses' negative attitude, ranging from sheer indifference to outright insults, as their reason for quitting.

COMMUNICATION IS EVERYTHING

Effective communication is critical for managing people. From the top echelons of management to the bottom, robust lines of communication must be kept open. Otherwise, issues get lost in translation and people leave. Bear in mind that communication is a two-way street. Team leaders must listen to those who report to them, but also provide feedback.

I firmly believe that constant evaluations are a necessary part of growth for your employees, especially those in leadership roles. Casually dropping pearls of wisdom and giving sporadic inputs is not adequate. A formal evaluation meeting, with a blunt assessment of performance and behaviour, is more likely to result in course corrections and improvements than an offhand reprimand or suggestion. Offer an objective assessment of weaknesses, with suggestions on how they can be addressed.

Lack of feedback can result in underperformance by managers and that will have a cascading effect. The organizational structure will collapse.

In the interest of full disclosure, mentoring isn't always fruitful. Some people may become very good at their jobs, but lack the capacity for further progress. I once decided to promote a promising employee, only to find out that he was less invested in his advancement than I was.

'I have a great opportunity for you. We're sending you to the UK,' I told him.

He was obviously excited at the idea, but said, 'Let me think about it'.

Having expected him to jump at the offer, I was a bit surprised.

A couple of days later, he came back to me and said he'd decided against it.

'It's my wife, you know. She doesn't want to move. All her friends and family are here.'

'My dear fellow, it's a once-in-a-lifetime opportunity, and a question of your career. You're a salesperson. Sell it to your wife!'

'I'll talk to her,' he said.

I could read his ambivalence, and as I'd expected, he turned down the job. In listening to his wife rather than following his own instincts, he had done himself a disservice. Instead of weighing the pros and cons and taking a considered decision, he had allowed someone else to manipulate him. He hadn't been true to himself. That's something to look out for when hiring people.

Every company has a hiring strategy, geared to its organizational goals. At HCL, we needed qualified, creative and highly motivated people, especially in sales and leadership positions. We turned to George Koreth, a professor noted for his expertise in assessing and instilling 'business achievement drive'. An adherent of psychologist and Harvard professor David McClelland's Human Motivation Theory, he'd worked with DCM earlier. He designed a recruitment process for HCL, as well as a training programme.

The candidates were put through various challenges, like the Thematic Apperception Test (TAT), which involves writing an imaginative story on a particular subject. Based on the key words and concepts employed, we were able to determine each individual's primary motivation, broadly clubbed under the heads 'N Ach' (need for achievement), 'N Aff' (need for affiliation) and 'N Pwr' (need for control). Thereby, traits like ego drive, empathy, competitiveness, risk-aversion, collaborative skills and so on were assessed, and candidates selected accordingly. N Ach is the most important quality in a salesperson or a leader. Empathizing (N Aff) might get you close to the client, but the ultimate objective is to make the sale, and that demands a determination to close the deal, the will to achieve.

New sales trainees were told how the intrinsic human 'need for achievement' could impact them as individuals and the organization as a whole. Koreth imparted ways of enhancing and sustaining the 'achievement drive', by deploying persuasive power or taking control of a situation. His genius lay in making his trainees feel that they were being helped to grow and hone their skills, rather than being evaluated.

As CEO, I made it a practice to meet all the new sales employees when they joined. During training, I would take a class with them and share the company's vision. I often cited the Kennedy man-on-the-moon story. In 1961, US President John F. Kennedy vowed that his country would put a man on the moon before 1970, and it did (although he wasn't around to see it). The lesson is that sheer willpower can achieve any goal, however impossible it seems.

I continued the tradition of personally meeting new employees throughout my career. The idea was to touch their lives from the very outset of their association with the organization, and shape their mindset.

According to Jack Welch, 'if you pick the right people and give them the opportunity to spread their wings and put compensation as a carrier behind it, you almost don't have to manage them.'

That brings us to the question of getting the 'right' people. There's no such thing as the perfect employee, and it's okay to have a team of perfectly ordinary people. Provided that they work well together, they will outperform a group of geniuses most of the time. A person might be highly qualified but that's no guarantee that they will deliver.

At HCL, our slogan exemplified our people-centric ethos: 'Pride. Passion. Performance'. Only when employees have a passion for the job, as well as a feeling of ownership and a stake in the future of the company, will they perform at their best.

Hardware is a low-overhead, low-margin business. HCL's salaries weren't much higher than the industry average, but we were top-rated in terms of job satisfaction. Thanks to our people-first culture, we instilled passion and a sense of pride in working for the company. We were unique in that respect and it gave us an edge.

In the intensely competitive hardware segment, high performers were gold. Often, competitors would attempt to poach our star employees by offering inflated salaries. Most often, they would be rebuffed, because of the pride factor—the sheer prestige of working at HCL. Those who left invariably missed the ambience of camaraderie and the excitement of a shared journey.

I can recall several occasions when our people went above and beyond. For instance, the incredible effort put in by the team assigned to the Commonwealth Games project, as described in Chapter 6.

Nurturing leadership skills is an important part of the training process. Leading is, first of all, a test of decision-making and problem-solving abilities. It's not enough for leaders to lay out theoretical scenarios; they must get their hands dirty and demonstrate how it's done by solving the problem right under the noses of their team. The efficacy of the demonstration effect can't be overstated.

Above all, leaders inspire and excite their people. Only if you have a spark within, and every aspect of your demeanour reflects excitement, can you evoke enthusiasm in others and rally them around you. There's no point in having a team of smart people, unless you use them smartly. A company may have an excellent strategy in place, but if its execution is poor, the performance will be a resounding flop.

Hence, the criticality of inspired and inspiring leadership, and the maxim 'a team is only as good as its leader'. The reverse is also true. The captain of a cricket team can't win a match on his own; eleven people have to work together to triumph. But it is the captain's job to come up with a strategy, motivate players, infuse a winning spirit, and ensure that they are in harmony with each other.

SETTING THE FIELD

A leader must be proactive; only followers are reactive. For example, in a highly competitive sales situation, you must seize the initiative and set up a favourable scenario. Pre-emptively plant seeds in the mind of the receiver/buyer, to the effect that they have an urgent need for a product or service. Then, present a solution that will meet that need. Your competitors will now be scrambling to explain what it is that they can offer. But you have the first-strike advantage. By acting, you have reduced every other player to reacting.

My former boss, Shiv Nadar, used a cricket analogy to get the point across to team leaders.

'Do you guys like to bat or bowl?' he would ask.

Bat, most of them would respond. One in twenty might say bowl.

'Why is that?' Nadar would ask that twentieth person.

'I like bowling.'

'That's not an answer.'

He would go on to explain that the bowler sets the field. He knows where the ball will drop, how the batsman will respond and where he could give a catch. The bowler will have a player in place to take that catch, or an alert wicketkeeper ready to stump the batsman. So, while a bowler is proactive, a batsman is reactive.

In business, as in cricket, you set the field. Keep bowling until you get the desired result. This is particularly important in the fast-evolving IT industry, where the goalposts keep changing. The team must always play on the front foot.

To stay one step ahead of the field, managers must keep themselves updated about new developments. In the tech business, where you are constantly challenged by bright minds, you have to keep learning and acting on what you learn. If you don't know more than others, you won't be able to convince them, and you will fall behind.

Motivating the team is vital, particularly at a time when the company's fortunes take a downturn. If the employees' morale is in their boots, they won't deliver. To pep them up, I would screen inspirational sporting clips, like that of a batsman hitting a six off the very last ball, or a striker scoring a goal in injury time and saving the game.

Motivating employees means summoning a winning spirit. After all, sales—the crux of any business—is about winning the deal. A culture of competitiveness spurs employees to up their game, and this works to the company's advantage; provided it doesn't become toxic.

Setting time-bound targets is an effective strategy for enhancing output. At HCL, we introduced 'senior management trainees', culled from the Indian Institutes of Management (IIMs). They were given a project and told to deliver within eighteen months. Success would lead to an automatic upgrade to the next level, but failure would lead to the door. You had to shape up, or ship out. The combination of time pressure and the incentive of a fast-track appointment usually worked, provided there was an element of passion for the job.

Recognition, like peer pressure, is an important source of motivation. At our quarterly conference, I would hand out token awards to good performers—just a plaque or a certificate—but it meant the world to the recipient, and was far more effective than a monetary compensation.

I connected with employees and learnt what was happening on the ground by spending considerable time on the office floor, a strategy I later learnt was known as Management By Walking Around (MBWA). Video-conferencing, phone calls, and second-hand information routed through managers, doesn't cut it. For example, if you are based in New Delhi, you cannot understand the ground realities and the level of employee satisfaction in Coimbatore, unless you go there.

Political leaders on campaign trails make it a point to single out important community leaders in the crowd and greet them by name, be it a sarpanch or a school headmaster. The same applies to coworkers. I would emerge from my cabin and take a stroll around the office, acknowledging people with a wave or a hello. That automatically brought them closer to me and made them feel appreciated.

We had a monthly 'Coffee with Ajai', an idea proposed by my HR team. Every month, I would drop in on one of our various departments and chat with coworkers over a cup of coffee. They'd be delighted to host the boss and I would familiarize myself with their thought processes, learning what the problems and issues were, and how performance could be enhanced.

I took it to another level. The start of a new year was always a test of my physical stamina, because I would shake the hand of every single person in our office, from managers to janitors. At the end of that exercise, which took about two days because we had over a thousand employees, my arm would feel like it was falling off, but it was worth the effort. There's a case to be made for the occasional touchy-feely style of people management.

Patience is an essential virtue when dealing with coworkers. If you lose patience, you lose a valued coworker, or at least, you undermine their confidence. If they disagree with you, don't railroad them. Make the effort to bring them around. Convincing people is like solving a Rubik's Cube; you fiddle with it until you get it right.

I was always accessible to anyone who had an idea or a problem to share. Secretaries have a tendency to act as gatekeepers, sometimes from a misplaced determination to 'protect' their boss from distractions, but most often because it makes them feel self-important. My secretary was under firm instructions not to keep people out, from within or outside the organization. 'You represent me and if you speak harshly to anyone or put anyone off, it reflects poorly on me,' I told my personal staff.

In my experience, no CEO—or indeed, the head of any organization—can afford to live and work in an ivory tower, disengaged from all but a handful of senior managers. The soul of a company resides in its people, rather than its hardware or software. What you can get out of them depends on your effectiveness as a leader. To inspire them to do their absolute best and take the company to new heights, you need to figure out what makes them tick. You must know them, and grow them.

12

SALESMANSHIP, OR THE ART OF LIVING

'SELL ME THIS PEN. TAKE a minute, think about it, then sell it to me,' I said.

Across the table from me, a hapless interviewee squirmed in his seat, eyeing the pen I was holding up as if it were an unexploded grenade.

The 'pen challenge' was an essential part of interviewing sales people at DCM DP and HCL. It calls for creativity, imagination and the ability to think laterally, and on your feet. We were using it as an evaluation tool long before *The Wolf of Wall Street* made it famous.

To recap the scene, Jordan Belfort (Leonardo di Caprio) challenges his friend to sell him a pen.

The man is nonplussed. Jordan then turns to his buddy Brad.

'Show them how it's done,' he says.

Brad takes the pen. 'Do me a favour,' he says to Jordan, 'write your name down on that paper napkin.'

'I don't have a pen,' says Jordan.

'Exactly. Supply and demand, bro!'

The salesmanship motif is reprised in the closing moments of the film, when Jordan opens a seminar with the same provocative demand, 'sell me this pen'.

The first film to feature the pen challenge was actually the Ranbir Kapoor-starrer comedy I've mentioned earlier, *Rocket Singh: Salesman of the Year,* where the protagonist is asked by his employer to sell him a pencil for Rs 100. The script, I'm told, was penned by a former HCL employee, who got the idea from us.

Of course, a typical sales situation doesn't work that way. A salesperson never goes in blind; they know everything there is to know about the product and customers. What we were trying to assess was the applicant's drive and hunger to sell, and ability to think outside the box.

I had been in their shoes. In 1972, I was one of the ten people—among hundreds of applicants—that George Koreth hired for DCM DP's sales team. To this day, I don't know what he saw in me. Perhaps he sensed that I had a high need for achievement, the 'N Ach' factor, as he called it. I was by no means an extrovert, but that didn't stop me from having a successful career in sales. Indeed, one theory on salesmanship holds that introverts excel at sales because they are composed, passionate, persistent and good at building relationships.

In my experience, personality type is not the key determinant, because selling is a learned skill. You may have an aptitude for it, but it takes intensive training, coupled with a need for achievement and a dash of imagination, to develop sales competence. In business, there's no such thing as a natural-born salesperson. Selling is a step-by-step process; a science, rather than an art. If you sidestep the process, you are unlikely to succeed.

Who is a salesperson? Take a look in the mirror. Every person is a salesperson in their own walks of life. In all our roles, personal or professional, we need to engage, influence and convince other people. As a politician, you induce voters to buy into your election promises. As a teacher, you persuade students to learn their tables by heart. As a lover, you coax your sweetheart into saying 'yes' to your proposal.

'We are all salesmen every day of our lives. We are selling our ideas, our plans, our enthusiasms to those with whom we come in contact,' American tycoon Charles M. Schwab has said. In sum, salesmanship is a valuable life skill.

At HCL, we took the recruitment and training of our sales personnel with the utmost seriousness. The trainees practiced relentlessly. We put them through role play exercises, in which they alternately played buyer and seller. Both actors learnt how to be better salespersons. Expressions are important, so it helps to practice your pitch in front of a mirror.

TRY AND TRY AGAIN

In business, there's no role more important than sales. All business forecasts begin and end with sales. Successful CEOs sell every day of their professional lives. At the outset of my career in sales, I was fortunate to have accomplished mentors/instructors. One of them advised me to read *Salesmanship* by Charles Atkinson Kirkpatrick. It had been published in 1971, and was very current at the time.

I remember one particular anecdote, which I've recounted to everyone I have taught and trained. It is told through a series of squares on a single page. In the first square, a salesperson tells their boss that they didn't get the order. Their boss tells them to try again. The salesperson goes back to the client, but fails to bring them around. They tell their boss that the prospect still hasn't panned out, so what should they do? The boss' reply: 'Keep going until you get it'. The lesson is that persistence pays; you never take 'no' for an answer.

Another must-read in those days was Thomas Harris' bestseller *I'm OK–You're OK*, a guide to transactional analysis. The theory was applied to business settings, and taught at DCM as a form of sales communication. Simply put, the salesperson analyses the mindset of the customer and adjusts technique accordingly: as though they are in a student-teacher relationship, a parent-child relationship, etc.

Sales trainees were taught to develop their powers of perception. For instance, when you walk into a customer's premises, take a quick but penetrating look at every object in the room: books, magazines, plaques and awards, furniture and furnishings, CDs, pictures, icons. Ask yourself what insights they offer into the customer's personality and mind, and take your cue from your conclusions.

Plunging directly into a sales pitch is a poor strategy. It is important to build a rapport by initiating a conversation on a subject of interest to the customer, which you should have sussed out before the meeting, or within moments of walking in. You might congratulate them on an award, or talk about a book or film that you have spotted on their shelf. If nothing else, discuss the weather. The initial chat will go a long way towards mellowing the customer and enabling the sale.

The takeaway is that you need to know your customer. These days, thanks to Google, social media and networking sites like LinkedIn, information is easy to find. So, prepare for the meeting by doing some research to gain an insight into their personality. Armed with it, you have a better chance of making the sale.

Being a good listener is a very important quality in a salesperson. Great talkers don't make sales, good listeners do. That's the advantage of being an introvert, because you tend to listen more and talk less. Glib patter will not get you very far, because sales is a serious business that calls for effective communication. Only then will you get the order.

Bear in mind that when you first meet a prospective client—a 'prospect' in sales lingo—it is for you to make them a customer. You must approach them with confidence, communicate clearly and negotiate politely but firmly. Ensure regular follow-ups thereafter.

A salesperson must also have range. One may be meeting with a textile company in the morning, a boiler manufacturer in the afternoon and a pharmaceutical major in the evening. One has to learn about a whole spectrum of businesses, to offer solutions to different customers.

Objection handling is another bit of know-how that every salesperson must cultivate. Sales objections can, and will, occur at some point in the process. From 'the cost is too high' and 'I don't really need this product' to 'your competitor's offering a better deal' and 'I don't like the colour', you will hear it all. Objection is another way of knowing if the customer is really interested.

Henry Ford, when asked why his Model T—the world's first mass-market car—couldn't come in different colours, famously responded, 'any customer can have a car painted any colour that he wants, so long as it is black'. But if you don't have the luxury of a unique product, you will need to proceed with tact and empathy to overcome hesitation and banish doubt. If your prospect says they are busy, describe how your product will ease their pressures. If they're already talking to someone else, show them that your deal is better.

On one occasion, we were bidding for a very big deal in Mumbai, against a host of strong competitors. I called a strategy meeting which carried on past midnight.

'We can't win this deal,' was the consensus.

'Let's raise the price,' I said.

Everyone was stunned. They thought I'd lost my marbles. 'That amounts to throwing in the towel', they said.

'Raise the price,' I insisted.

'Why?'

'It shows confidence,' I replied.

The following day, we went back with a quote 10 per cent higher than the original. We won the deal.

How you position yourself is critical for success. As a salesperson, take a leaf out of *The Godfather* and 'make them an offer they can't refuse.' That's being pro-active.

Salespersons are valued for their ability to close deals. An accomplished closer is someone who can finalize a difficult sale. As the saying goes, they can sell ice to an Eskimo. A closer is pro-active, sets the agenda and has a repertoire of tactics on command. In a presumptive close, for instance, the closer may cut the dilly-dallying short with, 'so, when will you need delivery?'. The assumption that the deal is done and dusted makes it difficult for the customer to backpedal.

At HCL, we created models for presumptive selling, so as to pre-empt objections and delays. One such model was the 'pre-installation survey', basically a form with a list of questions for the prospect. The idea was to get the prospect to fill the form. Once it was done, the deal was in the bag.

With all the skills and tactics at your command, selling is still hard work. My first-hand experience with the blood, sweat and tears that go into making a sale, during my years with DCM DP, are described earlier in this book.

If I became very successful at sales, it was because I learnt from the masters, among them Shiv Nadar, Arjun Malhotra and Yogesh Vaidya. I also read a number of books and passed on my learnings to others. The more you teach, the more you learn.

That said, the sales paradigm has shifted. David Scott's *The New Rules of Sales and Service* explains how online content and social media have become the main drivers of commerce. Rich in examples, the book outlines the success of new modes of selling that reduce time and costs. The Australian firm, Atlassian, sells software tools in the B2B area, without a single salesperson! The strategy is simple; the customer downloads a sachet from the website, gets hooked, and comes back for more.

As a CEO, it is important to understand the psychology of salespeople, in order to manage them effectively. Bear in mind that the one thing salespersons dislike the most is having to write a report. Insist on it, because you need to know just how they are spending their time. If they have had less than six hours of face-to-face time with a customer on any given day, they are not doing their job.

I find that CEOs often make the mistake of assuming that they can improve sales by hiring the best team that money can buy. But great teams have to be built and managed by someone who knows sales. Otherwise, anybody can take you for a ride. Some salespersons have a penchant for fudging reports, and create long lists of potential customers, none of which ever translate into orders. I had one such specimen, who sent wonderfully detailed reports, but—as I found out—never went out of his house. I had to show him the door.

I had a term for the impressive line-up of prospects who were always on the verge of placing orders, but never did: life partners. I dubbed the extravagant but ultimately meaningless reports as 'the-future-is-bright list' or the FIB factor. I'd tell those who served it up: 'A sales funnel has to be dynamic, not static. Chuck your list and look for new customers.'

Several companies had developed harsh models to motivate salespeople. One leading multinational, for example, did not have a tables for its sales force. They were given drawers to store their files, but no place to sit. At HCL, if salespersons were seen lounging at their desks, they were effectively doing nothing.

As a leader, you need to know three things: first, how to proactively set the agenda—or in cricket terminology, 'set the field'—in sales situations; second, how to create barriers for the competition, so that you can win the deal; third, you must set goals for your sales team. If you are creating a company, you will have benchmarks, such as achieving a hundred-million-dollar valuation in two years. At the end of the day, it is your sales force that will achieve those targets.

In the bigger deals, there are two strategies that I like to follow. The first is a 'brain map'. Basically, it involves putting your entire sales strategy on a single page, in graphic form. It looks something like a flow chart, and details, step by step, the process of winning the deal. I taught the concept to everyone who worked with me. The second is putting together a strong team. Big deals are all about teamwork.

You might wonder why salesmanship tends to get a bad rap. In public perception, the salesperson is still the individual sitting outside a doctor's office with a briefcase full of free samples. The media tends to portray successful salespersons as deceitful and ruthless. In *Wall Street*, Gordon Gekko (Michael Douglas) is the personification of greed. In the sitcom *House of Lies*, Marty Kaan (Don Cheadle) is the most sought after closer in the business, and will resort to all manners of trickery to make the sale. But they are the exception rather than the rule.

Most salespersons will convince a prospect to get the deal, but will also put themselves on the same side of the table. They are deeply invested in the customer because they understand that the customers success is their success. The salesperson positions themselves as a problem-solver, who can help the customer win. An unhappy customer is a retention risk, and will decrease referrals.

The fact is, the world needs salespersons in every field. The entire economy is driven by sales. When I mentor start-ups, I tell them that no matter how good their product is, it has no value if it doesn't sell. Sales create business, not manufacturing alone.

In terms of geopolitics, too, a country's soft power is all about salesmanship. Its global influence is not merely economic, but is predicated on its cultural exports, thought-leadership and contributions in various fields, which must be appropriately marketed. A classic instance was the United Nations' recognition of International Yoga Day in 2014.

A great leader must also be a great salesperson. In my view, one of the best salespersons in the world is Prime Minister Narendra Modi. By building relationships—with the Middle-East, for example—and showcasing yoga and ayurveda as well as India's space programme, pharma industry (particularly during the pandemic) and software excellence, he has enhanced the country's standing in the world.

Indeed, everyone can benefit from sales training. Whether you are a teacher or a student, a job-seeker, a social media influencer, a military commander, a bureaucrat, a media professional or football coach, you must know how to sell your ideas to 'win friends and influence people'. That is the essence of salesmanship.

13

TEACH A MAN TO FISH

GIVING BACK TO SOCIETY IS a part of the Indian ethos and has its roots in our spiritual traditions. The *Bhagavad Gita* (17.20-22) describes daan (charity) as a moral duty, but cautions against indiscriminate donations. The recipient must be worthy and the donation given at the proper time and place, and in the correct spirit.

In the last decade, I have devoted considerable time, energy and resources towards philanthropic endeavours. But I take my cue from the *Gita*, in that I am not a passive giver. Cutting a cheque is easy, but making sure that the funds are utilized for the public good is tough. It calls for evaluation of potential donees as well as mentoring and monitoring. I insist on documentation and photographs to assess the progress of a project, which in any case is a requirement under CSR rules. In effect, it involves an investment of time, which for many people is harder to donate than money!

Be clear about your objectives when giving. If you are guided solely by the feel-good factor, then your altruism becomes a form of self-indulgence. Only if your donation is outcome-oriented are you a genuine giver. Only then can you make a difference and give back to the society.

Personally, I look for sustainability. I fund programmes that can create productive assets or build capacities. My philanthropy is informed by two maxims. The first is: 'If you give a man a fish, you feed him for a day. If you teach a man to fish, you feed him for a lifetime.' In keeping with that spirit, I named my foundation Swayam, which loosely translates to self-actuated (it was my daughter-in-law, Minakshi, who came up with the name).

In India, nothing is more transformative than education. It lifts people out of poverty, allows for upward mobility, opens doors and changes perspectives. I can cite scores of examples, most of them fairly close to home.

That brings us to my second maxim: Charity begins at home. So, I began my philanthropic journey by financing the education of the children of my domestic staff, on the strict understanding that it was contingent on performance. Fail to measure up, and I would stop your funding.

The very first beneficiary was Rosie, the maid who had helped bring up my younger son, Akshay, in Singapore (and remains with us to this day). The second was Satya, our house-help in Delhi. I put their children, and in Rosie's case grandchildren as well, through school and college. The results were gratifying. Rosie's granddaughter found a good job at a call centre in Bengaluru, while Satya's son Naveen joined Amazon and later moved to Google.

Equally dramatic was the success story of my driver, Mithilesh Mishra. He had two sons, one of whom went on to get an BBA while the other studied computer science. The older one, Rajesh, joined HCL's sales division, taking advantage of a company policy that offered employment to children of veteran staffers. I mentored him until he found his feet. He then fell in love with a bright young colleague and married her.

The younger one, Mukesh, who is exceptionally bright, also trained with HCL. I got him a much-coveted spot in our Aadhaar project, the largest we had ever undertaken. It added considerable weight to his resume, and helped him get a job with Genpact. Thereafter, he moved to Ernst & Young.

Support doesn't necessarily mean fees and books alone. Another of our drivers, Kanhaiya, was diagnosed with cancer a year or so after he had joined. We funded his treatment, which prolonged his life, but couldn't cure him.

Kanhaiya's son is an excellent cricketer. Akshay, who is keen on cricket, bought him a full kit and encouraged him to practice. I've seen the boy in action and can honestly say he's a talented pace bowler, who clocks an amazing 150 kmph! I hope he manages to break into the IPL in the not-too-distant future, or at least, finds a spot as a net bowler so that his talent is recognized.

I extended my education programme to the bottom rungs of the HCL hierarchy as well. At one time, I was funding close to seventy children. My assistant, Lalita Gurnani, oversaw the programme with great dedication, monitoring the children's results to ensure that they were performing up to their potential. Sadly, it was discontinued after I left. Just as well, perhaps, because I found a sense of entitlement setting in among the beneficiaries. Often, taking resources for granted is inversely proportional to the will to achieve.

I have great hopes for another young scholar I've been supporting. Some four years ago, I had heard of Siddharth Kumar, a promising student at the Manav Rachna School, whose parents didn't have the funds to continue his education. My wife and I decided to support him, and he hasn't let us down. He is now in the ninth grade and I speak to him often, not just about academics, but his life in general. I believe that children perform better when they have a sense of being cared for.

POWER TO THE PEOPLE

Overall, my experiment in transforming lives through education was a success. Since then, I have expanded the scope of my philanthropic endeavours. Having been brought up in a small town in a middle-class family, I have a fair idea of the gaps in public services and delivery. That's where I direct my efforts.

In the villages around Jabalpur, I took up a project that combined my engineering and altruistic instincts, in that it was aimed at helping them achieve energy self-sufficiency. The nodal person, and indeed the instigator, was my late friend Rajnikant Yadav. He was a gifted photographer, and had a strong connect with the villages around the city.

'Some of these villages have no electricity. I'd like to help them out,' he told me. We decided on a pilot project in solar lighting in a village called Khamkhera. Ironically, although it is located right next to the Bargi dam and the hydel power station—which occupy land acquired from Khamkhera—the homes in that village were still lit by kerosene lamps.

Rajnikant combined artistry and dexterity with a scientific bent. He found an NGO with experience in solar power projects, and with its help, designed the system from the ground up. He set up a lab on the first floor of his home and manufactured the gadgets and components himself. The result was village-appropriate technology. The solar panels were designed so that they could be fixed on the roofs of the huts, each of which had three solar lights. Large LED solar lamps were installed at the chaupal (village square).

I was asked to attend the launch of the solar power system, and it was one of the nicest experiences I've had. We rolled up in Rajnikant's car and found a crowd waiting for us. We were garlanded and escorted to the chaupal by a procession of women singing and clapping. Seated on a makeshift dais, I was asked to press the button that would bring the system to life. And lo, there was light.

The denouement was a cultural show followed by a delightful meal comprising local dishes, served in community fashion with all of us sitting on the floor in a row, in the light of our solar lamps.

We extended the project to five neighbouring villages, and kept improving with experience. My only caveat was that the system should be maintained by the village denizens themselves. 'You spend money on kerosene to light your lamps and walk miles to buy it,' I said. 'Put that money, let's say ten rupees per head, in a box at the panchayat office and use it to buy replacement batteries when they run out.'

Rajnikant taught the village youth the basics of maintenance. He got children from various local schools together, gave them solar kits, and educated them on solar energy and how to harvest it. At his insistence, we also set up a training programme for fabrication of solar-powered gadgets. The project was not only successful, but sustainable.

As mentioned earlier, I funded an auditorium for my alma mater, JEC. My old school, Christ Church, is well-funded and has excellent facilities, so I've found other ways to contribute, for instance towards the activities of the alumni association. In 2020, Christ Church Boys' Senior Secondary School had its sesquicentennial (150th year) celebration, to which my friend, actor Sharat Saxena, and I were invited. To me fell the task of announcing gold medals for the top students. I was also given a rather impressive plaque.

In smaller cities like Jabalpur, children are not exposed to global trends, and miss out on opportunities as a result. So, I have twice been invited to talk to the students on 'jobs of the future', and advise them on their career choices. Many of the kids now follow me on Facebook.

THE GOOD SAMARITAN

Studies say that emotion is a powerful driver of charitable behaviour. I like to think that my funding decisions are rational, based on the efficacy of the proposed programme and the quantum of financing, but there's often a strong element of emotion involved. So it was in the winter of 2012.

A young woman and her friend boarded a bus in South Delhi on the night of 16 December. The six men already on board knocked her companion unconscious, then raped and brutalized her. The victims were thrown off the bus and lay on the street until the police arrived. So bestial was the assault, so terrible the wounds inflicted, that she died a fortnight later.

The story of 'Nirbhaya', as she came to be known in the vernacular, left me shattered, like millions across India. One aspect that struck me was the delay in medical intervention. Would she have survived with timely medical care? That question haunted many citizens. Enter Piyush Tewari, CEO of the SaveLIFE Foundation. The media quoted him as saying that people may have come forward to help, if there had been a Good Samaritan law in India. Bystanders, he said, were afraid to touch the victim or call for help lest they become liable to police interrogation.

I was impressed by this observation and the speaker, so I invited him over. He told me that some 150,000 people die in road accidents every year, half of them because the first responders don't reach the victims in time. I offered to support his campaign for a Good Samaritan law, and accepted his invitation to join SaveLIFE's board as a trustee.

The advocacy effort was a success. In 2016, the Supreme Court gave the force of law to guidelines for the protection of Good Samaritans. These were later included in the Motor Vehicles Act of 2019. Thereafter, we launched a series of radio spots to disseminate the Good Samaritan statute, as well as training programmes for first responders on how to handle road accident victims.

In 2021, SaveLIFE and Swayam collaborated with the Delhi government and the Traffic Police to launch an exercise in 'Tactical Urbanism' that involves low-cost interventions in urban design, transportation planning and infrastructure. The objective is to improve road safety at accident-prone intersections for vulnerable road users, like pedestrians and cyclists. The first such project was at Bhalswa Chowk in Delhi and the second at Rajghat, which averages nine to ten accidents a year.

YOU CAN DO ANYTHING

A philanthropist can bring more to the table than just funding. My particular skill set has been of value to the Population Foundation of India (PFI). This venerable institution, set up by a consortium of industrialists including J.R.D. Tata and Bharat Ram, works on population issues from the perspective of women's empowerment.

My friend Kiran Karnik was on the board of PFI and approached me on its behalf. 'The organisation's doing good work, but it's very deficient in technology,' he said, asking me if I'd be willing to advise it.

Next thing I knew, the inimitable Poonam Muttreja, executive director of PFI, was on the phone. 'We're planning to air an edutainment TV series as a form of social and behaviour change communication,' she said.

The idea was to use entertainment to change perspectives on family planning and contraception, child marriage, domestic violence and the rights of women. My role was to leverage technology to build an effective communications strategy.

I was invited to a meeting of some thirty people, including the distinguished US-based academician Arvind Singhal. He pointed out that sloganeering alone cannot induce behavioural change; the narrative format—storytelling—has greater impact. He cited the example of South Africa, which had used audio-visual presentations in a campaign against AIDS.

The director of the show, to be telecast on Doordarshan and titled *Main Kuchh Bhi Kar Sakti Hoon* (MKBKSH), was to be Feroz Abbas Khan, best known for his theatre musical *Mughal-e-Azam* (featuring the lovely Priyanka Barve in the lead role of Anarkali). The plot centred around Sneha, a young doctor who practices in a village. Gender discrimination, child marriage, lack of healthcare, sex selection, nutrition, drug abuse, sanitation and a host of regressive social practices are addressed.

I was asked to make a presentation on tech interventions that could make the series successful. The first measure I suggested was an

Interactive Voice Response System (IVRS) to allow viewer feedback. I introduced PFI to a start-up called Gram Vani, which had come up with a suitable product, and it came on board.

PFI received over 1.7 million calls. Viewer response spiked after actor Farhan Akhtar appeared on the show. He also collaborated with PFI through his non-profit, Men Against Rape and Discrimination (MARD), and participated in talk shows on their combined efforts.

I suggested a social media campaign to target viewers in villages and, Tier III and IV cities. 'Do it ahead of time,' I said. 'Be the first to use social media for creating awareness on population stabilisation.' I saw MKBKSH as a trans-media venture accessible on multiple platforms, so I proposed a version for radio, which had an enormous reach in India. Abbas altered the script to suit the radio format, and it was broadcast on over 150 channels, including All India Radio and FM stations.

Another innovation was the chatbot, SnehAI, 'a chatbot hosted on Facebook Messenger that provides a non-judgemental and secure space for young people to access information related to their sexual and reproductive health'. To further extend our reach, Sneha Centres were set up in several districts.

MKBKSH went on to bag multiple awards and make waves globally. Surveys have indicated positive outcomes, in terms of altering perspectives on social evils. I'm happy to have contributed my mite by transforming PFI's mode of functioning. Overnight, they went from zero tech to a Hinglish chatbot!

The series has been running for three seasons. The first and second were supported by global donors, and the third through a collaboration with the Swachh Bharat campaign, which leveraged the impact of MKBKSH for its sanitation mission. We are hoping to find backers for a fourth season.

Social interventions do not need to be on a large scale. Swayam has invested in a number of localized initiatives and relief efforts, either to support ongoing activities or new projects. For example, in Goa's Moira village, where I spent a lot of time, I addressed the garbage collection problem by donating a Mahindra Maxi truck to the village panchayat. The outcomes were immediate and visible!

We are a family of dog lovers, so it was only natural that Swayam would engage with an NGO working with street dogs: the Noida-based House of Stray Animals runs a free dispensary for injured or sick dogs. It feeds tens of thousands of strays, conducts sterilization drives and cremates the animals who don't make it. Swayam also made a donation to Friendicoes SECA, to meet the expenses for fodder, medicine and care for horses it rescued from a stud farm in Aligarh, Uttar Pradesh.

In keeping with my interest in democratizing education, Swayam extended help to a non-profit working with children in Delhi's slum areas. Its activities include classes for the children and vocational training for adults. It also brings out newsletters, and helps deprived and destitute children in various ways. Another initiative has been the distribution of laptops to beneficiaries of the Karm Trust, which mentors and upskills educated young women.

Awareness of rights is a big gap. Swayam collaborated on a project with the Atmashakti Trust to educate some 3,000 families in Odisha and Uttarakhand on the Mahatma Gandhi National Rural Employment Guarantee Act or MGNREGA. It arranged job cards for 95 per cent of those who applied for the scheme.

In the healthcare segment, Swayam has made significant contributions to NGOs working with cancer patients, including the Indian Cancer Society, Cankids–Kidscan (which provides holistic support to paediatric cancer patients and their families), and the Cuddles Foundation. The latter works with government and charity cancer hospitals across twenty-one cities to provide better nutrition to children fighting cancer, and trains paediatric oncology nutritionists.

Music and poetry are abiding interests of mine, so I was only too happy to make a donation to the Rekhta Foundation, which showcases Urdu literature and poets, past and present. It also holds the annual 'Jashn-e-Rekhta', a platform for contemporary litterateurs and artistes. Sanjiv Saraf, its founder, is passionate about reviving

Urdu (Rekhta is the old name for the language) and approached me for my father's works. He collected the entire corpus—books and music—which can now be found on Rekhta's website.

In the field of sports, Swayam has aided the Malabar Sports and Recreation Foundation, which is attempting to revive football in Kerala. Headed by a retired bureaucrat, it provides professional coaching and facilities to talented youngsters.

Among other recipients of funding from Swayam are Action for Autism, Missionaries of Charity and the Vidhi Centre for Legal Policy (towards their India Justice Report project). We also made relief efforts of various kinds during the COVID-19 pandemic.

THE INVISIBLES

India has made credible efforts towards poverty alleviation in recent years. Even so, an estimated hundred million people still live in ultra-poverty, struggling to survive without resources, healthcare, housing or adequate nutrition. These are 'the invisibles', existing in a twilight zone far from the mainstream, unseen and unheard.

Most people, policy-makers among them, go their entire lives without coming face to face with extreme poverty, with the result that the ultra-poor often fall through the cracks. The Nudge Institute, of which I am a founder angel, addresses precisely this segment.

The Bengaluru-based non-profit works towards poverty alleviation and sustainable livelihoods through its centres for rural development, social innovation, and skill development and entrepreneurship. Led by the dynamic Atul Satija, who was introduced to me by my friend Arun Seth, it has partnered with governments and the private sector on a variety of programmes and has adopted the 'graduation' approach created by Building Resources Across Communities (BRAC) in Bangladesh. Sequential interventions have brought families in over three-hundred villages out of ultra-poverty.

Encouraged by these results, Nudge has set itself a target of alleviating poverty in India in the next twenty-five years. I was captivated by the idea. So, when Atul suggested that funders go on a field trip to villages near Ranchi in Jharkhand, I readily agreed. Our objective was to visit a few villages to see where we are and what it would take. It was an eye-opener.

Day One, Latehar: We set off for a village called Latehar, to meet the 'didis' with whom the Nudge team works. Atul, his colleague Srikanta Routa, and Anjuli Bhargava—an excellent journalist from Goa—accompanied us. It took us around three hours to reach the village. There, we sat down with the 'didis', as the women participating in the programme are called (their husbands are called 'dadas'). We discovered that they were pretty much at the end of the three-year graduation programme.

We kept shooting questions at them, and I was amazed at the confidence with which they replied. All of them had Aadhaar cards and bank accounts, and each family had least five members. The concept of population stabilization has little relevance when livelihoods are based on family labour, so the more the merrier.

Two major interventions had made all the difference in terms of their family income and nutritional status. First, Nudge had provided them with livestock—either pigs or goats. They had learnt how to rear and breed them, either for the market or for self-consumption.

Second, they had been trained in the cultivation of vegetables and food grains. Their small kitchen gardens, they said, yielded enough vegetables for their own use, as well as for sale. Part of the tiny landholding—usually around a tenth of an acre—was devoted to appropriate food grains. To ensure a balanced diet, they had been introduced to the concept of 'tiranga' (tricolour) foods: green for vegetables, yellow for dals and white for rice.

The dadas chip in, both in farming and maintaining the livestock. They also produce an excellent country liquor, made from the edible, self-fermenting flowers of the Mahua tree (*Madhuca longifolia*) in home stills. Tribal communities believe that the brew has therapeutic properties. We were told that Mahua gave them the energy to work!

The didis revealed that their primary source of income prior to the Nudge programme was the brick kilns, where they worked for six months of the year and were at the mercy of the agents who took them there. It was hard work, in terrible conditions, and the agents often took away a hefty chunk of their wages, so that the Rs 10,000 they were promised every month never materialized.

Thanks to Nudge, they now had the means to earn a livelihood and sustain their families. Self-sufficiency has given them the confidence to live their lives with dignity and set the terms of employment. I came away with the feeling that I had been privileged to contribute to a worthwhile cause.

Day Two, Gumla and Beyond: On the following day, we spent time with stakeholders in Gumla, and then drove deep into the forests over treacherous roads. We found ourselves deep in Naxal territory, close to the Chhattisgarh border. We were accompanied by Mary Surin, a highly dedicated member of the Nudge team. Among my companions were two of the other founders: Shwetank Mishra of Paul Hamlyn Foundation and Anand Sahay, Global CEO of Xebia Duke. It turned out that Anand was once with HCL Technologies in the US. So, we had plenty to talk about!

We wound up in a remote village at the bottom of a hill. Here, the participants were one year into the coaching programme, and had started their livestock breeding and kitchen garden projects. They too, had Aadhaar cards and bank accounts. They had access to free food grains through the public distribution system (PDS), but had to travel a long way to get it. Most felt that the 35 kg allocation per family was inadequate.

The journey back was a challenge; walking down the hill to the village had been tough. I was dismayed at the prospect of having to climb all the way back. One of the team members took pity on me—I was the oldest member, after all—so I rode pillion on his scooty. The small two-wheeler was barely up to the task of lugging us up the steep, uneven path, and we nearly fell off. That said, I would not have missed the trip for the world.

History attests to the ethical underpinnings of philanthropy. In ancient India, merchant-bankers, traders and guilds (called 'Sreni' in Sanskrit) spent vast sums on public works and supporting the poor and destitute. The tradition continued down the ages, motivated either by a sense of moral duty or by practical considerations, such as building social relationships or gratifying rulers.

In modern times, the spirit of 'pure' philanthropy was carried forward most notably by Jamsetji Tata. Today, private benefaction has become a trend, with an acceleration in both CSR funding and family (or individual) donations. Billionaire philanthropy is now the 'done' thing, institutionalized by Warren Buffett and Bill Gates's 'The Giving Pledge' initiative. It has, of course, raised questions about the socio-political impact of massive charitable donations.

The point here is that philanthropy, if done properly, can change lives. One does not necessarily have to think on the scale of the Rockefeller Foundation-powered Green Revolution. Touching a handful of lives, or just one life, is enough. It is a matter more of the heart, than of deep pockets.

14

SPHERES OF BEING

SUCCESSFUL CEOs TEND TO HAVE interests outside of work. Empirical evidence supports the theory that wide-ranging hobbies improve mental agility, prevent burnout and enable lateral thinking. That said, it is difficult to make time for one's enthusiasms while running a company.

Only after I quit HCL did I have the luxury to actively pursue my pet passions, foremost among which was music. A friend, who was learning to sing, sang paeans about his teacher, so I asked to speak with him. From 2015, I began to take classes, on and off. A couple of years later, I felt confident enough to join a singing group called 'Luttf' (which translates to enjoyment). It gave me the opportunity not only to sing, but to listen to and interact with other amateur singers.

The COVID-19 pandemic brought our musical sessions to a halt. As a techie, it naturally occurred to me that we could revive them over Zoom, and that's how Zuttf (Luttf over Zoom, obviously) was born. The group would meet virtually every Friday to celebrate our mutual passion for music.

At first, it was a disaster, as we struggled with outages of sound, awry frequencies and so forth. One time, I had invited a noted musician to join us, but the glitches in the system reduced his performance to a cacophony.

Eventually, we fixed the bugs. The result was a series of fantastic sessions (more than seventy-five). We called it Lockdown Luttf. Each of us had to have a new song on Friday, based on a theme, be it Kishore Kumar or Rafi or Dev Anand, or songs of spring. On Wednesday, I would call my teacher and practice relentlessly. I recorded my performance and played it back over and over, so that I could fix my errors and enhance my rendition.

Some thirty members of the Luttf league were regular singers, so the competition was intense. I quite enjoyed the gruelling practice sessions, and in the process, my repertoire of songs expanded from ten to sixty. I challenged myself ruthlessly, stepping out of my comfort zone into uncharted musical territory under the tutelage of my teacher Inderprasad ji, who has dramatically improved my singing.

For example, I picked six or seven comic numbers from Kishore Kumar's oeuvre. His seemingly effortless delivery is deceptive; these deliciously funny songs are actually very difficult and testify to Kishore's virtuosity. Among them was '*Yaar tum shadi mat karna*', and I am happy to say my audience was hugely entertained.

I essayed an extremely difficult song from a Dilip Kumar film. It was recitative, similar to the Sprechstimme (German for speech-voice) technique, and involved adhering to the melodic contours of the composition through speech, rather than singing. I also attempted some of Manna Dey's off-beat, complex songs, which were not a part of his film discography.

Occasionally, Luttf invited celebrities to participate. One particularly enjoyable session featured the legendary Mukesh's son, Nitin, and actor-grandson, Neil Nitin Mukesh. They were politely appreciative of our renditions of Mukesh.

A singular blessing was the presence of Neelam Kohli, singer, music coordinator and compere par excellence. She built an enchanting narrative around the theme of the day, interspersed with songs contextualized through her encyclopaedic knowledge of music, singers, actors and directors.

Over time, I and other members of Luttf have upgraded to high-end equipment, including mixers, microphones and headphones, all in the interest of enhancing sound quality. I invested in a condenser microphone and an iPad-based mixer, which stand right next to my desk at all times.

I may never be pitch perfect, but every degree of improvement is uplifting. When I am 'filled with music', as George Eliot said, 'life seems to go on without effort'.

HABIB KE NAGHME

My sons are avid music-lovers, so I decided to connect them with their grandfather's legacy of poetry. I got in touch with Bollywood music director Deepak Pandit, who had started his career as a violinist accompanying ghazal king Jagjit Singh. He is himself a supremely gifted vocalist.

I sent him my father's book, an anthology of his compositions, and asked him to select eight or ten pieces. 'My request is that you set them to tunes. I want to create an album in my father's memory,' I said. To my delight, he agreed to compose and curate an album. He would send each of the ghazals, sung by him, to me on WhatsApp, and I would forward them to my sister, Indu, in Australia. After we'd heard the piece, we would confer and take a call on whether to include it in the album. For the most part, we agreed that the work was excellent.

Once all the pieces were ready, I asked Deepak to arrange for top-notch singers. Each ghazal in the album is rendered by a different artiste: '*Mere dil mein*' by Shreya Ghoshal; '*Kabhi taavil*' by Kaushiki Chakraborty and Deepak Pandit; '*Aaj taabeer khwabon ki*' by Shankar Mahadevan, '*Ummeed-e-deed*' by Talat Aziz and so on. The cover art was created by my niece, Aditi, a professional designer in Australia.

To mark the launch of the album, titled *Habib ke Naghme*, I decided to republish my father's book. Originally in Urdu, it had been transliterated to Hindi to make it more accessible. I decided on a private function, and invited Deepak Pandit to release the album in the presence of my entire family and our closest friends, including sitar maestro Shujaat Khan.

On a balmy September evening at the India International Centre in New Delhi, my dream was realized and my father's opus commended to the public. I persuaded my brother to say a few words about his life and work. The event also featured a music concert and a recital by eminent danseuse Astha Dixit, who performed to some of the pieces from the album.

One of the most memorable musical events I have attended was the World Sufi Festival at Nagaur, near Jodhpur in Rajasthan, at the initiative of the maharaja of Jodhpur. It was a magical night, with the fort bathed in the light of a thousand diyas. The maharaja is well-known to my wife's family and invited Akshay to perform at a temple the next morning. Along with a fellow musician, he put up a mesmerizing show.

Yet another sublime experience was Mark Knopfler's show in Paris in 2019, part of his Down the Road Wherever tour, to promote the album of that name. The Accor Arena was packed to capacity, and to my delight, he sang a few of the Dire Straits' hits.

Kunkun and I revived her late grandmother's tradition of baithaks. One time, we hosted the Pakistani artiste Farida Khanum. I had to strain every nerve to get her a visa. Like a typical denizen of Delhi, I called up someone I knew, who in turn called someone he knew and so on, until the fourth member of the chain showed up at the Indian High Commission in Islamabad and secured the visa. She arrived at the very last minute, and when she launched into '*Aaj jaane ki zid na karo*', I knew it had been worth every bit of effort. On another occasion, we had Rajasthani Manganiyar folk musician Mir Mukhtiar Ali, and also Shujaat Khan.

Of late, I have developed an interest in retro technology. Turntables and vinyl are back, so I have a record player and discs at my homes in Goa and Delhi. I also acquired a vacuum-tube amplifier, because, as any music aficionado will tell you, the purest sound comes from tubes, not from transistors.

In my bedroom in Delhi, I have an artefact of absolute beauty, the acme of cutting-edge audio tech: an egg-shaped Devialet Gold speaker. Why gold? Because the rose-gold bling on the exterior is literally 22-carat gold. So, Kunal, who sent it to me from Singapore for my seventieth birthday, had to pay through the nose when it got stuck at customs.

That said, it is worth its weight in gold. Rated as the best wireless speaker on the planet in terms of sound quality and design aesthetics, it has a bass that, to quote one review, 'knocked off our socks, pants, underwear, flesh, skeleton, and immortal soul'.

Akshay, an accomplished musician and composer, has imparted his skills to his children, both of whom show great musical promise. In honour of my seventieth birthday, my son and my grandchildren, Arhan and Ronen, created a special recital for me. It was a wonderful gift.

NEVER-ENDING STORIES

I was able to turn to my long-pending reading list when I finally had time to myself. Not that I had ever stopped reading, but the priority had always been to keep up with the latest developments in my field. At HCL, we subscribed to a host of technical journals: *Dataquest*, *PC World*, *Siliconindia*, *Computer World*, *Digit* and *Popular Electronics*. So much so that I took a course in speed-reading, which allows me to take in whole sentences at a glance, rather than words. Other than magazines, I read articles and research papers online.

In boyhood, I made friends with books and ever since, they have been the best of companions. They have kept me informed and entertained, cheered me in my darkest hours, helped me find solutions to knotty problems, given me some of my best ideas and relentlessly pointed out my mistakes.

Most of all, they freed my mind. Like the dragon unchained in countless fantasy novels, my imagination took wing and soared. Reading, unlike watching a film, is not a passive exercise. It engages you entirely, forcing your mind to work and visualize the worlds and characters it describes in words. Long after you turn the last page, the question of 'what happens next?' lingers in your mind. A book is a never-ending story.

On my travels, books always kept me company. Robert Ludlum, David Baldacci, Stieg Larsson, Dan Brown and a host of others enlivened my journeys and relaxed my mind. I had travelled the world through books long before I got onto my first flight. Many years later, I went to all the places that I had read about, and picked out landmarks, restaurants and streets that I had first seen within the pages of a book.

To this day, I find books are the best stress-busters and sleeping aids. I cannot sleep until I have read for at least an hour. Conversely, if I have book around, I never suffer from insomnia.

Soon after the Kindle was introduced, I bought one. If a Kindle can be said to be bursting at its seams, mine is. I don't download indiscriminately, however. I tend to read sample chapters before I buy a book. While I read a lot on Kindle and on my tablet while travelling, I love analogue books.

The sheer weight and solidity of the book in your hands, the crisp new-book smell and the joy of browsing through the shelves in a store has no parallel in the digital world. Plus, a room with books has a friendly feel.

My tastes have always been eclectic, so I'm stumped when someone asks me what I read. There's no specific genre that I can point to; I read what I like, usually fiction. I have read the *Harry Potter* series and action thrillers with equal enjoyment. I also pick up books on subjects that interest me or those authored by interesting people, like Bill Gates, Satya Nadella, Kevin Maney, Vijay Mahajan, Alfred Paul Ries and Andy Grove.

My reading list is long and varied. No sooner have I read one than I look forward to the next. A quote attributed to an anonymous book-lover has remained stuck in my mind: 'The only thing that can replace a good book is the next one.'

THE SPACE ECONOMY

My reading includes the latest developments in space technology, the stuff of my youthful daydreams. That's partly why I've chosen to invest in the space sector. But there's also the fact that the space economy is growing exponentially and is expected to touch one trillion dollars by 2040. As an investor, I honestly feel it is the next big thing.

Space research and technology have come a long way since the 1970s, when satellites first revolutionized communications, navigation and meteorology. Today, Elon Musk's Starlink, a constellation of several thousand satellites, provides high-speed broadband internet across the globe. Airtel has recently bought into OneWeb, a similar initiative backed by the UK government, which has obtained a licence to provide broadband from space services in India. One of the start-ups I am working with will benefit from the move.

Space tech spinoffs are a legion. Memory foam, fire resistant materials, wireless headsets, long-lasting batteries and cordless tools are among the utilitarian items that were initially created for astronauts. Food preservation techniques developed for space are applied in grocery stores and food processing plants. NASA's experiments on thermal insulation have yielded commonly used products like the space blanket, ceramic microspheres and aerogels, while the need for miniaturization led to micro-electronic-mechanical devices (MEMs), used in inkjet printers, pressure sensors and mobile phones. In medicine, the byproducts of space tech include lasers used in heart surgery, implantable insulin pumps and cochlear implants for the hearing-impaired.

Space has permeated our planet, fuelling dreams of inter-planetary travel. Space tourism is now a thing. I think the real game-changer has been the entry of private players into the space sector, notably Musk's SpaceX, Jeff Bezos's Blue Origin and Richard Branson's Virgin Galactic. Their stated objective is to make space travel cheaper and more accessible. In that respect, 2021 was a milestone year, with Branson and Bezos blasting off in their respective privately-built spacecrafts. I watched as Bezos's New Shepard made it past the Karman Line (one hundred kilometres above ground, or the 'edge' of space).

Thus, the cultural, scientific and economic impacts of the Moon landing have reverberated down the decades, changing our everyday lives.

India began its space journey under Prime Minister Jawaharlal Nehru, who set up the Indian National Committee for Space Research (INCOSPAR) in 1962, helmed by physicist-astronomer Vikram Sarabhai. India was already involved in space-related research, thanks to Sarabhai and Homi Jehangir Bhabha. The following year, India's first sounding rocket was launched from the Thumba Equatorial Rocket Launching Station.

For me, nothing symbolized India's great leap of imagination—and faith—more than the fact that the rocket components and payloads were transported on bicycles by scientists, whose laboratory was the cattle shed of a Catholic Church! Likewise in 1981, the Indian Space Research Organisation's first communication satellite, Apple, was transported on a bullock cart. The web series *Rocket Boys* documents the incredible contributions made by Sarabhai and Bhaba.

INCOSPAR became ISRO and in 1975, India's first satellite, Aryabhata, was launched courtesy of the Soviet Interkosmos programme. The collaboration with the Soviet Union also enabled Wing Commander Rakesh Sharma to become the first Indian citizen in space in 1984.

ISRO has a phenomenal track record. The Antrix Corporation, set up in 1992 as the commercial wing of ISRO, is a leading launch service provider and has placed hundreds of satellites into orbit for thirty-three countries.

It was the first space agency to detect water on the Moon, a finding later confirmed by NASA. It has one of the world's largest constellations of remote-sensing satellites, has developed indigenous cryogenic rocket technology and satellite navigation systems, and sent a probe to Mars (Mangalyaan)—the first Asian nation to do so. I look forward to Gaganyaan, the first indigenous human spaceflight mission.

I believe that ISRO's success owes itself to the fact that it answers directly to the PM of India and is free from bureaucratic interference. It also has the advantage of a much lower cost of development and access to highly skilled manpower. Repeated US sanctions on India have been a mixed blessing, prompting rapid indigenization of space technology. For example, after the US nixed the transfer of Russian cryogenic rocket technology to India in 1991, ISRO developed its own. I had recommended the same model for the National Electronics Mission in my Task Force Report of 2009. Sadly, it was not implemented.

Like all space agencies, ISRO serves the needs of the military. After the Gulf War, satellite-based reconnaissance and surveillance became a defence imperative. The Indian armed forces have several dedicated satellites, in addition to those for dual use. The dependence of the military, and indeed, of the civilian infrastructure, on satellite-based communication, navigation and intelligence, has underlined the need for counterspace capabilities.

After China demonstrated its anti-satellite (ASAT) weapon in 2007, ISRO initiated its own programme. With Mission Shakti in 2019, India became one of the only four nations with demonstrated ASAT capability. This was followed by the setting up of the Defence Space Agency and the Defence Space Research Organization (DSRO).

REACHING FOR THE MOON

Ten years ago, I had the opportunity to get involved in a space project. A start-up in Bengaluru, Axiom Research Labs, had decided to compete for Google's Lunar XPRIZE, a competition to land a rover on the moon, which was open only to privately funded teams.

The CEO, in whom I immediately recognized a fellow space buff, told me they'd registered for the challenge under the name TeamIndus. Obviously, they needed funding and were approaching anyone and everyone who might contribute. I gave them Rs 25 lakhs.

They designed two rovers and a lunar lander, but needed ISRO's PSLV to actually get them to the moon. ISRO, as a government agency, couldn't offer them a free ride, so a contract was drawn up for a paid launch in 2017. Only five teams remained in the running at this point. TeamIndus ran out of money and couldn't launch by the deadline. None of the teams did, and the competition ended without a winner.

My dream of being part of a Moon mission died, but it reinforced my fascination with space research. I spoke of the TeamIndus effort when receiving an award from PM Modi in 2014. He picked up on that and observed that space technology start-ups were eminently desirable. It wasn't just lip service; the Indian government has since made definitive moves to liberalize the space sector.

The setting up of INSPACe (Indian National Space Promotion and Authorization Centre) in 2020 has allowed private start-ups to access ISRO's space resources. The Indian Space Association (ISpA) followed a year later, with the intent of boosting India's share of the space economy from 2-3 per cent to 9 per cent.

Currently, start-ups in India are involved in multiple aspects of space technology, from high-speed communications (Astrogate Labs) and hyperspectral imaging (Pixxel), to launch vehicles (Skyroot Aerospace and Agnikul Cosmos, incubated by IIT Madras). One of them, Valles Marineris (named after a vast canyon on Mars), is partnering with Glavkosmos to promote space tourism.

The Indian Angel Network Fund, where I am on the investment committee, has invested in Dhruva Space, which aims to provide integrated satellite manufacturing, launch and ground station services. The company created waves at the Dubai International Astronautical Congress in 2021 (where all the major global space actors meet). As chairperson of FICCI's start-ups committee, I encourage Indian start-ups to participate.

Dhruva designs and manufactures small satellites according to specifications, including assembly, integration, testing and qualification, constellation design and disruption tolerant networking (to avoid delays and disruption when data is transmitted over vast distances). In addition, Dhruva has a team working on satellite launch services for deployment of CubeSats and small satellites. In terms of ground services, it will set up mission control and operations, with remotely operable terminals.

Pawan Goenka, whom I know, was recently named the chairperson of INSPACe. When I introduced Dhruva to him, he readily agreed to visit them. Knowing Pawan, I'm sure he'll bring his private-sector skills to bear, and work closely with ISRO to facilitate space sector start-ups.

The impact of policy changes on India's space industry is already visible. Earlier this year, Spacetech Analytics, in a 2021 report, put the number of space start-ups in India at 368. Starry-eyed entrepreneurs are delving into navigation and mapping, manufacturing, communication, remote sensing, space medicine and yes, space travel and tourism. The possibilities are as immense as space itself.

THE SHAPE OF THINGS TO COME

Another long-standing area of interest for me, as mentioned earlier, is futurology. I firmly believe that humankind will conquer death and disease, time and space. A brilliant future awaits humans—or 'posthumans'—provided we're still around to enjoy it.

Contemporary futurists extrapolate trends in scientific research to anticipate the shape of things to come, using predictive tools as far removed from crystal-gazing as alchemy is from nuclear fusion. I follow their work closely, particularly that of Ray Kurzweil and Peter Diamandis.

Central to Kurzweil's theories is the singularity (of the technological kind, as opposed to gravitational). It is the point at which the growth of technology will become exponential and irreversible, radically altering human civilization and humans themselves. His 'law of accelerating returns' postulates technological progress at ever-increasing speeds, leading not only to ultra-intelligent machines, but 'transhumans' with enhanced biological and cognitive abilities. Cyborgs, if you will. At singularity, which he believes will arrive by 2045, machines and humans will meld and become indistinguishable.

Technological breakthroughs are coming hard and fast, we don't need a Kurzweil to tell us that. Compare the progress of the last hundred years with the rest of human history. In the last quarter century or so, our civilization has been transformed by the World Wide Web, search engines, social media, e-commerce, cloud computing and AIs. Today's handheld computer, the smartphone, is millions of times faster than the truck-sized Apollo Guidance System that helped put man on the Moon.

Quantum computers—a billion-fold more powerful than today's supercomputers—are the next giant leap forward. Google demonstrated a 53-qubit system in 2019; it can execute a task in 3.3 minutes that would have taken a classical computer 10,000 years. By 2021, Chinese researchers had announced a 66-qubit processor. Given the accelerating rate of progress, the probability of a machine achieving human intelligence is high. As I've said in my lectures on the subject, it's no longer a question of 'if', but of 'how soon'.

AI has been around since the late 1950s, but it wasn't until the early 1980s that it attracted serious funding. Interest burgeoned after IBM's Deep Blue beat the Russian Grandmaster and reigning world chess champion, Garry Kasparov, in 1997 (just as Kurzweil had predicted). Today, AI is everywhere, used by companies like Apple (Siri), Amazon (Alexa), Netflix and Tesla to improve customer experience.

Singularitarians—futurists who believe superintelligence is nigh, be it machine, human, or machine-human hybrid—fall into two categories: those who fear AI and those who don't. Elon Musk, Vernor Vinge (the guy who conceptualized Singularity) and the late Stephen Hawking belong to the former. Needless to say, Kurzweil and Diamandis belong to the latter.

Can AI pose an existential threat? The same fears were raised vis-à-vis advances in biotechnology, but thirty years on, what's apparent is the benefits in medicine and commerce. No doomsday scenario has materialized, in the form of bioterrorism or unethical gene manipulation (unless you buy into the theory that the SARS-CoV-2 virus was cooked up in a lab). The same could well be true of AI. On the other hand, the sheer power of this technology calls for caution. Personally, I think that while technology itself is fundamentally neutral, a regulator for AI is necessary.

In terms of extinction level events, 'climate emergency'? poses a real and present danger. As an optimist, I believe societies will rise to the challenge by skewing lifestyles towards low consumption, intensive recycling, remanufacturing and carbon neutrality. Technology will help in a variety of ways, by enabling a near-total shift to renewable energy, for example. There is no time to lose, if we are to avoid conflicts over natural resources—wars that would be fought by robots, drones and remote-controlled weapons!

Diamandis' seminal book, *The Future Is Faster Than You Think*, expands on Singularity. He points out that the convergence of technologies—AI, robotics, virtual reality, digital biology, 3D printing, blockchain, quantum computing and global gigabit networks—will profoundly transform society, global governance and industry. Technology is progressing at ever-accelerating speeds. The culture shock that a Rip Van Winkle who slept through the last four decades will experience on waking up is nothing compared to what we're going to feel twenty years on.

Take the metaverse, for instance. In July 2021, Mark Zuckerberg delineated his company's mission: 'to bring the metaverse to life.' He was referring to a future iteration of the internet, in the form of 3D virtual spaces linked to a virtual universe, with a unified VR and AR platform. It would be a completely immersive virtual experience shared by a whole community, a place to work and play and travel. Sort of like the massively multiplayer online games (MMOs) available today, but more immersive.

The term metaverse first appeared in Neal Stephenson's 1992 book *Snow Crash*, but was foreshadowed in William Gibson's *Neuromancer* (1984), in which he conceived a VR dataspace, or cyberspace, known as the Matrix. Remember, this was before the World Wide Web and just a year after the TCIP/IP-enabled internet. The idea was further developed in the dystopian *Matrix* films and the gamer-fantasy *Ready Player One*.

Far-fetched? It only sounds that way. AI and the metaverse can be safely described as high-probability, high-impact events. Increasingly, Kurzweil and Diamandis, who cofounded the Singularity University in 2008, are being taken seriously. SingularityU's Executive Program attracts corporate leaders who want to get ahead of future trends, while their Global Solutions Program caters to a younger demographic, comprising those who want to learn about emerging technologies and their business applications: airborne/autonomous cars, hyperloops, quantum computing, VR and AR, 3D printing, blockchain and so on.

Circling back to the future, I firmly believe that the revolutionary changes in computer technology will be nothing compared to the wonders that convergence of technology and the life sciences will bring. Michael Crichton, best known for *The Andromeda Strain*, *Congo* and *Jurassic Park*, has explored this idea in some of his books.

Advances in molecular biology, cloning and gene editing have inspired researchers to attempt a 'resurrection' of the woolly mammoth from recovered DNA. Or at least, to create a mammoth-elephant hybrid. From that perspective, the resurrected-dinosaurs of *Jurassic Park* don't sound quite so unlikely.

Can human consciousness can be liberated from its 'cage of flesh'? Cloned or synthetic avatars animated with 'downloaded' human consciousness may seem like a bit of a stretch, although James Cameron used the idea to excellent effect in *Avatar*, as did the TV series *Altered Carbon*. At this point, I feel we know too little about the nature of cognition, consciousness and sentience to make a prediction.

Equally intriguing are emerging fields like bionanotechnology, at the intersection of nanotechnology and biology, which forms the basis of Crichton's novel, *Prey*, and of the dystopian film, *Transcendence*. Both are cautionary tales on the perils of AI and nanotechnology, which are linked to the notion of human immortality. This poses its own problems. Students often ask me, at the end of a lecture about the future, what will happen if everybody lives forever? I have no answer. The ethical, practical and psychological dimensions of immortality deserve serious consideration. No one can predict just how things will pan out.

Futurology is an inexact science, given the number of variables involved. It's a question of probabilities. One can't factor in an Albert Einstein, who shattered our comfortable notion of reality in one stroke. We have the mathematics and data to make ballpark predictions on, say, when humans will set foot on Mars and genetically engineered humans who can live there. Beyond that, it's like predicting the weather.

For instance, I was caught in a freak storm in Goa in the summer of 2021. Cyclone Tauktae had been predicted, but no one knew that wind speeds would hit a frightening 180 kilometres per hour, taxing my cyclone-resistant windows way beyond their limit. So, as with meteorology, futurology calls for broad brushstrokes.

As Arthur C. Clarke said: 'Trying to predict the future is a discouraging and hazardous occupation ... The only thing we can be sure of about the future is that it will be absolutely fantastic.'

15

MY FAMILY, AND OTHER HUMANS

'O LORD, THAT LENDS ME life, lend me a heart replete with thankfulness!' wrote William Shakespeare in *Henry VI*.

On my seventieth birthday, I was presented with an elegant coffee-table book on my life. It was my wife's brainchild and involved enormous effort on her part, in combing through family albums to unearth long-lost photographs, getting family and friends to write testimonials, penning an introductory narrative, and working with designers to put it all together. I didn't have the slightest hint that she was working on it. Simply titled *Ajai*, it was the best present I could have received on my platinum anniversary.

As I leafed through the pages that spanned my life, I was hard put to select the most meaningful moments. My engagement (the last family function that my father graced), the wedding itself, the birth of my sons and their graduations, becoming a grandfather for the first time ... it has been a veritable caravan of joys.

Conventional wisdom has it that fulfilment is found in a work-life balance. I'm inclined to the view that work and life are an integrated whole, a circle rather than opposing aspects that must be balanced. It accords with the uniquely Indian holistic take on life, that all human endeavour is informed by the trivarga (three aims) of artha, kama and dharma.

Success should be seen in terms of self-development rather than wealth alone, and the family plays an important role in this respect. As a member of a collective, you learn to be other-regarding, and to strive not merely in service of your own ambition, but for society as a whole.

When you are building a career, your family is your support 'system'. Practically speaking, you can ride out to slay dragons only if you know that your loved ones will keep the home fires? burning while you are away. A high-powered, adrenalin-fuelled career is all very well, but it is your partner who makes it possible for you to have that. So do not take them for granted.

Kunkun, my wife, has been the ideal partner in our family enterprise. I struggle to describe just how much she means to me. She is my anchor, my rock, the wind beneath my wings, the algorithm that drives my life. A safe haven when times are bad and a delightful companion when they are good. These may be platitudes, but every one of them is true. Quite simply, she is the most important person in my life (although my granddaughter Aavienda may dispute that).

Kunkun's sense of humour is easily tickled and highly infectious, which makes for a cheerful atmosphere in our home. She combines good humour and empathy with a sharp mind, so all of us—the domestic staff included—turn to her for advice. Her aesthetic sensibilities are flawless, and find expression in our beautiful homes in Delhi and Goa. Over the years, I've acquired a healthy respect for her managerial abilities; she runs households with a seamless efficiency that CEOs would envy.

When I look back on my life, there has been so much to celebrate, and my proudest and happiest moments are owed to my family. Every single day, I count my blessings. I appreciate the grace of God and the people around me, who decorate my life and bring me joy.

My sons have five children between them, and like all doting grandfathers, I think each one is special. None more so than the eldest, Aavi. When Kunkun and I visited Singapore, she insisted on staying with us for a couple of days. She delighted in waking up her grandmother in the mornings with a chirpy, 'Let's go have breakfast!'.

Her younger sibling, Raahil, is tech-crazy, which is a source of delight for me. We have long conversations on what he calls 'tech stuff'. Rishaan, the baby of the trio, is his grandmother's pet. He pretends to be a master chef and cooked for us virtually, all through the pandemic, when we had to make do with video calls.

I also spend a lot of time with my grandsons, Arhan and Ronen, in Goa. Arhan is smart and studious, like his mother Neha. Ronen, a chip off the old block, breezes through school like his father. My job as grandfather is playmate-cum-storyteller-in-chief. I play carrom and table tennis with them, read books out aloud and tell them endless stories: incidents from my life, anecdotes about their fathers growing up (and how mischievous they were) and fanciful tales made up on the spot.

As time goes on, there will be more to discuss, in terms of academic and career choices. I have already told their parents that they must learn coding, a useful skill no matter what profession they choose. If there's one thing I've learnt, it is that your job as a parent is never done. Your children will always turn to you, even when they have become parents themselves. There's a special joy in that.

SAYING GOODBYE

Even as my family has expanded, the ranks of the older members has attenuated. In 2020, I lost my mother-in-law, who had been such an important part of our lives. She had decided to return to Ranchi, overcome with a yearning to see her beautiful home. Given her erratic state of health, Kunkun and her siblings decided that one of them would have to stay with her at all times. A wise decision, because a few months later, she fell ill.

We got a call at around 10 p.m., informing us that she had collapsed and was in urgent need of medical intervention. But she had made us all promise that we would not take her to a hospital under any circumstances. What was to be done? I reached out to the only person who could help, my friend Rajiv Mathur, who runs a firm called Critical Care Unified. As the name implies, it is a healthcare firm that provides critical care outside the hospital.

'Rajiv, my mother-in-law's in Ranchi. She should be in an ICU, but her one request was that she should not be taken to a hospital, come what may,' I told him.

'We don't have a facility in Ranchi, unfortunately,' he replied.

'I know, but I am at my wit's end. I didn't know who else to call.'

'Let me see what I can do.'

Two hours later, he called back to say that all the arrangements had been made. On the following day, a critical care team flew to Ranchi with all the requisite medical equipment and by 1 p.m., a fully functioning ICU had been set up at home. Thanks to Rajiv, we had a few more precious months with her. I'm glad she passed on in her own home, able to look out on her garden, orchards and fields, rather than in city surroundings.

During the COVID-19 pandemic, my older sister Pammi, to whom I was very close, fell gravely ill. She had a heart ailment, but hospitals and healthcare workers were overwhelmed with COVID patients at the time, and I couldn't get her a room anywhere. I turned to my friends Ganesh and Meena, who run Portea, the largest 'medical delivery at home' service in India, and they arranged for nurses to look after her at home.

Her condition deteriorated, and I knew I had to get her into a hospital somehow. I called a friend, who introduced me to Sangita Reddy of Apollo Hospitals. She was kind enough to accommodate my sister in the ICU, and intervened yet again to get her a room. I was able to arrange for my nephew to visit her, but as a senior citizen, I was advised to stay away from the hospital. So, I wasn't able to meet her before she slipped into her final rest.

Arranging the funeral was tough, as the high COVID death toll had put crematoriums in Delhi under enormous pressure. So, I went online and found an agency which was willing to organize the final rites. But it was Lalita Gurnani who undertook the arrangements. A flower-bedecked ambulance took my sister from the hospital to the Lodhi Road crematorium, where Kunkun and I waited in a car. Disallowed from joining the throng of mourners, we said our final goodbyes from there.

Soon after, we lost Billy Maasi, Kunkun's aunt. She had stayed with us in Goa, where we had managed to shift during the height of the pandemic, for several months. I had loved her dearly. In the space of a few months, I had lost the three maternal figures in my life. I'm grateful for the time I had with them, and for the fact that I had the means to care for them.

BEING THANKFUL

Being able to help others is a blessing. As Swami Vivekananda said, to be able to serve mankind is a privilege, for that is the summum bonum (highest good) of our lives. My father created an atmosphere of loving kindness wherever he was, a function of his humility, generosity of spirit, tolerance and forgiving nature. I never heard him say a bad word about anyone. These were the 'sanskaras' (values) I received from him: seeing the best in everyone and helping out, unconditionally, whenever possible.

That approach creates bonds which are emotional rather than transactional, and brings people into your extended family. You look after them with the same familial spirit as you do your blood relations. For instance, when I returned from Singapore in 1990, I inherited my secretary, Cynthia, from my predecessor. I had a hard time settling down, given the contrast between the efficiency of Singapore and the chaos of India. Cynthia's assistance was invaluable. So, when she fell ill and had a difficult time performing her duties, I couldn't bring myself to let her go. For a long time, I did her work for her, until I simply couldn't handle it any more.

Likewise, when Rosie—a second mother to Akshay—fell ill while visiting a relative in Bengaluru, I was alarmed to hear that she was in a bad way and not receiving proper care. So, I arranged for her to be brought to Goa, where the doctors literally pulled her back from the brink. That said, there's no way I can repay Rosie for all that she has done for us, and am grateful to have her with us.

I'm also thankful for Mishraji, who has graduated from being a driver to managing all our properties. He is in charge of repairs and maintenance and his designation is that of administrative manager. He enjoys my confidence because he has proved equal to any challenge thrown at him. There are many others to whom I am indebted. My friends in the medical profession bear special mention: Dr Harsh Mahajan, Dr Naveen Sakhuja and Dr S.P.S. Puri. The latter is an eminent homoeopath, our go-to for ailments minor and major. All of them are kind enough to answer my calls 24×7.

Then there's Rakesh Jain and his associate, Shikha. They managed my investments scrupulously in the decades when I was with HCL, and couldn't spare the time for more than a cursory glance at my portfolio. They have become friends and advisers.

Over the years, Kunkun and I have forged lasting friendships with other couples, among them Gita Chaddha and her husband Nick Wilshaw. Through Ali and Kinny, our friends from Singapore (Kinny has since passed away), we met Arvind 'Bindo' Nanda. Our 'Dinner Friends' group includes Gautam and Shobhi Suri, Tarun and Anu Bakshi, Ramji and Benu Bharany, and Sonu and Sohrab Dalal. We also have close relationships with the delightful Tinoo and Poonam Mehra, Rajeev and Rita Bakshi, and Monica and Kanwar Palta. We've had some great holidays together with some of them; our group excursions to South America, Budapest,

Germany, Russia, New Zealand, Japan and Antarctica were pure fun, from start to finish.

There's no greater blessing in life than having good people around you, because only an environment of mutual support and affection can engender compassion, patience, a lack of envy and a positive attitude. Philosophers may see happiness as an elusive concept, but spiritual leaders have no such doubts—happiness is all about helping others, to the best of your ability. However unfashionable these sentiments may be in times of postmodernist pessimism, they have shaped my life.

A BRIDGE TO YOUTH

Friends of your youth see you in a way that no else does, not even your family. They look right past the accretions of years to the lad you used to be. They call you by an old nickname, tell an inside joke or share a memory, and the decades roll back.

Chintan Sagreiya, Suresh Sundaram and Sharat Saxena are the bridge to my youth. They knew me in my formative years, and were privy to my dreams and foibles, secrets and passions, flaws and strengths. Though our paths diverged across latitudes and longitudes, and we each found new friends, we remained in the backdrop of each other's lives.

After I left Jabalpur, Chintan achieved his ambition of setting up his own business and Suresh went on to work in several companies, winding up as head of customer support—a job that suited him to a T. He still collects music, and over the years, has made it a habit to send us all his playlists, first on CDs and then on flash drives. He still recalls my stint in Bombay, at the Sangita Apartments in Santacruz. He even remembers the names of the girls next door, Clara and Assumption.

Sharat, of course, went on to star in some 250 films. He's muscle-bound even at 71, and to this day, few people know that he is an engineer by training. His hits include *Mr India* and *Bajrangi Bhaijaan*, not to mention the role of Kichaka in the TV series *Mahabharata*. When we visited Christ Church school together, he was naturally the star attraction among the students.

All of them contributed to the 'book of Ajai'. Their accounts were by and large accurate, with the exception of Sharat, who spun a story as fanciful as any of his Bollywood scripts. Given that the write-ups were for my platinum jubilee, my boyhood buddies felt the need to be laudatory, but the best compliment of all was from Chintan. Among my many attributes, he said, was my salesmanship. 'He could sell a comb, even to a BALD me,' he wrote. I don't know about the selling a comb part, but he does have less hair than a newborn.

Yes, our hair has thinned even as our waistlines have thickened (except for Sharat), but when we get together, it's yesterday once more. There's no joy quite like it. We try to make it a point to meet in August every year, because by some quirk of providence, all our birthdays fall in that month: the first, fifth, eighteenth and twenty-ninth.

LOVE, UNCONDITIONAL

Dogs are among the best people I know, more humane than humans. For 30,000 years, dogs and humans have shared home and hearth, and a bond of love and loyalty. The exchange has been unequal, because no human can adequately reciprocate the unconditional love and selfless devotion a canine companion offers.

It was not until Kunkun and I had a permanent home in Delhi that we were able to include a dog in our family. By then, we had two sons, and all of us doted on the lovely Labrador pup we adopted. He enlivened our home for ten years, until the nightmarish day when our driver reversed a car over him. His legs crushed, he was immobilized and in great pain. Compassion lay in putting him to sleep.

For two years, Kunkun mourned him and refused to consider adopting another dog. Eventually, I persuaded her to accompany me to a breeder in Delhi Cantonment, just to look at some Labrador pups. From the moment we opened the doors of our car, our fate was sealed.

A bunch of ebullient puppies rushed up to us, yapping, sniffing, tongues lolling, tumbling over each other. Knee-deep in puppies, we found ourselves laughing in sheer joy. There was no question: one of these beauties was coming home with us.

But which one? The breeder agreed to let us take two of them home with us, so that our vet could check them out and help us decide. The next day, I went off to work, leaving Kunkun to take them to the vet, pick a pup and then return the other one.

That evening, when I came home, I said: 'Am I seeing double? There are two pups.'

'I'm keeping both,' she said, in a tone that brooked no argument.

And that was how Rusty and Cindy took over our home.

Rusty was your typical cuddly, snuggly Lab, an inveterate attention-seeker who slept on our bed. Cindy was self-contained, had a bit of a temper and rarely came up to our first-floor bedroom. She spent most of her time with Rosie, our maid, in the kitchen.

After several happy years came the inevitable—and dreaded—moment of parting. Rusty closed his eyes for the last time on a hot August day. Cindy followed him a few months later. We were bereft, and determined not to suffer the anguish of losing a beloved pet ever again.

Famous last words, as it turned out, because the next person to join our family was a dog-lover. Neha, my daughter-in-law, had lived in Singapore until she married Akshay. She had always longed for a dog. When the newlyweds moved in with us, Neha tentatively suggested adopting one, but Kunkun, still grieving over Rusty and Cindy, put her foot down.

One morning, as I was reading the newspaper, Akshay called out to me. 'Come in here, please,' he said, and I went to the next room, and there was Neha, holding a puppy—a gift from Akshay.

'He looks a bit strange,' I said, looking at the pup's short coat and folds of loose, wrinkled skin.

'This is a Chinese Shar Pei,' Neha replied, all smiles.

I had never heard of them, but was about to get chapter and verse on the breed. The Shar Pei originated in China, and was a popular hunting and guarding dog under the Han dynasty (200 BCE). It endured for 2,000 years, until the People's Republic of China, established in 1949, systematically discouraged dog ownership. During the Cultural Revolution (1966–76), dogs were slaughtered in thousands.

Only a few score remained by the late 1970s, mainly in Hong Kong and Taiwan, from where they were taken to the US. The American Kennel Club urged the public to help save the Shar Pei and a cross-bred version became hugely popular. They were rare in India, but Akshay had tracked down a breeder in Amritsar and found a pup for Neha.

Obviously, it fell to me to bring Kunkun around. Neha swore that she would keep the dog downstairs and out of our way. I didn't have the heart to refuse her.

Dexter was her first baby. He shared her bed, and not once did she complain about his very sharp claws. His vision was poor, so he kept bumping into things, but followed his nose to the kitchen, where Rosie welcomed him with choice tidbits. He grew fat, but that didn't stop him from making forays upstairs to our bedroom.

When my grandson, Arhan, was born, we had a serious case of sibling rivalry on our hands. Dexter didn't like Neha handling the baby, so he was ousted from her bedroom. Deeply upset, he began to spend more time upstairs. He won me over completely. I loved his grave, adorable face and bristly coat, his weird way of sliding across the room like a hip-hop dancer, his habit of licking my ears, and even his bursts of bad temper when someone stepped on his toes. His vulnerability, the poor eyesight that made it hard for him to avoid obstacles, made him even dearer to me.

Dexter made my life whole, filling an empty space I didn't know I had. He was more than a dog, or a friend; he was my soulmate. An unfailing source of joy, he made me feel that all was right with the world. He exemplified the maxim, 'you don't own a dog; the dog owns you'. So, when the time came for Neha and Akshay to move into a home of their own, the family sat down to discuss the most important aspect of the big shift: the custody of Dexter.

After several rounds of discussion, we worked out a shared custody arrangement. Every alternate day, Dexter would come to us. I tried to put up a brave face, but I just couldn't imagine being without him. Sensing how upset I was, the children decided to leave him with us. It was the best gift that I have ever received.

An eye operation eventually rectified Dexter's sight, which made it easier for him to negotiate unfamiliar environments. Just as well, because every winter, the family moved to Goa, and that included Dexter. He would travel in style, in a first-class coupe with two attendants. I discovered that train tickets for dogs were based on their weight. Dexter was a model passenger. At every third or fourth station, he would disembark, briskly relieve himself and then hop back on. He spent five winters in Goa, the last in our new house, acquired when Akshay and Neha decided to move there permanently.

Dexter fell ill at the worst possible time, in the midst of the COVID-19 pandemic. All the veterinary hospitals and clinics were closed, and given our age, we were forbidden from leaving the house. We found a vet, and sent him over in the car, but none of the pills and shots seemed to have an effect.

One night, Dexter was very restless. I sat with him on the floor, trying to ease his discomfort the only way I could, with gentle rubbing and affectionate whispers. I don't know when he slipped away. My one consolation was that he went after a lifetime of being loved, lying next to the person who loved him best.

We put Dexter to rest in our garden and for many months, I put fresh flowers on his grave every day. Wherever he is, Dexter is happy, because—as dog-lovers know—all dogs go to heaven.

Neha was devastated and wrote a eulogy of her own for Dexter, produced alongside.

Dexter

When I was growing up, there was nothing I wanted more than a puppy. Living in an apartment in Singapore, coupled with the mobile nature of my father's job, meant that my parents never felt fully ready to commit to owning a pet. So, when I got married, I remember telling Akshay, my husband, that I knew exactly what I wanted as my wedding gift—a puppy!

I will never forget the day I first saw him. I was on the way out of the house to work when Akshay surprised me with a basket in which, curled up in a tiny orange and white ball, was Dexter. A tiny, perfect Shar Pei, Dexter quickly become the centre of our lives. Quirky, sweet, temperamental and adorable, you could always find him nuzzled up in my shoulder or sleeping with me in my bed. He made the sweetest little grunting sounds when he was happy, but could also be adorably grumpy and moody and would sulk in his own little corner.

As he grew older, I loved watching him run circles around our living room, chasing Akshay around couches and behind the coffee-table. He'd spend hours in the garden, sniffing his way around the bushes and flowers, looking for insects and little lizards to terrorize. He would climb up and down the stairs of our home, looking for my father-in-law and spend lazy hours with him watching television or staring out of the window.

When Dexter left us, I remember thinking how we would never, ever, have a dog quite like him again.

Dexter was funny and strange, distinguished and dignified—all in one furry orange package. I miss him more than I can say.

Kunkun was so hard-hit by Dexter's passing that it took me years to convince her to get another one. The most difficult thing about having a dog in your life is knowing that you'll have to say goodbye. No one can take Dexter's place, but there's room enough in my heart for a whole pack. We have eight dogs in Goa, two of whom were part of a litter rescued by Neha and Akshay. They were orphaned when their mother was crushed by a car in a horrible accident near our home.

Beaux, as fair and lovely as the dawn, has just barged into my study and wants attention. I must attend to the all-important business of scratching his ears, so I'll sign off with a quote by dog-lover and author Charles Yu: 'If I was half the person my dog is, I would be twice the person I am.'

16

AN EPIC JOURNEY BEGINS

'MODIJI, THERE SHOULD BE A single window system for all approvals,' I said earnestly. As advisor to the Gujarat government on IT, I had sought a meeting with the then chief minister, Narendra Modi, to present a proposal for bringing semiconductor fabrication to the state.

A US-based manufacturer had shown interest in setting up operations, and the Gujarat Industrial Development Corporation, back then helmed by IAS officer Maheshwar Sahu, was on board. The US team was to visit Gujarat, to scout for locations.

The CM smiled. '*Yahan single window nahin hota hai. Single room hota hai*' (There isn't a single window but a single room here), he said. All the ministers and officials concerned would sit down with the US team in a room and thrash out the matter then and there.

I was surprised and gratified. In those days of bureaucratic over-regulation and endless delay in approvals, India was consistently ranked in the bottom fifty in the World Bank's 'ease of doing business' index (years later, the 'Modi effect' was to raise the country's ranking, from 142 in 2014 to 63 in 2020).

It was my first encounter with Narendra Modi. There was a dash of pepper in what was then a close-cropped beard, and a boatload of magnetism in his piercing gaze. I was impressed with his formidable communication skills and even more so by his fathoms-deep grassroots connect. He had a grasp of ground realities, and this informed his pragmatic yet determined approach to problem-solving.

The next time I met him, he was on the cusp of becoming PM, and had taken time out from his packed schedule to present me with Cybermedia's lifetime achievement award. I was asked to deliver a speech to the flower of India's ICT industry, and two of the things I mentioned appeared to pique his interest.

First, I made a pitch for self-reliance in electronics design and manufacture. Second, I talked about an Indian space start-up that was competing for the Google Lunar X Prize. In his address, he made it a point to say that he was happy to learn about entrepreneurship in the space sector. Imagine my gratification when, a few years later, the Government of India launched programmes aimed at enhancing India's share in the space economy, and adopted initiatives towards volume manufacturing in hardware.

My third encounter with Modi was at a meeting of the IITs, comprising chairpersons and directors of all the institutions. He gave a cracking good speech on how engineering and science were driving the country's progress. Here's someone with vision, I thought to myself.

One of the Modi government's first steps was based on the scheme for volume manufacturing that I had mooted way back. It is now called the production-linked incentive or PLI scheme. The localization of manufacture has yielded visible results, from thirty billion dollars in 2014 to seventy five billion dollars in 2019.

Mobile phone manufacturing has boomed on the strength of PLI, creating jobs and boosting exports. On the flip side, Chinese companies have taken full advantage by manufacturing in India, while using their own components and distribution networks. As a result, Indian brands are now all but dead.

India continues to lag behind on design and domestic value addition—although, ironically, Indian engineers have designed chips for global giants! The problem of a lack of depth remains, in the absence of a hardware manufacturing ecosystem in India. We have greater width in manufacturing, but the much-needed depth has not been achieved.

Consequently, while the demand for electronics and indigenous manufacturing are both growing, so is external reliance. Around 46 per cent of electronic products are imported (the value of imports stood at fifty four billion dollars in 2019-20) and of the 54 per cent that are locally manufactured, half are Chinese. The value addition in India is not more than 10–15 per cent.

HARD SOLUTIONS

Being proved right is not always a source of satisfaction. My 2009 prediction, that India's electronics import bill would exceed that of oil, was repeated ad nauseum in government, media and industry circles, but no one did anything about it, even as imports of electronics rose inexorably.

The policy paralysis may have owed, at least partially, to a preoccupation with the fantastic growth of India's software exports. Whatever the underlying causes, hardware was on the backburner. The lack of an enabling environment from the late 1990s onwards drove many indigenous manufacturers into oblivion. Small wonder there were few start-ups in the digital hardware space, and virtually no funding. HCL itself moved out of hardware after I left.

While I waited for things to change, I lobbied relentlessly—as a member of various government committees and industry bodies, as chairperson of the Electronic Sector Skills Council of India (ESSCI), as a talking head on TV channels and a columnist in newspapers. Time and again, I warned anyone who would listen that India had effectively become a colony of China, with local electronics brands disappearing and being replaced by those from China and South Korea. I had cautioned against import dependence and its economic and national security implications.

In 2011, I received an invitation from the Principal Scientific Adviser to cochair the core advisory group for R&D in the electronic hardware sector (CAREL). Our key recommendation was to promote indigenous innovation through a 'design challenge'. The IT ministry could invite designs for high-volume products like tablets, low-end mobile phones, CCTV cameras, smart metres and micro-ATMs, which could then be shared with manufacturers to enable 'Make in India'.

My rationale was that depth in electronics manufacture is contingent to designing in India. Then, as now, decisions on component manufacture for the Indian market were taken by companies based in China, the US or South Korea. I argued that if the accent is on indigenous design and manufacture, then it becomes feasible for the domestic industry to define and use locally sourced components. There will always be some that need to be imported, but the objective is to minimize the quantum of imports. Our report, unfortunately, went the way of all the others.

By then, India had already missed successive opportunities to become self-sufficient in electronics. Regardless, my vision of a thriving electronics industry did not dim and I continued to provide policy inputs and serve on various panels. I cochaired the working group for development of innovation and intellectual property in the electronics system design and manufacturing (ESDM) sector, and am currently part of a team headed by V.K. Saraswat, NITI Aayog member and former head of the Defence Research & Development Organisation (DRDO), which aims to bring large data centres to India.

Saraswat also drafted me into the semiconductor task force. This brings us to the heart of the problem. As mentioned earlier, it was in 2006 that I had first written a policy paper on indigenous manufacture of semiconductors; the 'heart' of virtually any electronic device you can think of.

For decades, the fabless versus fab debate had droned on, with most experts in favour of India as a 'fabless wonder'. 'Fabless', as the term implies, means outsourcing fabrication to a manufacturer. Most of these foundries are located in Taiwan, the US and China.

Chips serve as a meta-resource for diverse industries, and as such, India's external dependence in this respect must be reduced, especially in the current geopolitical scenario, where an increasingly assertive China has prompted strategic partnerships among democratic nations. We simply cannot afford the leverage that China currently enjoys. For example, ninety-two crore LED bulbs are manufactured annually in India, but all of them source chips from a single Chinese supplier. In 2021, the price of the chip more than tripled.

China continues to invest heavily in semiconductor fabs. According to *Bloomberg*, China was the biggest market for chip-manufacturing equipment in 2020 and 2021. To offset China, the US has floated the Chip-4 alliance, comprising Japan, Taiwan, South Korea and the US.

Given the criticality of semiconductors, cybersecurity is a major concern. While the focus tends to be on software and networks, hardware is at equal if not greater risk of being compromised. The possibility of electronic trapdoors and spyware built into Chinese-made chips cannot be taken lightly. To quote former US Senator Ben Sasse, 'Modern wars are fought with semiconductors'.

The truth of that statement was borne out when the global semiconductor shortage impacted 169 industries across India in 2021-22, slowing the economy as a whole. Then, on 15 December 2021, came the long-awaited moment. For fifteen years, I had clung to the dream of a vibrant electronics industry, and for the first time, I could see the outlines taking shape. In a seminal move, the Government of India approved a Rs 76,000-crore scheme for creating a semiconductor and display manufacturing ecosystem in India.

Life has come full circle, and I have picked up where I left off in Gujarat. I am once again an adviser, this time to the National Semiconductor Mission, which accords perfectly with my long-held dream of India becoming a global electronics hub.

As a member of the IT ministry-constituted advisory panel of experts that will steer objectives and provide guidance towards a sustainable semiconductor and display ecosystem, I believe the initiative will go a long way in developing our design and manufacturing capabilities.

The mission involves four key schemes: semiconductor fabs; display fabs; compound semiconductors/silicon photonics/sensors fab and semiconductor assembly, testing, marking and packaging (ATMP) facilities in India; along with a design-linked incentive (DLI) component.

Personally, I think it is a fantastic policy. Of course, we have a lot of catching up to do, in terms of building resilient supply chains and promoting investments, financing mechanisms and global engagement, besides research and innovation. Our sole fabrication facility, SCL Mohali, was handed over to the IT ministry by the Department of Space in 2022.

Today, India aspires to be a leading global power and to this end, envisions a five-trillion-dollar economy built on the strength of 'Make in India'. The Ministry of Electronics and Information Technology (MeitY) projects the share of the electronics sector in this scenario at 400 billion dollars. Bain & Company estimates that export manufacturing in six critical sectors—electronics, pharmaceuticals, industrial machinery, chemicals, automotive and textiles—will reach one trillion dollars by 2028.

All this is contingent on an enabling environment and timely action. Windows of opportunity are typically narrow, and a slow-and-steady approach doesn't cut it.

I firmly believe that this is our 'carpe diem' moment. We must seize the day. Why? First, the global trust deficit around China. Second, the shortage of chips in the wake of COVID and the Ukraine war. Both have prompted the world to look for alternative, resilient supply chains for products. This presents an opportunity for made-in-India hardware and semiconductors, and I'm convinced that we can emerge as a 'reliable partner' for the world.

India is ideally placed to enter the plus-one space, and in this context, the policy push around manufacturing came at a critical juncture. Granted that Vietnam has leveraged low costs, tax incentives and altered trade conditions to become a favoured destination for electronics manufacture, but India has so much more to offer. Our unique advantages include a vast domestic market, proximity to Africa, the Middle-East and Europe, and most of all, unmatched human resources.

We have a large pool of highly trained engineers and design specialists, and so, upstream activities involving design and production need not be located overseas. Our capacity for innovation, given the right environment, is unquestionable. Consider the India Stack, for instance, comprising Aadhaar and UPI, which has ushered millions of people into the digital economy. Our Unified Payments Interface, developed by the National Payments Corporation of India, has attracted kudos from global tech giants, and is now second only to cash as a payment method, and is being adopted by other nations. India accounted for the largest number of real-time transactions in 2021.

The Aadhaar identity management programme, unparalleled in the world, has revolutionized the financial sector and enabled Direct Benefit Transfer (DBT) of subsidies and entitlements directly into the beneficiaries' Aadhaar-seeded bank accounts, thereby reducing leakages and enhancing efficiency. It has also allowed the rollout of Ayushman Bharat, the world's largest public health scheme.

Countless apps, scores of unicorns and start-ups focused on developing innovative products testify to Indian ingenuity. Unicorns have raised ninety-four billion dollars in funding and have a combined valuation of 344 billion dollars. The McKinsey Global Institute Digital Adoption Index estimates India to be the second-fastest digitizing economy among seventeen leading economies globally. In sustainable ideas, too, we are ahead of others and by 2030, 50 per cent of our required energy will be generated from non-fossil fuels.

At the end of the day, the Indian mind is what sets us apart. We are heading towards a world where talent will be prized above capital, and we have it in bucket-loads. For millennia, our tradition of superb craftsmanship drove world trade; those incredible creative skills must now be brought to bear on the digital space.

AN EPIC 'MAKE IN INDIA' PROJECT

After decades of advising the government and industry on electronics hardware, I decided it was time to take the bull by the horns. So, with the objective of strengthening the Indian electronics sector, Arjun Malhotra, semiconductor industry veteran Satya Gupta and I launched the Electronics Products Innovation Consortium, or EPIC Foundation, in April 2022.

Our aim is precisely what I have been advising all along: real 'atmanirbharta' in electronics, from design to manufacturing of all products, including semiconductor chips. Set up as a Section 8 non-profit, EPIC will work closely with all the industry associations, academia, industry and government towards a forty-five-billion-dollar market for Indian electronic products. As Satya Gupta said: 'We conceived the foundation with the intent to revive Indian electronics products and brands with indigenous design and manufacturing.'

Apart from the three of us, the board comprises MAIT president emeritus Nitin Kunkolienker and IIT Kanpur director Abhay Karandikar. On board as advisers are luminaries like Vinod Dham, father of the Pentium chip, and V.K. Saraswat. I serve as chairperson.

It's a unique, industry-led initiative that will leverage CSR funds to further innovation in affordable, quality products for the mass market. The strategy is to create indigenous electronics products and brands in high-impact/high-volume categories, and to drive demand for semiconductor chips by scaling the volume for these Indian electronics products. My contention is that if we design in India and create products in India, from chips to systems, only then can we create the requisite demand for semiconductor fab in the country.

I firmly believe that we cannot put the cart before the horse. By creating demand well before semiconductor plants are up and running, we can ensure they stay in business. To do so, the government can aggregate demand from the central and state governments, and give preferential market access to indigenous products with a domestic value addition of 20 to 50 per cent. In my meetings with government departments prior to the launch of EPIC, I was happy to find a realization that ESDM must be brought back to India, so I am hopeful of their support.

We have identified ten key high-volume products that are doable, like tablets, surveillance cameras, STBs, Wi-Fi routers, LED lights, chargers, drones and passport chips. The top five manufacturers in each of these product segments are Chinese. If EPIC unfolds as planned, we anticipate billions of dollars in forex savings and lakhs of new jobs. We have signed memoranda of understanding with the governments of Delhi and Odisha, and with IIT Kanpur and IIT Madras. The objective is to design products, including semiconductors, here in India, and partner with Indian firms who can manufacture them.

For the ten products mentioned above, of the sixteen billion dollars' worth of demand, India has a share of only 1.25 billion. I can say with absolute confidence that EPIC can ensure an indigenously designed and manufactured tablet comparable with Lenovo and Samsung in terms of quality, at a much lower price.

We announced two products at the outset. The first is a 10.1-inch tablet for education, which will be manufactured in India and will have AI and machine learning-based inter-lingual translation for Indian languages, including both voice-to-voice and text-to-text translation. It will also have 'unique features' of repairability and upgradability. We are aiming at ten million indigenous tablets in the first phase.

At the launch, in keeping with our philosophy of creating equitable internet access for all, including differently abled fellow citizens, the EPIC foundation donated 20 Milky Way (Aakash-Ganga) Tablets each to The Blind Society of India and the Deaf Society for Women; a notable feature being that the EPIC logo on the device is in Braille.

The second product is an indigenous LED bulb driver chip. The value of the Indian LED lighting market stood at 2.754 billion dollars in 2021, and the IMARC Group projects that it will reach 9.658 billion dollars by 2027. We plan to enable the manufacture of 700 million LED chips, supported by the industry consortium Electric Lamp and Component Manufacturer's Association (ELCOMA). This will automatically create demand for upcoming semiconductor ATMP units in India and the SCL Fab.

It must be kept in mind that the chips required for most generic products are fairly low-level. The semiconductor shortage brought home the importance of the trailing-edge spectrum of chip technology. It is these low-powered chips used for pedestrian functions that command large volumes.

As Satya observed: 'The educational tablet project and LED chip project ... addresses social empowerment of 1.3 billion Indians and ... puts the wings to India's Semiconductor Mission.'

EPIC is exactly in tune with the government's policy objectives. We are dedicated to the future of Indian electronics, and especially, to its applications in the social sector—in education, environment, healthcare, agriculture and smart cities. One of our first steps was to sign an MoU with the Delhi government for setting up an Electronics City in the capital.

We produced a policy paper on ESDM in Delhi, where the share of electronics consumption is one of the highest in the country. Our SWOT analysis pointed out that despite high land and labour costs, Delhi has the advantages of high demand, preponderance of higher-education institutions, human resources, superior infrastructure and a thriving if unorganized Reuse-Repair-Refurbish (R-R-R) ecosystem. The city-state is thus well placed to take the lead in ESDM design and manufacture.

Our suggestions included talent development, nurturing hardware start-ups, a robust manufacturing infrastructure and a product design ecosystem. The latter prompted another policy paper, on electronic design and start-up villages. Academic institutions can set up or support incubators for start-ups and independent design houses, providing mentorship and access to VC funding. We facilitated discussions towards this end between IIIT Delhi and the Electropreneur Park (currently located at Delhi University).

EPIC is also working with other state governments for developing electronics product design and manufacturing ecosystems. Given that strong partnerships with academia are essential, our foundation has signed MoUs with IIT Kanpur and IIT Madras. Industry associations, too, are critical to this exercise, and several of them including IESA, ELCINA, MAIT, ESSCI and ELCOMA have extended support for our mission.

I am optimistic about the prospects for the industry and look forward to a time when India will design and manufacture not only to meet domestic requirements, but those of the world.

When aspiration meets vision, the result is electrifying.

EPILOGUE

ONE OF THE HAZARDS OF being seen as a grey eminence of the Indian tech industry is that I'm often asked, 'If Indians are so smart, how come we don't have a Google or a Microsoft?'.

What they're really asking is why India, with all its wealth of talent, does not have superbrands of its own. Earlier, I may have said, 'It's complicated ... perhaps we were overly focused on services, or on B2B models, rather than brand creation'. Today, my answer is we're getting there.

In the software space, TCS is an acknowledged superbrand. Software As A Service (SAAS) companies like Zoho and Freshworks are making waves globally and software products from India like IFLEX, FINACLE and TCS Financial have been adopted by financial institutions the world over. NASSCOM, the industry body behind the software boom, estimates that Indian software product sales could hit thirty billion dollars by 2025.

I expect a similar natural progression in the hardware sector. I have always believed that software services and products, and hardware manufacturing and products, are both critical to an Indian technology leadership position. We need to be a product nation in every field we choose, be it software, hardware or electric vehicles (EVs).

Electronics manufacturing and exports are expected to catch up with software, by generating 300 billion dollars by 2026. These days, news portals are replete with headlines asking if India can emerge as a smartphone/semiconductor/EV/tech superpower.

The answer is yes, to all four. Yes, we can. In the previous chapter, I've talked about leveraging India's unique strengths and the market opportunities afforded by recent geopolitical shifts. Increasingly, I see Indian enterprises accelerating technology adoption and innovation, and strategizing for a sustainable and competitive future.

What do we need to become a hardware product nation, while simultaneously meeting environmental goals and social imperatives? How can we up our game in terms of indigenous design and manufacture to the point where 'designed and manufactured in India' becomes a byword for quality and reliability?

As with any other sector, the primary requirements are skill, capital and a conducive policy framework. Fostering innovation and skill-building are the prerequisites. To that end, I have suggested a slew of measures, such as setting up fifty to a hundred design centres associated with academic research facilities, introducing B.Tech. curricula focused on product development, incentivizing designing in India and planning 500 global products in verticals like electronics, med-tech, EVs, pharma and industrial, and semiconductor machinery, in the next five years.

The Electropreneur Parks set up by the MeitY in Delhi and Bhubaneswar should be embedded within academic institutions with knowledge of hardware design, VLSI design and AI/ML. Bear in mind that the future of products is a mix of hardware and software. India already has great software capability, so additional innovations in hardware will enable us to create world-beating products.

Start-ups will play a major role in creating products, thereby reducing imports (for instance, 80 per cent of med-tech products are currently imported) and enhancing exports, just as they did for software in the 1990s. The scope for consumer electronics, from tablets to servers to networking, is vast. For instance, no sooner was the import of drones from China banned than start-ups began working on drones and their components.

In effect, we need to recapture the spirit of COVID-based innovation, with industry, academia and the government all working together. I am in favour of public-private partnership in product development, with funds earmarked for private companies and non-profits for the purpose. The Centre (and state governments) can also support indigenously developed products by giving them priority in procurement. For example, it procured and distributed some 370 million LED bulbs under the Ujala scheme over seven years.

A significant enabler for start-ups would be establishing product validation and certification centres all over the country, with a mandated fast-track turnaround. Rapid innovation is impossible if one has to wait a year or more for a government lab to test and certify a product. Global certification centres that offer the CE Mark or FDA should also be accessible, with a view to facilitating exports.

A major gap that needs to be addressed is logistics. A stronger component supply chain is needed if we are to reduce the dependence on China. Today, we are one of the worst as far as logistics efficiencies and the ratio of cost of logistics to manufacturing is concerned. Consider the fact that there is no direct shipping from the major component supply centres located in Southeast Asia to India. We need at least one trans-shipment port, as both inbound and outbound logistics are critical for the growth of exports.

In addition, our electronics manufacturing clusters need access to multimodal transport hubs, and should be located accordingly. The new logistics policy launched by PM Modi (focused on process reengineering, digitization and multimodal transportation) is downright visionary—if implemented in a timely manner, it will bring down the cost of logistical overheads from 13 or 14 per cent to single digits.

An important factor to consider is the skewed nature of our technology landscape. South India dominates in both software and hardware services and products. While the National Capital

Region and parts of Western India do participate in the software segment, electronics and semiconductors are mainly concentrated in Tamil Nadu and Karnataka, and more recently, in Uttar Pradesh's Noida region.

States like Madhya Pradesh need to diversify from agriculture to manufacturing. Back in 2003–04, when the Union IT minister Arun Shourie called for promotion of the hardware industry, MP was one of the states that expressed interest, but failed to attract investment. Whatever the reasons then, there's no time like the present for states to aggressively pursue IT hardware and create the right ecosystem to draw investments. After all, electronics offers the largest global market as well as a very large domestic market.

The electronics industry, too, needs to pull up its socks. While the software space has just one major association, hardware has a score of them. NASSCOM succeeded because it brought all stakeholders—global and Indian companies, MSMEs and start-ups—on to one platform. The unified approach resulted in software overtaking hardware, with several hardware companies morphing into software giants. Today, several engineering service providers (ESPs) under the NASSCOM umbrella do hardware/VLSI design work, and are involved in embedded software design and engineering (companies such as HCL have created hardware products and designed chips for major customers globally).

As of now, there are some twenty electronics hardware associations, each with their own members and specific agenda, all tugging in different directions. In the absence of a unified voice, the government encounters a cacophony of lobbying for vastly divergent policies. Time and again, ministers and secretaries have adjured me to 'get everyone to speak in one voice'.

Some fifteen years ago, an attempt was made to form an overarching representative body. I was asked to chair it, but to be honest, I balked at the idea of having to manage a medley of vested interests and expectations. I hope that all the associations will unite, because we need to work together to create a global electronics industry.

Take semiconductor manufacturing; we need indigenously designed products and companies using Indian components and semiconductors. So, MAIT and ICEA need to work closely with ISEA and ELCINA to use domestically produced components/semiconductors for their products. Also, in the interest of long-term sustainability, original equipment manufacturers and contract manufacturers need to upgrade to the original design manufacturers, as was the case in Taiwan. Ideally, the hardware industry should have ensured at the very outset that PLI schemes included design incentives. If we don't design and add value in India, how can we become globally competitive?

Today, we see a strong push towards large data centres, given the rise in data consumption and cloud adoption. Microsoft, for instance, announced the setting up of the Hyderabad data centre region in 2022. India has the capacity to attract data centre investments from all over the world, just as Singapore is doing. However, we need a comprehensive policy in this regard, which includes manufacturing the entire hardware component of the data centre infrastructure.

On the tricky issue of capital, a supporting ecosystem of angel investors and VCs for hardware is unfortunately missing. They must be incentivized to do so, and a clear policy formulated in this regard. Asking successful entrepreneurs to assist and mentor hardware start-ups, as NASSCOM has done for software, would make a big difference. Both Ratan Tata and Azim Premji have invested in a slew of start-ups. The government's 'Startup India Stand Up India' campaign promotes bank financing and incentives for entrepreneurs, but more needs to be done.

My colleagues at the Indian Angel Network and I have formed a special interest group for hardware, but the government will need to step in. For example, the Department of Biotechnology gave biotech start-ups a leg up through the Biotechnology Industry Research

Assistance Council (BIRAC), and this encouraged private investors to follow suit.

Another crucial step that we must take is to create special relationships with countries like Taiwan, Korea and Japan. Taiwan is ideally placed from our perspective, because it needs to diversify its investments away from China to a 'safe' friendly country like India, where there is abundant design talent, and now, great incentives for semiconductor and electronics manufacturing, as well as a large domestic market. In terms of creating deep design and R&D capability, the best option would be to partner with Taiwan's Industrial Technology Research Institute (ITRI), one of the world's leading applied research institutions. The one big gap in our current semiconductor policy is an R&D institute, and this can be bridged by partnering with Taiwan.

A HOLISTIC RIGHT TO REPAIR

Even as we strive towards a dominant position in product design and manufacturing, we have to keep sustainability in mind, by merging digital transformation with the environmental agenda. Of late, sustainability has received an institutional push, with the Securities and Exchange Board of India (SEBI) mandating an environmental, social and governance (ESG) overview. As a result, investments in ESG-themed funds rose from 275 million dollars in 2020 to 650 million dollars in 2021.

In the same spirit, PM Modi has emphasized India's Circular Economy Mission, calling on industry and citizens alike to reduce, recycle, reuse, redesign, recover and remanufacture; as opposed to the linear economy, based on take-make-dispose. The Ellen MacArthur Foundation estimates that the circular economy will lead to savings of forty trillion dollars annually by 2050, while reducing greenhouse gas emissions by 44 per cent.

Jaideep Prabhu of the Judge Business School, University of Cambridge, believes that India, with its millennia-old tradition of 'aparigraha' (non-attachment to materialistic possessions), can lead the way in shifting to a circular economy. India has a head-start in the three pillars of circularity: resource-sharing; self-made goods; and reuse, repair and recycling.

Another argument in favour of circularity is the fact that many of the materials used in electronics and renewable energy equipment are in short supply. The World Bank's Minerals for Climate Action reports that the transition to clean energy would deplete rare minerals. Thus, the critical need for conservation, circularity, repair, reuse and recycling.

Electronics is the world's largest and most rapidly growing industry, producing the fastest growing waste stream. India, as the third largest producer of e-waste, needs to recycle rather than stuff landfills (particularly as much of the waste is toxic and can leach into soil and ground water). The NITI Aayog is currently developing action plans for eleven categories of waste under the Circular Economy Mission. For electronics, these include all the e-waste from electronic products and lithium-ion batteries, solar panels, etc. Apart from recycling domestically, we should export our services overseas, as a sure-shot way to achieve climate goals.

Given the exploding demand for electronics, recycling is not enough. India's growing GDP and digitization of the economy have created a huge demand for products. Indeed, electronics and digital technologies are essential if India is to emerge as a five-trillion-dollar economy. So, we must repair, refurbish and reuse in order to reduce the dependence on critical, imported raw materials and chips manufactured abroad.

Repairs and refurbishment offer great scope for both our domestic market and exports. In this context, I am in favour of the right to repair, which is also in keeping with India's cultural ethos. Why do we speak in terms of a 'right' to repair when, surely, it is a presupposition? Unfortunately, that is not the case.

Manufacturers tailor their strategies towards replacement (use-and-throw) rather than repair. All manner of tactics come into play, from product design to legal barriers to overpriced repair services. Across the industry, forced obsolescence is the norm. Printers contain chips that prevent ink cartridges from being used after they cross a certain threshold of use. Most earphones can't be repaired without permanent damage. The iPhone is a classic example. In 2020, Apple was fined heavily for creating software that slowed down old phones, thereby forcing the customer to buy a newer version.

Planned obsolescence reduces product life, ensuring more sales. For instance, when the LED TV I had bought for Rs 200,000 crashed within the year, I was told that the cost of repair would be Rs 70,000, as the screen would have to be replaced. Later, I was informed that it was not repairable!

In reaction to such pernicious practices, a right to repair movement has gained momentum around the world. In 2021, the European Parliament passed a resolution mandating that certain products like TVs must be freely repaired for a period of time. In 2017, the Swedish government introduced a 50 per cent tax break for using repair services on consumer items. US President Joe Biden passed an executive order limiting the manufacturer's ability to restrict independent repair of electronic goods.

Repurchases not only create e-waste but limit affordability, a critical factor in India, where replacing a product every couple of years is simply not feasible. Take the case of educational tablets, which dramatically reduce the digital divide. Without product longevity, a large-scale rollout of government schemes providing free tablets to students will have short-lived benefits. They must be repairable and upgradable, with a capacity to run on all software, and a replaceable battery, so that they last well beyond their current life of two to three years, and can be passed on from one student to the next. This is just one example. Similarly, we need LED bulbs designed in consonance with local weather and power supply conditions.

The Indian consumer is open to refurbishing, at least in mobile phones. While a large number of users upgrade their phones every couple of years, they are happy to buy refurbished products. The same strategy can be extended to other electronic products.

A holistic right to repair will not only lower costs for consumers by extending product longevity, but create massive job opportunities in the form of millions of small repair shops. An informal repair economy already exists, partly because companies like Apple have a very high cost of repair.

The Ministry of Consumer Affairs has taken the lead in drafting a right to repair law. India must show the way to the rest of the world in this field, rather than follow what other nations are doing.

Globally, the repair economy has been valued at 100 billion dollars and is expected to reach 188 billion dollars by 2026. India, with its large pool of engineers, can become an electronics repairs outsourcing hub, and is aiming at a generous slice of this market. MAIT believes positioning India as a repair hub would be a significant economic driver, adding fifteen billion dollars to the GDP annually from 2025 onwards. It will result in global investments, higher incomes and employment generation.

Creating jobs is an urgent necessity, given the persistently high rates of unemployment and underemployment. Overall employment in the IT industry, which accounts for 8 per cent of India's GDP (with a domestic revenue of 49 billion dollars and exports of 178 billion dollars) stood at five million in March 2022. Many more jobs are needed, and this is where ESDM comes in. It has the capacity to create jobs not just for qualified engineers but even for diploma holders and blue-collar workers.

An ESSCI report estimates that the number of jobs in the ESDM sector will almost double to eleven million by 2025, most of them in manufacturing, consumer electronics and IT hardware. The future of Indian electronics, then, is this: a thriving, climate-compliant ESDM ecosystem with the capacity to generate millions of jobs.

Software and hardware together will allow an unmatched positioning of India globally, enabling the creation of world-class products, while generating jobs for Indian citizens both at home and abroad. As the doyen of the Indian IT industry, N. Seshagiri, said: 'Software and hardware are two sides of the same coin.'

Another important social imperative is digital democracy, which mandates internet access for all. Indeed, it is a fundamental right in certain countries. The digital divide that showed up starkly during the pandemic must be bridged. Universal access to broadband, as well as inexpensive and reliable electronics, supports education, entrepreneurship and sharing of ideas. A research paper by Ericsson says that a 10 per cent increase in mobile broadband translates into a 0.8 per cent initial increase in GDP. As C.K. Prahalad once said, 'The poor are poor because they don't have information'.

Going forward, I see the digital sector, which has ensured continuity during the global crises of the recent past and is the substrate of industry, not only emphasizing sustainability and resource efficiency, but gearing towards digital inclusion and the needs of Mahatma Gandhi's 'last man'.

ACKNOWLEDGEMENTS

I WOULD LIKE TO THANK my agent, Preeti Gill, for guiding me from the moment I decided to write the book and for connecting me to HarperCollins. I would like to also thank Sachin Sharma at HarperCollins India for telling me what will work best when writing and guiding me on the flow and structure of the book. And Bhavdeep Kang for her painstaking research and ensuring correctness in each chapter. And of course, Lalita Gurnani for helping me get all the information from her archives and locating pictures for the book.

ABOUT THE AUTHOR

Ajai Chowdhry, one of the six founding members of HCL, began an exciting journey more than four decades ago, with a dream to give India its very own microcomputer. The pioneers of digital electronics in India, they scripted three major milestones of the IT industry: the PC revolution, mobile telephony and systems integration. Ajai, regarded as the 'father of Indian hardware', has been a relentless advocate of self-sufficiency in electronics. He has served, and continues to serve, on several government committees working towards making India the electronics hub of the world. Ajai is currently the chairman of the Mission Governing Board of the National Quantum Mission of India.

HarperCollins *Publishers* India

At HarperCollins India, we believe in telling the best stories and finding the widest readership for our books in every format possible. We started publishing in 1992; a great deal has changed since then, but what has remained constant is the passion with which our authors write their books, the love with which readers receive them, and the sheer joy and excitement that we as publishers feel in being a part of the publishing process.

Over the years, we've had the pleasure of publishing some of the finest writing from the subcontinent and around the world, including several award-winning titles and some of the biggest bestsellers in India's publishing history. But nothing has meant more to us than the fact that millions of people have read the books we published, and that somewhere, a book of ours might have made a difference.

As we look to the future, we go back to that one word—a word which has been a driving force for us all these years.

Read.

Harper Collins

4th

HARPER FICTION

HARPER NON-FICTION

HARPER BUSINESS

HarperCollins *Children's Books*

HARPER DESIGN

Harper Sport

HARPER PERENNIAL

HARPER VANTAGE

हार्पर हिन्दी